The Lutheran Catechism: Law, Gospel, Discipleship

A Six-Month Daily Devotional

with Questions and Prayers

Edited by

Jon Alan Schmidt

Just and Sinner
Ithaca, NY 14850
www.JSPublishing.org

The Lutheran Catechism: Law, Gospel, Discipleship
Original German Texts by Martin Luther
English Translations by William Hermann Theodore Dau
Introduction, Arrangement, Questions, and Prayers by Jon Alan Schmidt
Copyright 2023 by Jon Alan Schmidt
ISBN: 978-1-952295-56-0

All rights reserved. No part of this publication may be reproduced, stored or transmitted in any form or by any means, electronic, mechanical, photocopying, recording, scanning, or otherwise without written permission from the publisher. It is illegal to copy this book, post it to a website, or distribute it by any other means without permission.

Table of Contents

Introduction	1
Readings with Questions and Prayers	6
Daily Prayers	386
Table of Duties	388

Introduction

About This Book

Contrary to common usage among Lutherans, the term *catechism*, strictly speaking, refers to neither of the two documents (Large and Small) first published by Martin Luther in 1529 and included in the *Book of Concord* in 1580. By the time of the Reformation, the term was well established in the Western church as designating the standard content for basic instruction in the faith: the Apostles' Creed, the Lord's Prayer, and the Ten Commandments, often in that order. Luther's most obvious innovation was revising this sequence, and he explained his rationale for doing so as follows in his 1522 *Personal Prayer Book* (from *Luther's Works*, American Edition, vol. 43, pp. 13–14):

> Three things a person must know in order to be saved. First, he must know what to do and what to leave undone. Second, when he realizes that he cannot measure up to what he should do or leave undone, he needs to know where to go to find the strength he requires. Third, he must know how to seek and obtain that strength. It is just like a sick person who first has to determine the nature of his sickness, then find out what to do or to leave undone. After that he has to know where to get the medicine which will help him do or leave undone what is right for a healthy person. Third, he has to desire to search for this medicine and to obtain it or have it brought to him.
>
> Thus the commandments teach man to recognize his sickness, enabling him to perceive what he must do or refrain from doing, consent to or refuse, and so he will recognize himself to be a sinful and wicked person. The Creed will teach and show him where to find the medicine—grace—which will help him to become devout and keep the commandments. The Creed points him to God and his mercy, given and made plain to him in Christ. Finally, the Lord's Prayer teaches all this, namely,

through the fulfilment of God's commandments everything will be given him. In these three are the essentials of the entire Bible.

Luther then added discussions of Holy Baptism, confession, and the Sacrament of the Altar, since these are the means by which the Great Physician dispenses the medicine of grace to those afflicted by the sickness of sin. These "six chief parts" together comprise *The Lutheran Catechism*, and its structure corresponds to this book's subtitle:

- The *law* instructs us how to think, speak, and act, and reveals our inability to do so perfectly as God the Creator demands.
- The *gospel* offers us forgiveness through the redemption of Jesus Christ, and new life through the sanctification of the Holy Spirit.
- *Discipleship* is our exercise of faith in constant prayer, daily repentance as a return to baptism, regular confession and reception of the Lord's Supper, and conscientious discharge of our various vocations at home and in the world.

As illustrated by the diagram on page vi, the first six petitions of the Lord's Prayer recapitulate key aspects of the Ten Commandments and the Apostles' Creed, while the Seventh Petition serves "as the sum of all" by asking God for deliverance from evil. The sacraments are then his efficacious answer.

Although it is now widely perceived to be a one-time doctrinal manual to prepare youths for the rite of confirmation, Luther advocated sustained employment of his Small Catechism by people of all ages. Each part is explicitly intended not primarily for pastors or other church workers, but "as the housefather should teach it in a simple way to his household." In sixteenth-century Germany, that would have included not only the housefather's own immediate and extended family, but also any servants or other employees, and perhaps even *their* families—a genuine "house church."

This book is designed to facilitate such consistent usage by pairing each item and explanation in the Small Catechism with passages from the corresponding section of the Large Catechism. The content is arranged to serve as a devotional for each day, with questions to prompt meditation—within one's own mind, through journaling, or

The Lutheran Catechism

perhaps in conversation with others—and brief accompanying prayers. The only exception is confession; since Luther did not include this as a distinct topic in the Large Catechism, those readings are instead from relevant portions of his 1537 personal confession of faith, the Smalcald Articles, which was also included in the *Book of Concord* in 1580.

"Week Zero" provides excerpts from Luther's prefaces that spell out his purposes in writing the Small and Large Catechisms, as well as his preferred strategy for teaching them. These seven entries are intended to serve as a helpful introduction and occasional refresher as needed; excellent resources for anyone wishing to delve deeper include *That I May Be His Own: An Overview of Luther's Catechisms*, by Charles P. Arand, and two books by John T. Pless: *Praying Luther's Small Catechism* and *Luther's Small Catechism: A Manual for Discipleship*. The catechism proper is spread out over twenty-six weeks, so that it can be reviewed in its entirety twice per year; by comparison, Lutheran pastors in the sixteenth century routinely preached on it as many as four times per year.

For ease of reference, the daily prayers for morning, evening, asking a blessing, and giving thanks are provided as an appendix along with the table of duties, organized by the days of the week to serve as a reminder of the "holy orders" that God has appointed for all Christians. Later additions to the Small Catechism that were left out of the 1580 *Book of Concord* are likewise omitted here. These include Andreas Osiander's 1531 insertion regarding "The Office of the Keys"; the table of duties entries on "What the Hearers Owe to Their Pastors" and "What Subjects Owe to the Magistrates," which only appeared in Latin editions; and "Christian Questions with Their Answers," which debuted in 1551, five years after Luther's death.

Luther strongly recommended memorizing not only the basic texts themselves, but also his short explanations in the Small Catechism. The reader is encouraged to take his advice, either as an initial step or over the course of the first six months. One helpful discipline for cementing the words in the mind is to recite the six chief parts in their entirety on a weekly basis—for example, the Ten Commandments on Monday, the Apostles' Creed on Tuesday, the Lord's Prayer on Wednesday, Holy Baptism on Thursday, Confession on Friday, and the Sacrament of the Altar on Saturday; perhaps appending "Christian

The Lutheran Catechism

Questions with Their Answers" on Sunday, as preparation for receiving the Lord's Supper.

This book is dedicated to my wife, Irene, my partner in all things, but especially in training up our children in the way they should go (Prov. 22:6); and to those children, Timothy and Cristina, to whom I have sought to teach *The Lutheran Catechism* in a simple way throughout their lives. May God richly bless them and all who use this book as they read, mark, learn, and inwardly digest the truths of his holy word, and then put them into practice as followers of the Lord Jesus Christ in the power of the Holy Spirit!

Jon Alan Schmidt

Olathe, Kansas

Lent 2023

The Lutheran Catechism

THE STRUCTURE OF MARTIN LUTHER'S SMALL CATECHISM

WORD			(3) Our Father	PRAYER
LAW	GOSPEL			
(1) Ten Commandments	(2) Apostles' Creed		Thy name be hallowed	Give us our daily bread
Fear God	God as Creator		Thy kingdom come	Forgive us our trespasses
Love God	God as Redeemer		Thy will be done	Lead us not into temptation
Trust in God	God as Sanctifier			

Summary: Deliver us from evil

(4) Holy Baptism
(5) Confession
(6) Lord's Supper

SACRAMENTS

5

The Lutheran Catechism

Week Zero - Sunday

Preface

Martin Luther, to all faithful and godly pastors and preachers:

Grace, mercy, and peace in Jesus Christ, our Lord.

The deplorable, miserable condition which I discovered lately when I, too, was a visitor, has forced and urged me to prepare this catechism, or Christian doctrine, in this small, plain, simple form. Mercy! Good God! What manifold misery I beheld! The common people, especially in the villages, have no knowledge whatever of Christian doctrine, and, alas! many pastors are altogether incapable and incompetent to teach.

A Christian, profitable, and necessary preface, and faithful, earnest exhortation of Dr. Martin Luther to all Christians, but especially to all pastors and preachers, that they should daily exercise themselves in the catechism, which is a short summary and epitome of the entire Holy Scriptures, and that they may always teach the same.

We have no slight reasons for treating the catechism so constantly and for both desiring and beseeching others to teach it, since we see to our sorrow that many pastors and preachers are very negligent in this, and slight both their office and this teaching. . . .

But for myself I say this: I am also a doctor and preacher, yea, as learned and experienced as all those may be who have such presumption and security; yet I do as a child who is being taught the catechism, and every morning, and whenever I have time, I read and say, word for word, the Ten Commandments, the Creed, the Lord's Prayer, the Psalms, etc. And I must still read and study daily, and yet I cannot master it as I wish, but must remain a child and pupil of the catechism, and am glad so to remain. [LC LP.0–1a, 7–8a]

The Lutheran Catechism

Meditation:
1. What motivated Luther to prepare his Small and Large Catechisms? Is the need for them any less today than in his time?
2. How often did Luther believe that pastors, preachers, and all Christians should review the catechism? Why?
3. How often did Luther himself review the catechism? Why? What are some specific benefits of studying such a concise summary of Christian doctrine?

Prayer:

Heavenly Father, thank you for your faithful servant, Martin Luther, and these texts that he prepared to summarize the basic truths of your holy word. Amen.

Week Zero – Monday

Preface

Nevertheless, all maintain that they are Christians, have been baptized, and receive the holy sacraments. Yet they cannot recite either the Lord's Prayer, or the Creed, or the Ten Commandments; they live like dumb brutes and irrational hogs; and yet, now that the gospel has come, they have nicely learned to abuse all liberty like experts.

Therefore I beg such lazy paunches or presumptuous saints to be persuaded and believe for God's sake that they are verily, verily! not so learned or such great doctors as they imagine; and never to presume that they have finished learning this, or know it well enough in all points, even though they think that they know it ever so well. For though they should know and understand it perfectly (which, however, is impossible in this life), yet there are manifold benefits and fruits still to be obtained, if it be daily read and practiced in thought and speech; namely, that the Holy Ghost is present in such reading and repetition and meditation, and bestows ever new and more light and devoutness, so that it is daily relished and appreciated better, as Christ promises, Matthew 18:20: "Where two or three are gathered together in my name, there am I in the midst of them."

Besides, it is an exceedingly effectual help against the devil, the world, and the flesh and all evil thoughts to be occupied with the word of God, and to speak of it, and meditate upon it, so that the First Psalm declares those blessed who meditate upon the law of God day and night. Undoubtedly, you will not start a stronger incense or other fumigation against the devil than by being engaged upon God's commandments and words, and speaking, singing, or thinking of them. For this is indeed the true holy water and holy sign from which he flees, and by which he may be driven away.

Now, for this reason alone, you ought gladly to read, speak, think, and treat of these things, if you had no other profit and fruit from them than that by doing so you can drive away the devil and evil thoughts. For he cannot hear or endure God's word. [LC LP.9–11a]

The Lutheran Catechism

Meditation:
1. What concerned Luther about the common people of his day? Why are we so easily tempted to abuse our liberty in Christ?
2. What are some specific reasons why every Christian should be able to recite the catechism from memory, yet still study it daily?
3. What three enemies of our faith did Luther identify here? How does the catechism help us in our battle against them?

Prayer:

Lord God, equip me daily with the basic truths of your holy word, so that I may employ them to stand against the devil, the world, and my flesh. Amen.

Week Zero – Tuesday

Preface

Therefore, I entreat you all for God's sake, my dear sirs and brethren, who are pastors or preachers, to devote yourselves heartily to your office, to have pity on the people who are entrusted to you, and to help us inculcate the catechism upon the people, and especially upon the young. And let those of you who cannot do better take these tables and forms and impress them, word for word, on the people, as follows.

And if this were not sufficient to admonish us to read the catechism daily, yet we should feel sufficiently constrained by the command of God alone, who solemnly enjoins in Deuteronomy 6:6ff that we should always meditate upon his precepts, sitting, walking, standing, lying down, and rising, and have them before our eyes and in our hands as a constant mark and sign. Doubtless he did not so solemnly require and enjoin this without a purpose; but because he knows our danger and need, as well as the constant and furious assaults and temptations of devils, he wishes to warn, equip, and preserve us against them, as with a good armor against their fiery darts and with good medicine against their evil infection and suggestion. . . .

And what else are such supercilious, presumptuous saints, who are unwilling to read and study the catechism daily, doing than esteeming themselves much more learned than God himself with all his saints, angels, prophets, apostles, and all Christians? For inasmuch as God himself is not ashamed to teach these things daily, as knowing nothing better to teach, and always keeps teaching the same thing, and does not take up anything new or different, and all the saints know nothing better or different to learn, and cannot finish learning this, are we not the finest of all fellows to imagine, if we have once read or heard it, that we know it all, and have no further need to read and learn, but can finish learning in one hour what God himself cannot finish teaching, although he is engaged in teaching it from the beginning to the end of the world, and all prophets, together with all saints, have been occupied with learning it, and have ever remained pupils, and must continue to be such? [LC LP.14, 16]

Meditation:

1. What did Luther urge pastors and preachers to do with the catechism? Why? How has your discipleship benefited from their teaching?
2. What did God command his people to do with his precepts? Why is it important that we do this constantly?
3. What attitude is evident in those who refuse to read and study the catechism daily? Why is it impossible for us ever to finish learning it?

Prayer:

Almighty God, remind me through your Holy Spirit to keep your word before me always, and forgive me for those times when I fail to do so. Amen.

Week Zero – Wednesday

Preface

In the first place, let the preacher above all be careful to avoid many kinds of or various texts and forms of the Ten Commandments, the Lord's Prayer, the Creed, the sacraments, etc., but choose one form to which he adheres, and which he inculcates all the time, year after year. For young and simple people must be taught by uniform, settled texts and forms, otherwise they easily become confused when the teacher today teaches them thus, and in a year some other way, as if he wished to make improvements, and thus all effort and labor is lost.

This sermon is designed and undertaken that it might be an instruction for children and the simpleminded. Hence of old it was called in Greek *catechism*, i.e., instruction for children, what every Christian must needs know, so that he who does not know this could not be numbered with the Christians nor be admitted to any sacrament, just as a mechanic who does not understand the rules and customs of his trade is expelled and considered incapable. Therefore we must have the young learn the parts which belong to the catechism or instruction for children well and fluently, and diligently exercise themselves in them, and keep them occupied with them.

Therefore it is the duty of every father of a family to question and examine his children and servants at least once a week and to ascertain what they know of it, or are learning, and, if they do not know it, to keep them faithfully at it. . . . However, for the common people we are satisfied with the three parts, which have remained in Christendom from of old, though little of it has been taught and treated correctly, until both young and old, who are called and wish to be Christians, are well trained in them and familiar with them. [LC SP.1–4, 6]

The Lutheran Catechism

Meditation:
1. What did Luther recommend about the texts of the catechism? Why is it important to select a single version and stick with it?
2. What kind of people did Luther identify as the primary audience for the teaching of the catechism? Why?
3. What kind of people did Luther identify as the primary teachers of the catechism? Why parents, rather than pastors?

Prayer:

Dear Lord, thank you for your word as summarized in the catechism. Help all Christian parents learn it for themselves and teach it to their children. Amen.

Week Zero – Thursday

Preface

Also our blessed fathers understood this well; for they all used the same form of the Lord's Prayer, the Creed, and the Ten Commandments. Therefore, we too should teach the young and simple people these parts in such a way as not to change a syllable, or set them forth and repeat them one year differently than in another.

Hence, choose whatever form you please, and adhere to it forever.... [T]each them, first of all, these parts, namely, the Ten Commandments, the Creed, the Lord's Prayer, etc., according to the text, word for word, so that they, too, can repeat it in the same manner after you and commit it to memory.

These are the most necessary parts which one should first learn to repeat word for word, and which our children should be accustomed to recite daily when they arise in the morning, when they sit down to their meals, and when they retire at night....

Now, when these three parts are apprehended, it behooves a person also to know what to say concerning our sacraments, which Christ himself instituted, baptism and the holy body and blood of Christ, namely, the text which Matthew 28:19ff and Mark 16:15f record at the close of their gospels when Christ said farewell to his disciples and sent them forth....

So much is sufficient for a simple person to know from the Scriptures concerning baptism. In like manner, also, concerning the other sacrament, in short, simple words, namely, the text of St. Paul....

Thus we would have, in all, five parts of the entire Christian doctrine which should be constantly treated and required, and heard recited word for word. For you must not rely upon it that the young people will learn and retain these things from the sermon alone. [LC SP.15-16a, 20, 22, 24]

The Lutheran Catechism

Meditation:
1. What are the three chief parts of the catechism? Why is it important to memorize them word for word?
2. How often did Luther advocate having children recite the catechism? Why? What tends to get in the way of maintaining such a practice?
3. What two sacraments are discussed in the catechism? Where is their institution by Christ recorded in Scripture? Why should we know this?

Prayer:

Heavenly Father, remind me that I am forever your child, and teach me to know and abide by your holy word accordingly. Amen.

Week Zero – Friday

Preface

In the second place, after they have well learned the text, then teach them the sense also, so that they know what it means, and again choose the form of these tables, or some other brief uniform method, whichever you like, and adhere to it, and do not change a single syllable, as was just said regarding the text; and take your time to it. For it is not necessary that you take up all the parts at once, but one after the other. After they understand the First Commandment well, then take up the Second, and so on, otherwise they will be overwhelmed, so as not to be able to retain any well.

When these parts have been well learned, you may, as a supplement and to fortify them, lay before them also some psalms or hymns, which have been composed on these parts, and thus lead the young into the Scriptures, and make daily progress therein.

However, it is not enough for them to comprehend and recite these parts according to the words only, but the young people should also be made to attend the preaching, especially during the time which is devoted to the catechism, that they may hear it explained, and may learn to understand what every part contains, so as to be able to recite it as they have heard it, and, when asked, may give a correct answer, so that the preaching may not be without profit and fruit. For the reason why we exercise such diligence in preaching the catechism so often is that it may be inculcated on our youth, not in a high and subtle manner, but briefly and with the greatest simplicity, so as to enter the mind readily and be fixed in the memory.

Therefore we shall now take up the above-mentioned articles one by one and in the plainest manner possible say about them as much as is necessary. [LC SP.25–28]

Meditation:

1. What did Luther recommend, once someone has learned the text of the catechism itself? Why are the sense and meaning as important as the words?
2. What supplemental aids did Luther identify for this? What are some other tools that can help fortify our understanding?
3. How can learning and singing psalms and hymns help people grasp the meaning of the catechism? How can hearing sermons help them?

Prayer:

Lord God, open my mind and heart so that I not only know your holy word, but also understand it and apply it properly to my daily living. Amen.

Week Zero – Saturday

Preface

In the third place, after you have thus taught them this short catechism, then take up the Large Catechism, and give them also a richer and fuller knowledge. Here explain at large every commandment, petition, and part with its various works, uses, benefits, dangers, and injuries, as you find these abundantly stated in many books written about these matters. And particularly, urge that commandment or part most which suffers the greatest neglect among your people.

Therefore I again implore all Christians, especially pastors and preachers, not to be doctors too soon, and imagine that they know everything (for imagination and cloth unshrunk fall far short of the measure), but that they daily exercise themselves well in these studies and constantly treat them; moreover, that they guard with all care and diligence against the poisonous infection of such security and vain imagination, but steadily keep on reading, teaching, learning, pondering, and meditating, and do not cease until they have made a test and are sure that they have taught the devil to death, and have become more learned than God himself and all his saints.

If they manifest such diligence, then I will promise them, and they shall also perceive, what fruit they will obtain, and what excellent men God will make of them, so that in due time they themselves will acknowledge that the longer and the more they study the catechism, the less they know of it, and the more they find yet to learn; and then only, as hungry and thirsty ones, will they truly relish that which now they cannot endure, because of great abundance and satiety. To this end may God grant his grace! Amen. [LC LP.19–20]

The Lutheran Catechism

Meditation:
1. What did Luther recommend, once someone has learned the entire Small Catechism? What are other potential sources of richer and fuller knowledge?
2. Which commandment or part suffers the most neglect among your people? Which one suffers the most neglect in your own life?
3. What effects do you hope that your study of the catechism using this book will have? How will you evaluate whether they come about?

Prayer:

Father, I am a sinner who cannot keep your commandments perfectly. Forgive me for the sake of Jesus Christ and sanctify me by the Holy Spirit. Amen.

Week One – Sunday

The Ten Commandments

1. Thou shalt have no other gods before me.
2. Thou shalt not take the name of the Lord, thy God, in vain.
3. Thou shalt sanctify the holy day.
4. Thou shalt honor thy father and mother.
5. Thou shalt not kill.
6. Thou shalt not commit adultery.
7. Thou shalt not steal.
8. Thou shalt not bear false witness against thy neighbor.
9. Thou shalt not covet thy neighbor's house.
10. Thou shalt not covet thy neighbor's wife, nor his manservant, nor his maidservant, nor his cattle, nor anything that is his.

Thus we have the Ten Commandments, a compend of divine doctrine, as to what we are to do in order that our whole life may be pleasing to God, and the true fountain and channel from and in which everything must arise and flow that is to be a good work, so that outside of the Ten Commandments no work or thing can be good or pleasing to God, however great or precious it be in the eyes of the world. Let us see now what our great saints can boast of their spiritual orders and their great and grievous works which they have invented and set up, while they let these pass, as though they were far too insignificant, or had long ago been perfectly fulfilled.

I am of the opinion, indeed, that here one will find his hands full to observe these, namely, meekness, patience, and love towards enemies, chastity, kindness, etc., and what such virtues imply. But such works are not of value and make no display in the eyes of the world; for they are not peculiar and conceited works, and restricted to particular times, places, rites, and customs, but are common, everyday domestic works which one neighbor can practice toward another; therefore they are not of high esteem. [LC I.311–13]

The Lutheran Catechism

Meditation:
1. What is the purpose of the Ten Commandments? Why is it important for us to know what God considers to be a good work?
2. What kinds of works are good in the eyes of the world, but not necessarily pleasing to God? Why?
3. What makes it difficult to behave as described here? Why does the world often fail to value such works?

Prayer:

Almighty God, teach me to shape and evaluate my own conduct in accordance with your true standards, rather than the false standards of the world. Amen.

The Lutheran Catechism

Week One – Monday

The Ten Commandments

1. Thou shalt have no other gods before me.
2. Thou shalt not take the name of the Lord, thy God, in vain.
3. Thou shalt sanctify the holy day.
4. Thou shalt honor thy father and mother.
5. Thou shalt not kill.
6. Thou shalt not commit adultery.
7. Thou shalt not steal.
8. Thou shalt not bear false witness against thy neighbor.
9. Thou shalt not covet thy neighbor's house.
10. Thou shalt not covet thy neighbor's wife, nor his manservant, nor his maidservant, nor his cattle, nor anything that is his.

But the other works cause people to open their eyes and ears wide, and men aid to this effect by the great display, expense, and magnificent buildings with which they adorn them, so that everything shines and glitters. There they waft incense, they sing and ring bells, they light tapers and candles, so that nothing else can be seen or heard. For when a priest stands there in a surplice embroidered with gilt, or a layman continues all day upon his knees in church, that is regarded as a most precious work which no one can sufficiently praise. But when a poor girl tends a little child and faithfully does what she is told, that is considered nothing; for else what should monks and nuns seek in their cloisters?

But see, is not that a cursed presumption of those desperate saints who dare to invent a higher and better life and estate than the Ten Commandments teach, pretending (as we have said) that this is an ordinary life for the common man, but that theirs is for saints and perfect ones? [LC I.314–15]

Meditation:

1. What are some examples of works that are approved by the world? What is an example of a truly good work that is easily overlooked?

2. Is there anything inherently wrong with buildings, adornments, incense, bells, candles, vestments, kneeling, etc.? What makes them problematic?
3. Why can there be no higher and better life and estate than the Ten Commandments teach?

Prayer:

Dear Lord, forgive me for thinking that I can invent higher and better ways of living than what you have already revealed to me in your holy word. Amen.

Week One – Tuesday

The Ten Commandments

1. Thou shalt have no other gods before me.
2. Thou shalt not take the name of the Lord, thy God, in vain.
3. Thou shalt sanctify the holy day.
4. Thou shalt honor thy father and mother.
5. Thou shalt not kill.
6. Thou shalt not commit adultery.
7. Thou shalt not steal.
8. Thou shalt not bear false witness against thy neighbor.
9. Thou shalt not covet thy neighbor's house.
10. Thou shalt not covet thy neighbor's wife, nor his manservant, nor his maidservant, nor his cattle, nor anything that is his.

And the miserable blind people do not see that no man can get so far as to keep one of the Ten Commandments as it should be kept, but both the Apostles' Creed and the Lord's Prayer must come to our aid (as we shall hear), by which that is sought and prayed for and received continually. Therefore all their boasting amounts to as much as if I boasted and said: To be sure, I have not a penny to make payment with, but I confidently undertake to pay ten florins.

All this I say and urge in order that men might become rid of the sad misuse which has taken such deep root and still cleaves to everybody, and in all estates upon earth become used to looking hither only, and to being concerned about these matters. For it will be a long time before they will produce a doctrine or estates equal to the Ten Commandments, because they are so high that no one can attain to them by human power; and whoever does attain to them is a heavenly, angelic man, far above all holiness of the world. Only occupy yourself with them, and try your best, apply all power and ability, and you will find so much to do that you will neither seek nor esteem any other work or holiness. [LC I.316–18]

Meditation:

1. Why is it impossible for any of us to keep even one of the Ten Commandments as it should be kept?
2. That being the case, why should we even bother to try? How do the Apostles' Creed and the Lord's Prayer come to our aid in this regard?
3. Why are we tempted to seek and esteem works that God has not commanded? Why is it foolish for us to boast of them?

Prayer:

Heavenly Father, thank you for your law that reveals the depth of my sin, and especially for your gospel that reveals the depth of your forgiveness. Amen.

The Lutheran Catechism

Week One – Wednesday

The First Commandment

Thou shalt have no other gods.

What does this mean?—Answer.

We should fear, love, and trust in God above all things.

That is: Thou shalt have me alone as thy God. What is the force of this, and how is it to be understood? What does it mean to have a god? or, what is God? Answer: A god means that from which we are to expect all good and to which we are to take refuge in all distress, so that to have a god is nothing else than to trust and believe him from the heart; as I have often said that the confidence and faith of the heart alone make both God and an idol. If your faith and trust be right, then is your god also true; and, on the other hand, if your trust be false and wrong, then you have not the true God; for these two belong together, faith and God. That now, I say, upon which you set your heart and put your trust, is properly your god.

Therefore it is the intent of this commandment to require true faith and trust of the heart which settles upon the only true God, and clings to him alone. That is as much as to say: "See to it that you let me alone be your God, and never seek another," i.e.: "Whatever you lack of good things, expect it of me, and look to me for it, and whenever you suffer misfortune and distress, creep and cling to me. I, yes, I, will give you enough and help you out of every need; only let not your heart cleave to or rest in any other." [LC I.1–4]

Meditation:
1. What does it mean to have a god? What does it mean to have the true God? How can we tell the difference?
2. What are some specific ways in which you fear God? love God? trust in God? Why are all three of these necessary to keep the First Commandment?
3. What are some specific things that you are tempted to fear, love, or trust above God? What might help you to resist such temptation?

Prayer:

Dear God, may your grace and mercy preserve us from fearing, loving, or trusting anything above you, through Jesus Christ our Lord. Amen.

Week One – Thursday

The First Commandment

Thou shalt have no other gods.

What does this mean?—Answer.

We should fear, love, and trust in God above all things.

This I must unfold somewhat more plainly, that it may be understood and perceived by ordinary examples of the contrary. Many a one thinks that he has God and everything in abundance when he has money and possessions; he trusts in them and boasts of them with such firmness and assurance as to care for no one. Lo, such a man also has a god, Mammon by name, i.e., money and possessions, on which he sets all his heart, and which is also the most common idol on earth. He who has money and possessions feels secure, and is joyful and undismayed as though he were sitting in the midst of Paradise. On the other hand, he who has none doubts and is despondent, as though he knew of no God. For very few are to be found who are of good cheer, and who neither mourn nor complain if they have not mammon. This sticks and clings to our nature, even to the grave.

So, too, whoever trusts and boasts that he possesses great skill, prudence, power, favor, friendship, and honor has also a god, but not this true and only God. This appears again when you notice how presumptuous, secure, and proud people are because of such possessions, and how despondent when they no longer exist or are withdrawn. Therefore I repeat that the chief explanation of this point is that to have a god is to have something in which the heart entirely trusts. [LC I.5–10]

Meditation:
1. What are two specific examples of gods that many people have, rather than the true God? What makes them so seductive?
2. What is mammon? Why are those who have it tempted to trust it above God? Why are those who lack it tempted to seek it above God?
3. Who is the source of every person's money, possessions, skills, prudence, power, favor, friendships, and honor? Why do we often forget this?

Prayer:
Lord, thank you for the many blessings that you have poured out upon me. Forgive me for so easily focusing on them, rather than on you. Amen.

Week One – Friday

The First Commandment

Thou shalt have no other gods.

What does this mean?—Answer.

We should fear, love, and trust in God above all things.

Besides, consider what, in our blindness, we have hitherto been practicing and doing under the papacy. If anyone had toothache, he fasted and honored St. Apollonia; if he was afraid of fire, he chose St. Lawrence as his helper in need; if he dreaded pestilence, he made a vow to St. Sebastian or Rochio, and a countless number of such abominations, where everyone selected his own saint, worshiped him, and called for help to him in distress. Here belong those also, as, e.g., sorcerers and magicians, whose idolatry is most gross, and who make a covenant with the devil, in order that he may give them plenty of money or help them in love affairs, preserve their cattle, restore to them lost possessions, etc. For all these place their heart and trust elsewhere than in the true God, look for nothing good to him nor seek it from him.

Thus you can easily understand what and how much this commandment requires, namely, that man's entire heart and all his confidence be placed in God alone, and in no one else. For to have God, you can easily perceive, is not to lay hold of him with our hands or to put him in a bag, or to lock him in a chest. But to apprehend him means when the heart lays hold of him and clings to him. But to cling to him with the heart is nothing else than to trust in him entirely. For this reason he wishes to turn us away from everything else that exists outside of him, and to draw us to himself, namely, because he is the only eternal good. As though he would say: Whatever you have heretofore sought of the saints, or for whatever you have trusted in mammon or anything else, expect it all of me, and regard me as the one who will help you and pour out upon you richly all good things. [LC I.11–15]

Meditation:
1. What common aspect of medieval piety is described here? What was wrong with it? What is the proper attitude that we should have toward the saints?
2. What appealing aspect of many false gods is impossible when we apprehend the true God? Why?
3. Why does God earnestly desire that we fear, love, and trust in him above all things? Why is it so easy for us to forget this?

Prayer:

Father, teach me to seek all that I need from you alone. Forgive me for instead relying all too often on myself and the things that I can control. Amen.

Week One – Saturday

The First Commandment

Thou shalt have no other gods.

What does this mean?—Answer.

We should fear, love, and trust in God above all things.

Lo, here you have the meaning of the true honor and worship of God, which pleases God, and which he commands under penalty of eternal wrath, namely, that the heart know no other comfort or confidence than in him, and do not suffer itself to be torn from him, but, for him, risk and disregard everything upon earth. On the other hand, you can easily see and judge how the world practices only false worship and idolatry. For no people has ever been so reprobate as not to institute and observe some divine worship; everyone has set up as his special god whatever he looked to for blessings, help, and comfort.

Thus, for example, the heathen who put their trust in power and dominion elevated Jupiter as the supreme god; the others, who were bent upon riches, happiness, or pleasure, and a life of ease, Hercules, Mercury, Venus, or others; women with child, Diana or Lucina, and so on; thus everyone made that his god to which his heart was inclined, so that even in the mind of the heathen to have a god means to trust and believe. But their error is this, that their trust is false and wrong; for it is not placed in the only God, besides whom there is truly no God in heaven or upon earth. Therefore the heathen really make their self-invented notions and dreams of God an idol, and put their trust in that which is altogether nothing. Thus it is with all idolatry; for it consists not merely in erecting an image and worshiping it, but rather in the heart, which stands gaping at something else, and seeks help and consolation from creatures, saints, or devils, and neither cares for God, nor looks to him for so much good as to believe that he is willing to help, neither believes that whatever good it experiences comes from God. [LC I.16-21]

The Lutheran Catechism

Meditation:
1. What is true honor and worship of God that pleases him? What kinds of things hinder you from offering it?
2. Why do you suppose that all peoples and cultures set up some sort of religious practices? What mistake do they make in doing so?
3. Why is idolatry ultimately empty? Why do people engage in it anyway? How have you sometimes fallen into that trap yourself?

Prayer:

Lord God, help me to honor and worship you rightly, as you have commanded, rather than inventing and exalting my own notions and dreams. Amen.

Week Two – Sunday

The First Commandment

Thou shalt have no other gods.

What does this mean?—Answer.

We should fear, love, and trust in God above all things.

Besides, there is also a false worship and extreme idolatry, which we have hitherto practiced, and is still prevalent in the world, upon which also all ecclesiastical orders are founded, and which concerns the conscience alone, that seeks in its own works help, consolation, and salvation, presumes to wrest heaven from God, and reckons how many bequests it has made, how often it has fasted, celebrated Mass, etc. Upon such things it depends, and of them boasts, as though unwilling to receive anything from God as a gift, but desires itself to earn or merit it superabundantly, just as though he must serve us and were our debtor, and we his liege lords. What is this but reducing God to an idol, yea, an apple-god, and elevating and regarding ourselves as God? But this is slightly too subtle, and is not for young pupils.

But let this be said to the simple, that they may well note and remember the meaning of this commandment, namely, that we are to trust in God alone, and look to him and expect from him naught but good, as from one who gives us body, life, food, drink, nourishment, health, protection, peace, and all necessaries of both temporal and eternal things. He also preserves us from misfortune, and if any evil befall us, delivers and rescues us, so that it is God alone (as has been sufficiently said) from whom we receive all good, and by whom we are delivered from all evil. Hence also, I think, we Germans from ancient times call God (more elegantly and appropriately than any other language) by that name from the word *good*, as being an eternal fountain which gushes forth abundantly nothing but what is good, and from which flows forth all that is and is called good. [LC I.22–25]

Meditation:

1. What is the focus of the false worship described here? Why is it wrong to seek help, consolation, and salvation in our own works?
2. Why do some people insist on earning whatever they might receive from God? What attitude toward him does this indicate?
3. What good things can we expect from God? Does this mean that Christians are guaranteed nothing but good in this life? Why not?

Prayer:

Heavenly Father, I praise you for the abundant goodness that you have bestowed upon me and ask you to deliver me whenever evil befalls me. Amen.

Week Two – Monday

The First Commandment

Thou shalt have no other gods.

What does this mean?—Answer.

We should fear, love, and trust in God above all things.

For even though otherwise we experience much good from men, still whatever we receive by his command or arrangement is all received from God. For our parents, and all rulers, and everyone besides with respect to his neighbor, have received from God the command that they should do us all manner of good, so that we receive these blessings not from them, but, through them, from God. For creatures are only the hands, channels, and means whereby God gives all things, as he gives to the mother breasts and milk to offer to her child, and corn and all manner of produce from the earth for nourishment, none of which blessings could be produced by any creature of itself.

Therefore no man should presume to take or give anything except as God has commanded, in order that it may be acknowledged as God's gift, and thanks may be rendered him for it, as this commandment requires. On this account also these means of receiving good gifts through creatures are not to be rejected, neither should we in presumption seek other ways and means than God has commanded. For that would not be receiving from God, but seeking of ourselves.

Let everyone, then, see to it that he esteem this commandment great and high above all things, and do not regard it as a joke. Ask and examine your heart diligently, and you will find whether it cleaves to God alone or not. If you have a heart that can expect of him nothing but what is good, especially in want and distress, and that, moreover, renounces and forsakes everything that is not God, then you have the only true God. If, on the contrary, it cleaves to anything else, of which it expects more good and help than of God, and does not take refuge in him, but in adversity flees from him, then you have an idol, another god. [LC I.26–28]

Meditation:
1. What do you have that you did not receive from God? Why is it sometimes difficult to keep this in mind?
2. Why do you suppose that God gives us so many of his good gifts through other creatures? Why is it a mistake to seek them elsewhere?
3. How can you ask and examine your heart to find whether it cleaves to God alone? If not, what can you do about it?

Prayer:

Gracious Lord, thank you for your many gifts to me, and for the creatures that you use to convey them to me. Help me not to seek them elsewhere. Amen.

Week Two – Tuesday

The First Commandment

Thou shalt have no other gods.

What does this mean?—Answer.

We should fear, love, and trust in God above all things.

Saul was a great king, chosen of God, and a godly man; but when he was established on his throne, and let his heart decline from God, and put his trust in his crown and power, he had to perish with all that he had, so that none even of his children remained.

David, on the other hand, was a poor, despised man, hunted down and chased, so that he nowhere felt secure of his life; yet he had to remain in spite of Saul, and become king. For these words had to abide and come true, since God cannot lie or deceive. Only let not the devil and the world deceive you with their show, which indeed remains for a time, but finally is nothing.

Let us, then, learn well the First Commandment, that we may see how God will tolerate no presumption nor any trust in any other object, and how he requires nothing higher of us than confidence from the heart for everything good, so that we may proceed right and straightforward and use all the blessings which God gives no farther than as a shoemaker uses his needle, awl, and thread for work, and then lays them aside, or as a traveler uses an inn, and food, and his bed only for temporal necessity, each one in his station, according to God's order, and without allowing any of these things to be our lord or idol. Let this suffice with respect to the First Commandment, which we have had to explain at length, since it is of chief importance, because, as before said, where the heart is rightly disposed toward God and this commandment is observed, all the others follow. [LC I.45–48]

Meditation:

1. What is the point of the contrast between Saul and David? Where did Saul go wrong? Why was it inevitable that David would become king?
2. Why is God intolerant of anything that threatens to take his place in our hearts? What is the proper use of every blessing that we receive from him?
3. Why is the First Commandment the most important one? In what sense do all the others follow from it?

Prayer:

Almighty God, preserve me from allowing the devil, the world, or my flesh to displace you as my true Lord with any gift that you have given me. Amen.

Week Two – Wednesday

The Second Commandment

Thou shalt not take the name of the Lord, thy God, in vain.

What does this mean?—Answer. We should fear and love God that we may not curse, swear, use witchcraft, lie, or deceive by his name, but call upon it in every trouble, pray, praise, and give thanks.

As the First Commandment has instructed the heart and taught faith, so this commandment leads us forth and directs the mouth and tongue to God. For the first objects that spring from the heart and manifest themselves are words. Now, as I have taught above how to answer the question, what it is to have a god, so you must learn to comprehend simply the meaning of this and all the commandments, and to apply it to yourself.

If, then, it be asked: "How do you understand the Second Commandment, or what is meant by taking in vain, or misusing, God's name?" answer briefly thus: "It is misusing God's name when we call upon the Lord God, no matter in what way, for purposes of falsehood or wrong of any kind." Therefore this commandment enjoins this much, that God's name must not be appealed to falsely, or taken upon the lips, while the heart knows well enough, or should know, differently; as among those who take oaths in court, where one side lies against the other. For God's name cannot be misused worse than for the support of falsehood and deceit. Let this remain the exact German and simplest meaning of this commandment. [LC I.50–52]

Meditation:

1. What is the connection between the First and Second Commandments? between the heart and the mouth?
2. What does it ordinarily mean to say that we did something "in vain"? How does that sense of the expression apply to our speaking of the Lord's name?
3. Besides lying under oath in court, what are some examples of calling upon God for purposes of falsehood or wrong?

Prayer:

O Lord my God, when I speak your name or even just invoke it within my mind, help me never to empty it of its meaning, but to call upon it in truth. Amen.

Week Two – Thursday

The Second Commandment

Thou shalt not take the name of the Lord, thy God, in vain.

What does this mean?—Answer. We should fear and love God that we may not curse, swear, use witchcraft, lie, or deceive by his name, but call upon it in every trouble, pray, praise, and give thanks.

From this everyone can readily infer when and in how many ways God's name is misused, although it is impossible to enumerate all its misuses. Yet, to tell it in a few words, all misuse of the divine name occurs, first, in worldly business and in matters which concern money, possessions, honor, whether it be publicly in court, in the market, or wherever else men make false oaths in God's name, or pledge their souls in any matter. And this is especially prevalent in marriage affairs, where two go and secretly betroth themselves to one another, and afterward abjure. But the greatest abuse occurs in spiritual matters, which pertain to the conscience, when false preachers rise up and offer their lying vanities as God's word.

Behold, all this is decking oneself out with God's name, or making a pretty show, or claiming to be right, whether it occur in gross, worldly business or in sublime, subtle matters of faith and doctrine. And among liars belong also blasphemers, not alone the very gross, well known to everyone, who disgrace God's name without fear (these are not for us, but for the hangman to discipline); but also those who publicly traduce the truth and God's word and consign it to the devil. Of this there is no need now to speak further.

Here, then, let us learn and take to heart the great importance of this commandment, that with all diligence we may guard against and dread every misuse of the holy name, as the greatest sin that can be outwardly committed. For to lie and deceive is in itself a great sin, but is greatly aggravated when we attempt to justify it, and seek to confirm it by invoking the name of God and using it as a cloak for shame, so that from a single lie a double lie, nay, manifold lies, result. [LC I.53–56]

Meditation:

1. In what two contexts is God's name commonly misused? Which is the greater type of abuse? Why?
2. In what sense is teaching false doctrine misusing God's name? What examples come to mind of people who claim to speak for God, but do not?
3. Do we normally think of misusing God's name as the greatest sin that can be outwardly committed? Why not?

Prayer:

God, guard my lips from speaking your name thoughtlessly or carelessly, and from claiming your authority for anything false. Amen.

Week Two – Friday

The Second Commandment

Thou shalt not take the name of the Lord, thy God, in vain.

What does this mean?—Answer. We should fear and love God that we may not curse, swear, use witchcraft, lie, or deceive by his name, but call upon it in every trouble, pray, praise, and give thanks.

For this reason, too, God has added a solemn threat to this commandment, to wit: "For the Lord will not hold him guiltless that taketh his name in vain." That is: It shall not be condoned to anyone nor pass unpunished. For as little as he will leave it unavenged if anyone turn his heart from him, as little will he suffer his name to be employed for dressing up a lie. Now, alas! it is a common calamity in all the world that there are as few who are not using the name of God for purposes of lying and all wickedness as there are those who with their heart trust alone in God.

For by nature we all have within us this beautiful virtue, to wit, that whoever has committed a wrong would like to cover up and adorn his disgrace, so that no one may see it or know it; and no one is so bold as to boast to all the world of the wickedness he has perpetrated; all wish to act by stealth and without anyone being aware of what they do. Then, if anyone be arraigned, the name of God is dragged into the affair and must make the villainy look like godliness, and the shame like honor. This is the common course of the world, which, like a great deluge, has flooded all lands. Hence we have also as our reward what we seek and deserve: pestilences, wars, famines, conflagrations, floods, wayward wives, children, and servants, and all sorts of defilement. Whence else should so much misery come? It is still a great mercy that the earth bears and supports us. [LC I.57–60]

Meditation:

1. What specific threat did God attach to the Second Commandment? What does this indicate about the seriousness of how we use his name?
2. Why is it nevertheless so common for people (including ourselves) to break this commandment, often without giving it a second thought?
3. What consequences are suggested here? Do you find it plausible to attribute so much of the evil in our world to this? Why or why not?

Prayer:

Lord, teach me always to honor and uphold your name as you have commanded. Forgive me whenever I fail to do so, deliberately or thoughtlessly. Amen.

Week Two – Saturday

The Second Commandment

Thou shalt not take the name of the Lord, thy God, in vain.

What does this mean?—Answer. We should fear and love God that we may not curse, swear, use witchcraft, lie, or deceive by his name, but call upon it in every trouble, pray, praise, and give thanks.

Therefore, above all things, our young people should have this commandment earnestly enforced upon them, and they should be trained to hold this and the First Commandment in high regard; and whenever they transgress, we must at once be after them with the rod, and hold the commandment before them, and constantly inculcate it, so as to bring them up not only with punishment, but also in the reverence and fear of God.

Thus you now understand what it is to take God's name in vain, that is (to recapitulate briefly), either simply for purposes of falsehood, and to allege God's name for something that is not so, or to curse, swear, conjure, and, in short, to practice whatever wickedness one may.

Besides this you must also know how to use the name aright. For when saying: "Thou shalt not take the name of the Lord, thy God, in vain," he gives us to understand at the same time that it is to be used properly. For it has been revealed and given to us for the very purpose that it may be of constant use and profit. Hence it is a natural inference, since using the holy name for falsehood or wickedness is here forbidden, that we are, on the other hand, commanded to employ it for truth and for all good, as when one swears truly where there is need and it is demanded. So also when there is right teaching, and when the name is invoked in trouble or praised and thanked in prosperity, etc.; all of which is comprehended summarily and commanded in the passage Psalm 50:15: "Call upon me in the day of trouble; I will deliver thee, and thou shalt glorify me." For all this is bringing it into the service of truth, and using it in a blessed way, and thus his name is hallowed, as we pray in the Lord's Prayer. [LC I.61–64]

Meditation:
1. Why is it especially important that we enforce the Second Commandment upon our young people?
2. Why do we need to recognize that it has a positive aspect, as well as a negative aspect? What is the opposite of taking God's name in vain?
3. What does it mean to call upon the name of the Lord? How is the Second Commandment connected with the Lord's Prayer?

Prayer:

Heavenly Father, thank you for giving me the privilege of calling upon your name, employing it for truth, and otherwise using it in a blessed way. Amen.

Week Three – Sunday

The Second Commandment

Thou shalt not take the name of the Lord, thy God, in vain.

What does this mean?—Answer. We should fear and love God that we may not curse, swear, use witchcraft, lie, or deceive by his name, but call upon it in every trouble, pray, praise, and give thanks.

Thus you have the sum of the entire commandment explained. And with this understanding the question with which many teachers have troubled themselves has been easily solved, to wit, why swearing is prohibited in the gospel, and yet Christ, St. Paul, and other saints often swore. The explanation is briefly this: We are not to swear in support of evil, that is, of falsehood, and where there is no need or use; but for the support of good and the advantage of our neighbor we should swear. For it is a truly good work, by which God is praised, truth and right are established, falsehood is refuted, peace is made among men, obedience is rendered, and quarrels are settled. For in this way God himself interposes and separates between right and wrong, good and evil. If one part swears falsely, he has his sentence that he shall not escape punishment, and though it be deferred a long time, he shall not succeed; so that all that he may gain thereby will slip out of his hands, and he will never enjoy it; as I have seen in the case of many who perjured themselves in their marriage vows, that they have never had a happy hour or a healthful day, and thus perished miserably in body, soul, and possessions.

Therefore I advise and exhort as before that by means of warning and threatening, restraint and punishment, the children be trained betimes to shun falsehood, and especially to avoid the use of God's name in its support. For where they are allowed to do as they please, no good will result, as is even now evident that the world is worse than it has ever been, and that there is no government, no obedience, no fidelity, no faith, but only daring, unbridled men, whom no teaching or reproof helps; all of which is God's wrath and punishment for such wanton contempt of this commandment. [LC I.65–69]

Meditation:
1. What is the key distinction between swearing that is prohibited and swearing that is permitted?
2. What are some examples of common situations when people swear, but should not have to do so? Why are we to avoid such behavior?
3. How does contempt for the Second Commandment lead to the kind of world that is described here? What can we do about it?

Prayer:

Dear Lord, help me to be the kind of person whose "yes" means "yes" and whose "no" means "no," such that swearing is unnecessary. Amen.

Week Three – Monday

The Second Commandment

Thou shalt not take the name of the Lord, thy God, in vain.

What does this mean?—Answer. We should fear and love God that we may not curse, swear, use witchcraft, lie, or deceive by his name, but call upon it in every trouble, pray, praise, and give thanks.

On the other hand, they should be constantly urged and incited to honor God's name, and to have it always upon their lips in everything that may happen to them or come to their notice. For that is the true honor of his name, to look to it and implore it for all consolation, so that (as we have heard above) first the heart by faith gives God the honor due him, and afterwards the lips by confession.

This is also a blessed and useful habit and very effectual against the devil, who is ever about us, and lies in wait to bring us into sin and shame, calamity and trouble, but who is very loath to hear God's name, and cannot remain long where it is uttered and called upon from the heart. And, indeed, many a terrible and shocking calamity would befall us if, by our calling upon his name, God did not preserve us. I have myself tried it, and learned by experience that often sudden great calamity was immediately averted and removed during such invocation. To vex the devil, I say, we should always have this holy name in our mouth, so that he may not be able to injure us as he wishes.

For this end it is also of service that we form the habit of daily commending ourselves to God, with soul and body, wife, children, servants, and all that we have, against every need that may occur; whence also the blessing and thanksgiving at meals, and other prayers, morning and evening, have originated and remain in use. [LC I.70–73]

Meditation:

1. What are some specific ways in which we can honor God's name with our lips? How can this lead to honoring God himself in our hearts?
2. What effect does calling upon God's name have on the devil? Why does this prevent him from injuring us as he wishes?
3. How can learning and reciting daily prayers (morning, evening, blessing, thanksgiving) help us cultivate the habit of commending ourselves to God?

Prayer:

Father, I commend myself, my family, and all things to you. Protect me from the devil, and help me to honor you in my heart and your name with my lips. Amen.

Week Three – Tuesday

The Second Commandment

Thou shalt not take the name of the Lord, thy God, in vain.

What does this mean?—Answer. We should fear and love God that we may not curse, swear, use witchcraft, lie, or deceive by his name, but call upon it in every trouble, pray, praise, and give thanks.

Likewise the practice of children to cross themselves when anything monstrous or terrible is seen or heard, and to exclaim: "Lord God, protect us!" "Help, dear Lord Jesus!" etc. Thus, too, if anyone meets with unexpected good fortune, however trivial, that he say: "God be praised and thanked; this God has bestowed on me!" etc., as formerly the children were accustomed to fast and pray to St. Nicholas and other saints. This would be more pleasing and acceptable to God than all monasticism and Carthusian sanctity.

Behold, thus we might train our youth, in a childlike way and playfully in the fear and honor of God, so that the First and Second Commandments might be well observed and in constant practice. Then some good might take root, spring up and bear fruit, and men grow up whom an entire land might relish and enjoy. Moreover, this would be the true way to bring up children well, as long as they can become trained with kindness and delight. For what must be enforced with rods and blows only will not develop into a good breed, and at best they will remain godly under such treatment no longer than while the rod is upon their back.

But this so spreads its roots in the heart that they fear God more than rods and clubs. This I say with such simplicity for the sake of the young, that it may penetrate their minds. For since we are preaching to children, we must also prattle with them. Thus we have prevented the abuse and have taught the right use of the divine name, which should consist not only in words, but also in practice and life, so that we may know that God is well pleased with this, and will as richly reward it as he will terribly punish the abuse. [LC I.74–77]

Meditation:

1. What kind of language do we tend to use upon seeing or hearing something monstrous or terrible? What should we say and do instead?
2. How often do we pause to praise and thank God when surprised by something good? Why would this be a good habit to develop?
3. How might we use kindness and delight to train children regarding the first two commandments, rather than always resorting to punishment?

Prayer:

Lord God, help me to delight in your commandments and recognize with thankfulness that I am in your hands under all circumstances. Amen.

Week Three – Wednesday

The Third Commandment

Thou shalt sanctify the holy day.

What does this mean?—Answer. We should fear and love God that we may not despise preaching and his word, but hold it sacred, and gladly hear and learn it.

The word *holy day* (*Feiertag*) is rendered from the Hebrew word *sabbath*, which properly signifies to rest, that is, to abstain from labor. Hence we are accustomed to say, to cease working, or sanctify the Sabbath. Now, in the Old Testament, God separated the seventh day, and appointed it for rest, and commanded that it should be regarded as holy above all others. As regards this external observance, this commandment was given to the Jews alone, that they should abstain from toilsome work, and rest, so that both man and beast might recuperate, and not be weakened by unremitting labor. Although they afterwards restricted this too closely, and grossly abused it, so that they traduced and could not endure in Christ those works which they themselves were accustomed to do on that day, as we read in the gospel; just as though the commandment were fulfilled by doing no external work whatever, which, however, was not the meaning, but, as we shall hear, that they sanctify the holy day or day of rest.

This commandment, therefore, according to its gross sense, does not concern us Christians; for it is altogether an external matter, like other ordinances of the Old Testament, which were attached to particular customs, persons, times, and places, and now have been made free through Christ. [LC I.79-82]

Meditation:
1. What was the meaning and purpose of the Sabbath day in the Old Testament? Which day of the week was it?
2. How did the Third Commandment specifically apply to the Jews? How were they observing it during the time when Jesus walked upon the earth?
3. Why do these aspects of the Third Commandment not apply to Christians? Which aspect still does apply to us today?

Prayer:

Heavenly Father, thank you for setting an example for us by resting on the seventh day. Help us to set apart the holy day accordingly. Amen.

Week Three – Thursday

The Third Commandment

Thou shalt sanctify the holy day.

What does this mean?—Answer. We should fear and love God that we may not despise preaching and his word, but hold it sacred, and gladly hear and learn it.

But to grasp a Christian meaning for the simple as to what God requires in this commandment, note that we keep holy days not for the sake of intelligent and learned Christians (for they have no need of it), but first of all for bodily causes and necessities, which nature teaches and requires; for the common people, manservants and maidservants, who have been attending to their work and trade the whole week, that for a day they may retire in order to rest and be refreshed.

Secondly, and most especially, that on such day of rest (since we can get no other opportunity) freedom and time be taken to attend divine service, so that we come together to hear and treat of God's word, and then to praise God, to sing and pray.

However, this, I say, is not so restricted to any time, as with the Jews, that it must be just on this or that day; for in itself no one day is better than another; but this should indeed be done daily; however, since the masses cannot give such attendance, there must be at least one day in the week set apart. But since from of old Sunday has been appointed for this purpose, we also should continue the same, in order that everything be done in harmonious order, and no one create disorder by unnecessary innovation. [LC I.83–85]

Meditation:

1. What two purposes are served by setting apart one day of the week? What does this suggest might happen if all days were treated the same?
2. What activities are mentioned here as especially appropriate for the day of rest? Why is it important that Christians gather regularly for worship?
3. Is there anything inherently special about Sunday? Why do most Christians continue to worship on that day?

Prayer:

Holy Lord, help me to recognize my need for weekly rest and worship. Thank you for the group of fellow believers with whom I am able to gather. Amen.

Week Three – Friday

The Third Commandment

Thou shalt sanctify the holy day.

What does this mean?—Answer. We should fear and love God that we may not despise preaching and his word, but hold it sacred, and gladly hear and learn it.

Therefore this is the simple meaning of the commandment: since holidays are observed anyhow, such observance should be devoted to hearing God's word, so that the special function of this day should be the ministry of the word for the young and the mass of poor people; yet that the resting be not so strictly interpreted as to forbid any other incidental work that cannot be avoided.

Accordingly, when asked, "What is meant by the commandment: Thou shalt sanctify the holy day?" answer: "To sanctify the holy day is the same as to keep it holy." But what is meant by keeping it holy? Nothing else than to be occupied in holy words, works, and life. For the day needs no sanctification for itself; for in itself it has been created holy. But God desires it to be holy to you. Therefore it becomes holy or unholy on your account, according as you are occupied on the same with things that are holy or unholy.

How, then, does such sanctification take place? Not in this manner, that we sit behind the stove and do no rough work, or deck ourselves with a wreath and put on our best clothes, but (as has been said) that we occupy ourselves with God's word, and exercise ourselves therein. [LC I.86–88]

Meditation:
1. What is the special function of the holy day? Why is it so important to hear God's word every week?
2. In what sense has every day been created holy in itself? What then does it mean for one day to be holy *to us*?
3. What are some specific ways of occupying ourselves with God's word? of exercising ourselves therein?

Prayer:

Almighty God, teach me to hear and learn your word on the appointed day at church, and to exercise myself in it throughout the week in every context. Amen.

Week Three – Saturday

The Third Commandment

Thou shalt sanctify the holy day.

What does this mean?—Answer. We should fear and love God that we may not despise preaching and his word, but hold it sacred, and gladly hear and learn it.

And, indeed we Christians ought always to keep such a holy day, and be occupied with nothing but holy things, i.e., daily be engaged upon God's word, and carry it in our hearts and upon our lips. But (as has been said) since we do not at all times have leisure, we must devote several hours a week for the sake of the young, or at least a day for the sake of the entire multitude, to being concerned about this alone, and especially urge the Ten Commandments, the Creed, and the Lord's Prayer, and thus direct our whole life and being according to God's word. At whatever time, then, this is being observed and practiced, there a true holy day is being kept; otherwise it shall not be called a Christians' holy day. For, indeed, non-Christians can also cease from work and be idle, just as the entire swarm of our ecclesiastics, who stand daily in the churches, singing, and ringing bells but keeping no holy day holy, because they neither preach nor practice God's word, but teach and live contrary to it.

For the word of God is the holy thing above all holy things, yea, the only one which we Christians know and have. For though we had the bones of all the saints or all holy and consecrated garments upon a heap, still that would help us nothing; for all that is a dead thing which can sanctify nobody. But God's word is the treasure which sanctifies everything, and by which even all the saints themselves were sanctified. [LC I.89–91a]

Meditation:

1. How often should we be engaged upon God's word? Why, then, is it necessary to set apart one particular day each week as holy?
2. What is it that makes any given day holy? How do many non-Christians, and even some Christians, tend to treat Sunday?
3. Why is the word of God the holy thing above all holy things? In what sense does it sanctify everything?

Prayer:

Father, help me daily to be engaged upon your word and at least weekly to be concerned about this alone, so that it sanctifies everything, including me. Amen.

Week Four – Sunday

The Third Commandment

Thou shalt sanctify the holy day.

What does this mean?—Answer. We should fear and love God that we may not despise preaching and his word, but hold it sacred, and gladly hear and learn it.

At whatever hour, then, God's word is taught, preached, heard, read, or meditated upon, there the person, day, and work are sanctified thereby, not because of the external work, but because of the word, which makes saints of us all. Therefore I constantly say that all our life and work must be ordered according to God's word, if it is to be God-pleasing or holy. Where this is done, this commandment is in force and being fulfilled.

On the contrary, any observance or work that is practiced without God's word is unholy before God, no matter how brilliantly it may shine, even though it be covered with relics, such as the fictitious spiritual orders, which know nothing of God's word and seek holiness in their own works.

Note, therefore, that the force and power of this commandment lies not in the resting, but in the sanctifying, so that to this day belongs a special holy exercise. For other works and occupations are not properly called holy exercises, unless the man himself be first holy. But here a work is to be done by which man is himself made holy, which is done (as we have heard) alone through God's word. For this, then, fixed places, times, persons, and the entire external order of worship have been created and appointed, so that it may be publicly in operation. [LC I.91b–94]

Meditation:

1. What are five specific ways in which God's word is used to sanctify people, days, and work? How often do you experience each of them?
2. In what sense does the word make saints of us all? What are the implications of this for our life and work?
3. What is the fundamental purpose for conducting worship at certain times and places? What are we missing when we choose not to attend?

Prayer:

Lord God, thank you for teachers, preachers, readers, writers, and thinkers who share your word with me and others, so that we may be made holy by it. Amen.

Week Four – Monday

The Third Commandment

Thou shalt sanctify the holy day.

What does this mean?—Answer. We should fear and love God that we may not despise preaching and his word, but hold it sacred, and gladly hear and learn it.

Since, therefore, so much depends upon God's word that without it no holy day can be sanctified, we must know that God insists upon a strict observance of this commandment, and will punish all who despise his word and are not willing to hear and learn it, especially at the time appointed for the purpose.

Therefore not only those sin against this commandment who grossly misuse and desecrate the holy day, as those who on account of their greed or frivolity neglect to hear God's word or lie in taverns and are dead drunk like swine; but also that other crowd, who listen to God's word as to any other trifle, and only from custom come to preaching, and go away again, and at the end of the year know as little of it as at the beginning. For hitherto the opinion prevailed that you had properly hallowed Sunday when you had heard a Mass or the Gospel read; but no one cared for God's word, as also no one taught it. Now, while we have God's word, we nevertheless do not correct the abuse; we suffer ourselves to be preached to and admonished, but we listen without seriousness and care.

Know, therefore, that you must be concerned not only about hearing, but also about learning and retaining it in memory, and do not think that it is optional with you or of no great importance, but that it is God's commandment, who will require of you how you have heard, learned, and honored his word. [LC I.95–98]

Meditation:
1. What would it mean to despise God's word? How would this manifest in someone's behavior?
2. Why is it necessary not only to attend worship, but also to listen carefully and learn God's word? What difference should it make in our lives?
3. Why is it advisable to memorize God's word? What are some ways in which you could go about doing so?

Prayer:

Dear Lord, forgive me for not always attending to your word, even when I am present at a worship service. Help me always to listen and learn. Amen.

Week Four – Tuesday

The Third Commandment

Thou shalt sanctify the holy day.

What does this mean?—Answer. We should fear and love God that we may not despise preaching and his word, but hold it sacred, and gladly hear and learn it.

Likewise those fastidious spirits are to be reproved who, when they have heard a sermon or two, find it tedious and dull, thinking that they know all that well enough, and need no more instruction. For just that is the sin which has been hitherto reckoned among mortal sins, and is called *akadia*, i.e., torpor or satiety, a malignant, dangerous plague with which the devil bewitches and deceives the hearts of many, that he may surprise us and secretly withdraw God's word from us.

For let me tell you this, even though you know it perfectly and be already master in all things: still you are daily in the dominion of the devil, who ceases neither day nor night to steal unawares upon you, to kindle in your heart unbelief and wicked thoughts against the foregoing and all the commandments. Therefore you must always have God's word in your heart, upon your lips, and in your ears. But where the heart is idle, and the word does not sound, he breaks in and has done the damage before we are aware. On the other hand, such is the efficacy of the word, whenever it is seriously contemplated, heard, and used, that it is bound never to be without fruit, but always awakens new understanding, pleasure, and devoutness, and produces a pure heart and pure thoughts. For these words are not inoperative or dead, but creative, living words. And even though no other interest or necessity impel us, yet this ought to urge everyone thereunto, because thereby the devil is put to flight and driven away, and, besides, this commandment is fulfilled, and is more pleasing to God than any work of hypocrisy, however brilliant. [LC I.99–102]

Meditation:
1. Why is it tempting for long-time Christians to think that they have mastered everything that they need to know? Why is this never really the case?
2. What danger lurks for those who become content with their knowledge? What is the only antidote?
3. How is God's word described here? How have you personally experienced its efficacy, fruitfulness, creativity, and life?

Prayer:

Heavenly Father, I praise you that your word is living and active. Make it part of my daily life, so that it bears fruit in me and the devil is put to flight. Amen.

Week Four – Wednesday

The Fourth Commandment

Thou shalt honor thy father and thy mother.

What does this mean?—Answer. We should fear and love God that we may not despise nor anger our parents and masters, but give them honor, serve, obey, and hold them in love and esteem.

Thus far we have learned the first three commandments, which relate to God. First, that with our whole heart we trust in him, and fear and love him throughout all our life. Secondly, that we do not misuse his holy name in the support of falsehood or any bad work, but employ it to the praise of God and the profit and salvation of our neighbor and ourselves. Thirdly, that on holidays and when at rest we diligently treat and urge God's word, so that all our actions and our entire life be ordered according to it. Now follow the other seven, which relate to our neighbor, among which this is the first and greatest. . . .

To this estate of fatherhood and motherhood God has given the special distinction above all estates that are beneath it that he not simply commands us to love our parents, but to honor them. For with respect to brothers, sisters, and our neighbors in general he commands nothing higher than that we love them, so that he separates and distinguishes father and mother above all other persons upon earth, and places them at his side. For it is a far higher thing to honor than to love one, inasmuch as it comprehends not only love, but also modesty, humility, and deference as to a majesty there hidden, and requires not only that they be addressed kindly and with reverence, but, most of all, that both in heart and with the body we so act as to show that we esteem them very highly, and that, next to God, we regard them as the very highest. For one whom we are to honor from the heart we must truly regard as high and great. [LC I.103, 105–7]

Meditation:
1. To whom do the first three commandments relate? What about the other seven? How does the Fourth Commandment serve as the transition?
2. In what sense is parenthood the highest of all estates? What does God uniquely command regarding our parents? Why?
3. In addition to love, what does honoring someone require? What are some specific ways of showing that we esteem our parents very highly?

Prayer:

Lord God, thank you for your very first gifts to me, my father and mother, by whom you conceived me and brought me into the world. Amen.

Week Four – Thursday

The Fourth Commandment

Thou shalt honor thy father and thy mother.

What does this mean?—Answer. We should fear and love God that we may not despise nor anger our parents and masters, but give them honor, serve, obey, and hold them in love and esteem.

We must, therefore, impress it upon the young that they should regard their parents as in God's stead, and remember that however lowly, poor, frail, and queer they may be, nevertheless they are father and mother given them by God. They are not to be deprived of their honor because of their conduct or their failings. Therefore we are not to regard their persons, how they may be, but the will of God who has thus created and ordained. In other respects we are, indeed, all alike in the eyes of God; but among us there must necessarily be such inequality and ordered difference, and therefore God commands it to be observed, that you obey me as your father, and that I have the supremacy.

Learn, therefore, first, what is the honor towards parents required by this commandment, to wit, that they be held in distinction and esteem above all things, as the most precious treasure on earth. Furthermore, that also in our words we observe modesty toward them, do not accost them roughly, haughtily, and defiantly, but yield to them and be silent, even though they go too far. Thirdly, that we show them such honor also by works, that is, with our body and possessions, that we serve them, help them, and provide for them when they are old, sick, infirm, or poor, and all that not only gladly, but with humility and reverence, as doing it before God. For he who knows how to regard them in his heart will not allow them to suffer want or hunger, but will place them above him and at his side, and will share with them whatever he has and possesses. [LC I.108–11]

Meditation:

1. Why should we regard our parents as in God's stead? Who placed them into that role in our lives?
2. What kinds of conduct or failings on our parents' part make it difficult for us to honor them? What are some ways in which they can go too far?
3. How can we show our parents honor by works? What should we be willing to share with them as needed?

Prayer:

Heavenly Father, it is not always easy to honor my earthly parents as I should. Forgive me when I fail to do so, and help me to do better. Amen.

Week Four – Friday

The Fourth Commandment

Thou shalt honor thy father and thy mother.

What does this mean?—Answer. We should fear and love God that we may not despise nor anger our parents and masters, but give them honor, serve, obey, and hold them in love and esteem.

Secondly, notice how great, good, and holy a work is here assigned children, which is, alas! utterly neglected and disregarded, and no one perceives that God has commanded it, or that it is a holy, divine word and doctrine. For if it had been regarded as such, everyone could have inferred that they must be holy men who live according to these words. Thus there would have been no need of inventing monasticism nor spiritual orders, but every child would have abided by this commandment, and could have directed his conscience to God and said: "If I am to do good and holy works, I know of none better than to render all honor and obedience to my parents, because God has himself commanded it. For what God commands must be much and far nobler than everything that we may devise ourselves; and since there is no higher or better teacher to be found than God, there can be no better doctrine, indeed, than he gives forth. Now, he teaches fully what we should do if we wish to perform truly good works; and by commanding them, he shows that they please him. If, then, it is God who commands this, and who knows not how to appoint anything better, I will never improve upon it."

Behold, in this manner we would have had a godly child properly taught, reared in true blessedness, and kept at home in obedience to his parents and in their service, so that men should have had blessing and joy from the spectacle. However, God's commandment was not permitted to be thus commended, but had to be neglected and trampled underfoot, so that a child could not lay it to heart, and meanwhile gaped at the devices which we set up, without once giving reverence to God. [LC I.112–14]

Meditation:
1. What is the great, good, and holy work that the Fourth Commandment assigns to children?
2. Why are we tempted to invent our own ways of trying to please God, rather than simply doing as he has told us?
3. How does society benefit when children are properly taught, reared in true blessedness, and kept at home in obedience and service to their parents?

Prayer:

Dear Lord, help me always to remember that I am your child, and that I am my parents' child, so that I seek to please you by honoring them. Amen.

Week Four – Saturday

The Fourth Commandment

Thou shalt honor thy father and thy mother.

What does this mean?—Answer. We should fear and love God that we may not despise nor anger our parents and masters, but give them honor, serve, obey, and hold them in love and esteem.

Let us, therefore, learn at last, for God's sake, that, placing all other things out of sight, our youths look first to this commandment, if they wish to serve God with truly good works, that they do what is pleasing to their fathers and mothers, or to those to whom they may be subject in their stead. For every child that knows and does this has, in the first place, this great consolation in his heart, that he can joyfully say and boast (in spite of and against all who are occupied with works of their own choice): "Behold, this work is well pleasing to my God in heaven, that I know for certain." Let them all come together with their many great, distressing, and difficult works and make their boast; we will see whether they can show one that is greater and nobler than obedience to father and mother, to whom God has appointed and commanded obedience next to his own majesty; so that if God's word and will are in force and being accomplished, nothing shall be esteemed higher than the will and word of parents; yet so that it, too, is subordinated to obedience toward God and is not opposed to the preceding commandments.

Therefore you should be heartily glad and thank God that he has chosen you and made you worthy to do a work so precious and pleasing to him. Only see that, although it be regarded as the most humble and despised, you esteem it great and precious, not on account of our worthiness, but because it is comprehended in, and controlled by, the jewel and sanctuary, namely, the word and commandment of God. [LC I.115–17]

Meditation:
1. Where should youths look first if they wish to serve God with truly good works? Why?
2. Under what circumstances would children be subject to someone instead of their parents? Is there anyone whom you should honor accordingly?
3. Why is it comforting to know that honoring our parents is pleasing to God? How might this help us do so more consistently?

Prayer:

Lord God, thank you for giving me your word and commandments so that I know exactly what is pleasing to you. Help me to live accordingly. Amen.

Week Five – Sunday

The Fourth Commandment

Thou shalt honor thy father and thy mother.

What does this mean?—Answer. We should fear and love God that we may not despise nor anger our parents and masters, but give them honor, serve, obey, and hold them in love and esteem.

Oh, what a high price would all Carthusians, monks, and nuns pay, if in all their religious doings they could bring into God's presence a single work done by virtue of his commandment, and be able before his face to say with joyful heart: "Now I know that this work is well pleasing to thee." Where will these poor wretched persons hide when in the sight of God and all the world they shall blush with shame before a young child who has lived according to this commandment, and shall have to confess that with their whole life they are not worthy to give it a drink of water? And it serves them right for their devilish perversion in treading God's commandment underfoot that they must vainly torment themselves with works of their own device, and, in addition, have scorn and loss for their reward.

Should not the heart, then, leap and melt for joy when going to work and doing what is commanded, saying: Lo, this is better than all holiness of the Carthusians, even though they kill themselves fasting and praying upon their knees without ceasing? For here you have a sure text and a divine testimony that he has enjoined this; but concerning the other he did not command a word. But this is the plight and miserable blindness of the world that no one believes these things; to such an extent the devil has deceived us with false holiness and the glamour of our own works. [LC I.118–20]

Meditation:
1. Why do you suppose that Carthusians, monks, and nuns were not able to be certain that the works they typically did were pleasing to God?
2. What are some contemporary examples of doing something to please God that he has not actually commanded?
3. Why should we always be joyful when going to work and doing what God has commanded? What hinders us from having such an attitude?

Prayer:

God Almighty, thank you for revealing your commands to us, so that we need not invent our own ways of pleasing you. Give us joy in obeying them. Amen.

Week Five – Monday

The Fourth Commandment

Thou shalt honor thy father and thy mother.

What does this mean?—Answer. We should fear and love God that we may not despise nor anger our parents and masters, but give them honor, serve, obey, and hold them in love and esteem.

Therefore I would be very glad (I say it again) if men would open their eyes and ears, and take this to heart, lest some time we may again be led astray from the pure word of God to the lying vanities of the devil. Then, too, all would be well; for parents would have more joy, love, friendship, and concord in their houses; thus the children could captivate their parents' hearts. On the other hand, when they are obstinate, and will not do what they ought until a rod is laid upon their back, they anger both God and their parents, whereby they deprive themselves of this treasure and joy of conscience, and lay up for themselves only misfortune. Therefore, as everyone complains, the course of the world now is such that both young and old are altogether dissolute and beyond control, have no reverence nor sense of honor, do nothing except as they are driven to it by blows, and perpetrate what wrong and detraction they can behind each other's back; therefore God also punishes them, that they sink into all kinds of filth and misery. As a rule, the parents, too, are themselves stupid and ignorant; one fool trains another, and as they have lived, so live their children after them. [LC I.121–24]

Meditation:
1. What are some lying vanities of the devil that have taken hold in our society? How can we counteract them with the pure word of God?
2. What are the benefits for both parents and children of obeying the Fourth Commandment? What are the consequences of disobeying it?
3. Why do children tend to live in accordance with the example set by their parents? What responsibility does this entail for parents?

Prayer:
Father, open my eyes to the lying vanities of the devil, the world, and my flesh. Help me to overcome them by always clinging to your pure word. Amen.

Week Five – Tuesday

The Fourth Commandment

Thou shalt honor thy father and thy mother.

What does this mean?—Answer. We should fear and love God that we may not despise nor anger our parents and masters, but give them honor, serve, obey, and hold them in love and esteem.

This, now, I say should be the first and most important consideration to urge us to the observance of this commandment; on which account, even if we had no father and mother, we ought to wish that God would set up wood and stone before us, whom we might call father and mother. How much more, since he has given us living parents, should we rejoice to show them honor and obedience, because we know it is so highly pleasing to the Divine Majesty and to all angels, and vexes all devils, and is, besides, the highest work which we can do, after the sublime divine worship comprehended in the previous commandments; so that giving of alms and every other good work toward our neighbor are not equal to this. For God has assigned this estate the highest place, yea, has set it up in his own stead, upon earth. This will and pleasure of God ought to be a sufficient reason and incentive to us to do what we can with good will and pleasure.

Besides this, it is our duty before the world to be grateful for benefits and every good which we have of our parents. But here again the devil rules in the world, so that the children forget their parents, as we all forget God, and no one considers how God nourishes, protects, and defends us, and bestows so much good on body and soul; especially when an evil hour comes, we are angry and grumble with impatience, and all the good which we have received throughout our life is wiped out. Just so we do also with our parents, and there is no child that understands and considers this, except the Holy Ghost grant him this grace. [LC I.125–28]

Meditation:
1. Why is it such a blessing to have a father and a mother? What challenges does a child face when one or the other (or both) is absent?
2. Why is honoring and obeying one's parents so highly pleasing to the Divine Majesty and all angels? Why is it so vexing to all devils?
3. What should our attitude be regarding our parents and all that they have done for us? Why do we so easily forget this?

Prayer:

God in heaven, thank you for all that you have given me, especially through my parents. Forgive me for not always being as grateful as I should be. Amen.

Week Five – Wednesday

The Fourth Commandment

Thou shalt honor thy father and thy mother.

What does this mean?—Answer. We should fear and love God that we may not despise nor anger our parents and masters, but give them honor, serve, obey, and hold them in love and esteem.

God knows very well this perverseness of the world; therefore he admonishes and urges by commandments that everyone consider what his parents have done for him, and he will find that he has from them body and life, moreover, that he has been fed and reared when otherwise he would have perished a hundred times in his own filth. Therefore it is a true and good saying of old and wise men: To God, to parents, and to teachers we can never render sufficient gratitude and compensation. He that regards and considers this will indeed without compulsion do all honor to his parents, and bear them up on his hands as those through whom God has done him all good.

Over and above all this, another great reason that should incite us the more is that God attaches to this commandment a temporal promise and says: That thou mayest live long upon the land which the Lord, thy God, giveth thee.

Here you can see yourself how much God is in earnest in respect to this commandment, inasmuch as he not only declares that it is well pleasing to him, and that he has joy and delight therein; but also that it shall be for our prosperity and promote our highest good; so that we may have a pleasant and agreeable life, furnished with every good thing. Therefore also St. Paul greatly emphasizes the same and rejoices in it when he says, Ephesians 6:2-3: "This is the first commandment with a promise: That it may be well with thee, and thou mayest live long on the earth." For although the rest also have their promises contained in them, yet in none is it so plainly and explicitly stated. [LC I.129-33]

Meditation:

1. What are some ways in which the world discourages children from honoring their parents? How can we counteract them?
2. Besides God and our parents, to whom can we never render sufficient gratitude and compensation? Why?
3. What specific promise did God attach to the Fourth Commandment? What is the connection between honoring parents and living long?

Prayer:

Lord, thank you for my parents and for all my teachers over the years. Help me to be properly grateful for them, and to express that gratitude to them. Amen.

The Lutheran Catechism

Week Five – Thursday

The Fourth Commandment

Thou shalt honor thy father and thy mother.

What does this mean?—Answer. We should fear and love God that we may not despise nor anger our parents and masters, but give them honor, serve, obey, and hold them in love and esteem.

Here, then, you have the fruit and the reward, that whoever observes this commandment shall have happy days, fortune, and prosperity; and on the other hand, the punishment, that whoever is disobedient shall the sooner perish, and never enjoy life. For to have long life in the sense of the Scriptures is not only to become old, but to have everything which belongs to long life, such as health, wife and children, livelihood, peace, good government, etc., without which this life can neither be enjoyed in cheerfulness nor long endure. If, therefore, you will not obey father and mother and submit to their discipline, then obey the hangman; if you will not obey him, then submit to the skeleton man, i.e., death. For on this God insists peremptorily: Either if you obey him, rendering love and service, he will reward you abundantly with all good, or if you offend him, he will send upon you both death and the hangman.

Whence come so many knaves that must daily be hanged, beheaded, broken upon the wheel, but from disobedience, because they will not submit to discipline in kindness, so that, by the punishment of God, they bring it about that we behold their misfortune and grief? For it seldom happens that such perverse people die a natural or timely death.

But the godly and obedient have this blessing, that they live long in pleasant quietness, and see their children's children (as said above) to the third and fourth generation. [LC I.134–37]

Meditation:
1. Why is observing the Fourth Commandment generally conducive to happy days, fortune, and prosperity?
2. Are these outcomes absolutely guaranteed to all people who seek to honor their parents? Why not?
3. What tends to happen to those who routinely disobey their parents when they become adults? Why?

Prayer:

Father, you desire my obedience for my own good. Help me to honor my parents and other authorities. Bless all who do so, as you have promised. Amen.

Week Five – Friday

The Fourth Commandment

Thou shalt honor thy father and thy mother.

What does this mean?—Answer. We should fear and love God that we may not despise nor anger our parents and masters, but give them honor, serve, obey, and hold them in love and esteem.

Thus experience also teaches that where there are honorable, old families who fare well and have many children, they owe their origin to the fact, to be sure, that some of them were brought up well and were regardful of their parents. On the other hand, it is written of the wicked, Psalm 109:13: "Let his posterity be cut off; and in the generation following let their name be blotted out." Therefore heed well how great a thing in God's sight obedience is, since he so highly esteems it, is so highly pleased with it, and rewards it so richly, and besides enforces punishment so rigorously on those who act contrariwise.

All this I say that it may be well impressed upon the young. For no one believes how necessary this commandment is, although it has not been esteemed and taught hitherto under the papacy. These are simple and easy words, and everybody thinks he knew them afore; therefore men pass them lightly by, are gaping after other matters, and do not see and believe that God is so greatly offended if they be disregarded, nor that one does a work so well pleasing and precious if he follows them. [LC I.138–40]

Meditation:
1. What does experience teach about families that fare well and have many children? Have you found this to be true in your own experience?
2. What do you think about the modern trend toward smaller families? How well do children generally honor their parents today?
3. Why is it tempting to pass lightly by the simple truths that we have already learned? Why is it important to revisit them over and over again?

Prayer:

Lord God, thank you for the blessings of parents and children. Help us to keep studying your word carefully, no matter how familiar it might become. Amen.

Week Five – Saturday

The Fourth Commandment

Thou shalt honor thy father and thy mother.

What does this mean?—Answer. We should fear and love God that we may not despise nor anger our parents and masters, but give them honor, serve, obey, and hold them in love and esteem.

In this commandment belongs a further statement regarding all kinds of obedience to persons in authority who have to command and to govern. For all authority flows and is propagated from the authority of parents. For where a father is unable alone to educate his child, he employs a schoolmaster to instruct him; if he be too weak, he enlists the aid of his friends and neighbors; if he departs this life, he delegates and confers his authority and government upon others who are appointed for the purpose. Likewise, he must have domestics, manservants and maidservants, under himself for the management of the household, so that all whom we call masters are in the place of parents and must derive their power and authority to govern from them. Hence also they are all called fathers in the Scriptures, as those who in their government perform the functions of a father, and should have a paternal heart toward their subordinates. As also from antiquity the Romans and other nations called the masters and mistresses of the household housefathers and housemothers. So also they called their national rulers and overlords fathers of the entire country, for a great shame to us who would be Christians that we do not likewise call them so, or, at least, do not esteem and honor them as such. [LC I.141–42]

Meditation:
1. What is the basis of all earthly authority? What are the implications of this for keeping the Fourth Commandment?
2. What are some other authorities, besides our parents, that we are required to honor? How are they similar to and different from parents?
3. What would change about our attitudes and actions toward supervisors, government officials, and so forth if we thought of them more like parents?

Prayer:

Almighty God, you rule the universe yet invite us to call you Father. Help us to honor all authorities that you place over us as we honor our parents. Amen.

Week Six – Sunday

The Fourth Commandment

Thou shalt honor thy father and thy mother.

What does this mean?—Answer. We should fear and love God that we may not despise nor anger our parents and masters, but give them honor, serve, obey, and hold them in love and esteem.

Now, what a child owes to father and mother, the same owe all who are embraced in the household. Therefore manservants and maidservants should be careful not only to be obedient to their masters and mistresses, but also to honor them as their own fathers and mothers, and to do everything which they know is expected of them, not from compulsion and with reluctance, but with pleasure and joy for the cause just mentioned, namely, that it is God's command and is pleasing to him above all other works. Therefore they ought rather to pay wages in addition and be glad that they may obtain masters and mistresses to have such joyful consciences and to know how they may do truly golden works; a matter which has hitherto been neglected and despised, when, instead, everybody ran, in the devil's name, into convents or to pilgrimages and indulgences, with loss and with an evil conscience.

If this truth, then, could be impressed upon the poor people, a servant-girl would leap and praise and thank God; and with her tidy work for which she receives support and wages she would acquire such a treasure as all that are esteemed the greatest saints have not obtained. Is it not an excellent boast to know and say that, if you perform your daily domestic task, this is better than all the sanctity and ascetic life of monks? And you have the promise, in addition, that you shall prosper in all good and fare well. How can you lead a more blessed or holier life as far as your works are concerned? For in the sight of God faith is what really renders a person holy, and alone serves him, but the works are for the service of man. There you have everything good, protection and defense in the Lord, a joyful conscience and a gracious God besides, who will reward you a hundredfold, so that you are even a nobleman if you be only pious and obedient. But if not, you have, in the first place, nothing but the wrath and displeasure of God, no peace of heart, and afterwards all manner of plagues and misfortunes. [LC I.143–48]

Meditation:

1. How should servants behave toward their masters? What is the application of this to the modern employee-employer relationship?
2. Why is performing our daily domestic tasks better than all the sanctity and ascetic life of monks? What specific vocations are you living out right now?
3. What renders a person holy in the sight of God? For whose benefit, then, do we do good works?

Prayer:

Dear Lord, thank you for the roles to which you have called me at this time in my life. Help me to find joy in serving my neighbors in them. Amen.

Week Six – Monday

The Fourth Commandment

Thou shalt honor thy father and thy mother.

What does this mean?—Answer. We should fear and love God that we may not despise nor anger our parents and masters, but give them honor, serve, obey, and hold them in love and esteem.

Whoever will not be influenced by this and inclined to godliness we hand over to the hangman and to the skeleton man. Therefore let everyone who allows himself to be advised remember that God is not making sport, and know that it is God who speaks with you and demands obedience. If you obey him, you are his dear child; but if you despise to do it, then take shame, misery, and grief for your reward.

The same also is to be said of obedience to civil government, which (as we have said) is all embraced in the estate of fatherhood and extends farthest of all relations. For here the father is not one of a single family, but of as many people as he has tenants, citizens, or subjects. For through them, as through our parents, God gives to us food, house and home, protection and security. Therefore, since they bear such name and title with all honor as their highest dignity, it is our duty to honor them and to esteem them great as the dearest treasure and the most precious jewel upon earth.

He, now, who is obedient here, is willing and ready to serve, and cheerfully does all that pertains to honor, knows that he is pleasing God and that he will receive joy and happiness for his reward. If he will not do it in love, but despises and resists or rebels, let him also know, on the other hand, that he shall have no favor nor blessing, and where he thinks to gain a florin thereby, he will elsewhere lose ten times as much, or become a victim to the hangman, perish by war, pestilence, and famine, or experience no good in his children, and be obliged to suffer injury, injustice, and violence at the hands of his servants, neighbors, or strangers and tyrants; so that what we seek and deserve is paid back and comes home to us. [LC I.149–51]

Meditation:

1. What role do civil authorities have in enforcing the Fourth Commandment? Why is it so important that we take it seriously?
2. What are some examples of things that God provides to us through our parents and other authorities? How should we respond accordingly?
3. With what attitude should we obey the authorities that God has placed over us? What do we risk otherwise?

Prayer:

Father, teach me to recognize the good gifts that you provide through parents and other authorities. Give me joy in obeying and serving them. Amen.

Week Six – Tuesday

The Fourth Commandment

Thou shalt honor thy father and thy mother.

What does this mean?—Answer. We should fear and love God that we may not despise nor anger our parents and masters, but give them honor, serve, obey, and hold them in love and esteem.

If we would ever suffer ourselves to be persuaded that such works are pleasing to God and have so rich a reward, we would be established in altogether abundant possessions and have what our heart desires. But because the word and command of God are so lightly esteemed, as though some babbler had spoken it, let us see whether you are the man to oppose him. How difficult, do you think, it will be for him to recompense you! Therefore you would certainly live much better with the divine favor, peace, and happiness than with his displeasure and misfortune. Why, think you, is the world now so full of unfaithfulness, disgrace, calamity, and murder, but because everyone desires to be his own master and free from the emperor, to care nothing for anyone, and do what pleases him? Therefore God punishes one knave by another, so that, when you defraud and despise your master, another comes and deals in like manner with you, yea, in your household you must suffer ten times more from wife, children, or servants.

Indeed, we feel our misfortune, we murmur and complain of unfaithfulness, violence, and injustice, but will not see that we ourselves are knaves who have fully deserved this punishment, and yet are not thereby reformed. We will have no favor and happiness, therefore it is but fair that we have nothing but misfortune without mercy. There must still be somewhere upon earth some godly people because God continues to grant us so much good! On our own account we should not have a farthing in the house nor a straw in the field. All this I have been obliged to urge with so many words, in hope that someone may take it to heart, that we may be relieved of the blindness and misery in which we are steeped so deeply, and may truly understand the word and will of God, and earnestly accept it. For thence we would learn how we could have joy, happiness, and salvation enough, both temporal and eternal. [LC I.152–57]

Meditation:

1. What kinds of rewards are associated with obeying the Fourth Commandment? Why?
2. What kinds of punishments are associated with disobeying the Fourth Commandment? Why?
3. Why are we tempted to pursue joy, happiness, and salvation in our own ways rather than God's? What is the outcome when we do so?

Prayer:

Lord, thank you for granting me so much good, despite my tendency to seek it apart from you. Help me to understand and accept your word and will. Amen.

Week Six – Wednesday

The Fourth Commandment

Thou shalt honor thy father and thy mother.

What does this mean?—Answer. We should fear and love God that we may not despise nor anger our parents and masters, but give them honor, serve, obey, and hold them in love and esteem.

Thus we have two kinds of fathers presented in this commandment, fathers in blood and fathers in office, or those to whom belongs the care of the family, and those to whom belongs the care of the country. Besides these there are yet spiritual fathers; not like those in the papacy, who have indeed had themselves called thus, but have performed no function of the paternal office. For those only are called spiritual fathers who govern and guide us by the word of God; as St. Paul boasts his fatherhood 1 Corinthians 4:15, where he says: "In Christ Jesus I have begotten you through the gospel." Now, since they are fathers, they are entitled to their honor, even above all others. But here it is bestowed least; for the way which the world knows for honoring them is to drive them out of the country and to grudge them a piece of bread, and, in short, they must be (as says St. Paul, 1 Corinthians 4:13) as the filth of the world and everybody's refuse and foot rag.

Yet there is need that this also be urged upon the populace, that those who would be Christians are under obligation in the sight of God to esteem them worthy of double honor who minister to their souls, that they deal well with them and provide for them. For that, God is willing to add to you sufficient blessing and will not let you come to want. But in this matter everyone refuses and resists, and all are afraid that they will perish from bodily want, and cannot now support one respectable preacher, where formerly they filled ten fat paunches. In this we also deserve that God deprive us of his word and blessing, and again allow preachers of lies to arise to lead us to the devil, and, in addition, to drain our sweat and blood. [LC I.158–63]

Meditation:

1. What three kinds of fathers are included in the Fourth Commandment? What is the primary role of our spiritual fathers?
2. Who have been your spiritual fathers during the course of your life? Who are your spiritual fathers right now?
3. What are some specific ways in which we can honor our spiritual fathers? Why does the world resist doing so?

Prayer:

Heavenly Father, thank you for giving me spiritual fathers to govern and guide me by your word. Help me to esteem them worthy of double honor. Amen.

Week Six – Thursday

The Fourth Commandment

Thou shalt honor thy father and thy mother.

What does this mean?—Answer. We should fear and love God that we may not despise nor anger our parents and masters, but give them honor, serve, obey, and hold them in love and esteem.

But those who keep in sight God's will and commandment have the promise that everything which they bestow upon temporal and spiritual fathers, and whatever they do to honor them, shall be richly recompensed to them, so that they shall have, not bread, clothing, and money for a year or two, but long life, support, and peace, and shall be eternally rich and blessed. Therefore only do what is your duty, and let God take care how he is to support you and provide for you sufficiently. Since he has promised it, and has never yet lied, he will not be found lying to you.

This ought indeed to encourage us, and give us hearts that would melt in pleasure and love toward those to whom we owe honor, so that we would raise our hands and joyfully thank God who has given us such promises, for which we ought to run to the ends of the world. For although the whole world should combine, it could not add an hour to our life or give us a single grain from the earth. But God wishes to give you all exceeding abundantly according to your heart's desire. He who despises and casts this to the winds is not worthy ever to hear a word of God. This has now been stated more than enough for all who belong under this commandment. [LC I.164–66]

Meditation:
1. What does it mean to keep in sight God's will and commandment? What is his promise to those who do so?
2. Can the world, on its own, really extend or improve our lives? What are some specific ways in which it attempts to do so?
3. What does God wish to give us? How can we be careful to keep our heart's desire in the right place?

Prayer:

Lord, teach me your will and commandment, and give me faith in your promise. Help me to share your word and the hope that it brings with others. Amen.

Week Six – Friday

The Fourth Commandment

Thou shalt honor thy father and thy mother.

What does this mean?—Answer. We should fear and love God that we may not despise nor anger our parents and masters, but give them honor, serve, obey, and hold them in love and esteem.

In addition, it would be well to preach to the parents also, and such as bear their office, as to how they should deport themselves toward those who are committed to them for their government. For although this is not expressed in the Ten Commandments, it is nevertheless abundantly enjoined in many places in the Scripture. And God desires to have it embraced in this commandment when he speaks of father and mother. For he does not wish to have in this office and government knaves and tyrants; nor does he assign to them this honor, that is, power and authority to govern, that they should have themselves worshiped; but they should consider that they are under obligations of obedience to God; and that, first of all, they should earnestly and faithfully discharge their office, not only to support and provide for the bodily necessities of their children, servants, subjects, etc., but, most of all, to train them to the honor and praise of God. Therefore do not think that this is left to your pleasure and arbitrary will, but that it is a strict command and injunction of God, to whom also you must give account for it.

But here again the sad plight arises that no one perceives or heeds this, and all live on as though God gave us children for our pleasure or amusement, and servants that we should employ them like a cow or ass, only for work, or as though we were only to gratify our wantonness with our subjects, ignoring them, as though it were no concern of ours what they learn or how they live; and no one is willing to see that this is the command of the Supreme Majesty, who will most strictly call us to account and punish us for it; nor that there is so great need to be so seriously concerned about the young. [LC I.167–71]

Meditation:

1. What needs to be preached to parents and masters? What danger always exists for those who have power and authority to govern others?
2. What is the most important responsibility of parents and masters? What are some specific ways of training others to honor and praise God?
3. How do some parents and masters view their children and servants? Have you observed such attitudes firsthand?

Prayer:

Gracious God, when I have authority over others, help me to exercise it in accordance with your will and for their benefit, not my own. Amen.

Week Six – Saturday

The Fourth Commandment

Thou shalt honor thy father and thy mother.

What does this mean?—Answer. We should fear and love God that we may not despise nor anger our parents and masters, but give them honor, serve, obey, and hold them in love and esteem.

For if we wish to have excellent and apt persons both for civil and ecclesiastical government, we must spare no diligence, time, or cost in teaching and educating our children, that they may serve God and the world, and we must not think only how we may amass money and possessions for them. For God can indeed without us support and make them rich, as he daily does. But for this purpose he has given us children, and issued this command that we should train and govern them according to his will, else he would have no need of father and mother. Let everyone know, therefore, that it is his duty, on peril of losing the divine favor, to bring up his children above all things in the fear and knowledge of God, and if they are talented, have them learn and study something, that they may be employed for whatever need there is.

If that were done, God would also richly bless us and give us grace to train men by whom land and people might be improved, and likewise well-educated citizens, chaste and domestic wives, who afterwards would rear godly children and servants. Here consider now what deadly injury you are doing if you be negligent and fail on your part to bring up your child to usefulness and piety, and how you bring upon yourself all sin and wrath, thus earning hell by your own children, even though you be otherwise pious and holy. And because this is disregarded, God so fearfully punishes the world that there is no discipline, government, or peace, of which we all complain, but do not see that it is our fault; for as we train them, we have spoiled and disobedient children and subjects. Let this be sufficient exhortation; for to draw this out at length belongs to another time. [LC I.172–78]

Meditation:

1. What is the connection between government and parenting? How do these reinforce each other, for better or for worse?
2. What is the primary purpose of teaching and educating children? Why do many parents focus instead on improving their worldly situation?
3. What are the consequences of poor parenting? What evidence do you see of this in the world today?

Prayer:

Father, help parents to bring their children up in the fear and knowledge of God, so that they grow up to become good citizens and government officials. Amen.

Week Seven – Sunday

The Fifth Commandment

Thou shalt not kill.

What does this mean?—Answer. We should fear and love God that we may not hurt nor harm our neighbor in his body, but help and befriend him in every bodily need.

We have now completed both the spiritual and the temporal government, that is, the divine and the paternal authority and obedience. But here now we go forth from our house among our neighbors to learn how we should live with one another, everyone himself toward his neighbor. Therefore God and government are not included in this commandment, nor is the power to kill, which they have, taken away. For God has delegated his authority to punish evildoers to the government instead of parents, who aforetime (as we read in Moses) were required to bring their own children to judgment and sentence them to death. Therefore, what is here forbidden is forbidden to the individual in his relation to anyone else, and not to the government.

Now this commandment is easy enough, and has been often treated, because we hear it annually in the Gospel of St. Matthew 5:21ff, where Christ himself explains and sums it up, namely, that we must not kill, neither with hand, heart, mouth, signs, gestures, help, nor counsel. Therefore it is here forbidden to everyone to be angry, except those (as we said) who are in the place of God, that is, parents and the government. For it is proper for God and for everyone who is in a divine estate to be angry, to reprove and punish, namely, on account of those very persons who transgress this and the other commandments. [LC I.180–82]

Meditation:
1. What was the focus of the first four commandments? What will be the focus of the remaining six commandments?
2. Why does the Fifth Commandment not strictly apply to governments? Does this mean that capital punishment is always justified?
3. What are some ways in which we can break the Fifth Commandment without actually killing someone?

Prayer:

Lord, grant grace and wisdom to those whom you have given authority to punish evildoers, that they may exercise such power carefully and justly. Amen.

Week Seven – Monday

The Fifth Commandment

Thou shalt not kill.

What does this mean?—Answer. We should fear and love God that we may not hurt nor harm our neighbor in his body, but help and befriend him in every bodily need.

But the cause and need of this commandment is that God well knows that the world is evil, and that this life has much unhappiness; therefore he has placed this and the other commandments between the good and the evil. Now, as there are many assaults upon all commandments, so it happens also in this commandment that we must live among many people who do us harm, so that we have cause to be hostile to them.

As when your neighbor sees that you have a better house and home, greater possessions and fortune from God than he, he is sulky, envies you, and speaks no good of you.

Thus by the devil's incitement you will get many enemies who cannot bear to see you have any good, either bodily or spiritual. When we see such people, our hearts, in turn, would rage and bleed and take vengeance. Then there arise cursing and blows, from which follow finally misery and murder. Here, now, God like a kind father steps in ahead of us, interposes and wishes to have the quarrel settled, that no misfortune come of it, nor one destroy another. And briefly, he would hereby protect, set free, and keep in peace everyone against the crime and violence of everyone else; and would have this commandment placed as a wall, fortress, and refuge about our neighbor, that we do him no hurt nor harm in his body. [LC I.183–85]

Meditation:

1. What is the cause and need of this commandment and all the others? In what sense do God's commandments come between the good and the evil?
2. What causes hostility between neighbors? Why are God's blessings upon his people all too often viewed negatively by the world?
3. What temptation do we face when someone is against us? What does God want to happen in such situations?

Prayer:

Dear God, forgive me for sometimes having hostility toward other people. Help me, as much as it is up to me, to live at peace with everyone. Amen.

Week Seven – Tuesday

The Fifth Commandment

Thou shalt not kill.

What does this mean?—Answer. We should fear and love God that we may not hurt nor harm our neighbor in his body, but help and befriend him in every bodily need.

Thus this commandment aims at this, that no one offend his neighbor on account of any evil deed, even though he have fully deserved it. For where murder is forbidden, all cause also is forbidden whence murder may originate. For many a one, although he does not kill, yet curses and utters a wish, which would stop a person from running far if it were to strike him in the neck. Now, since this inheres in everyone by nature and it is a common practice that no one is willing to suffer at the hands of another, God wishes to remove the root and source by which the heart is embittered against our neighbor, and to accustom us ever to keep in view this commandment, always to contemplate ourselves in it as in a mirror, to regard the will of God, and with hearty confidence and invocation of his name to commit to him the wrong which we suffer. Thus we shall suffer our enemies to rage and be angry, doing what they can, and we learn to calm our wrath, and to have a patient, gentle heart, especially toward those who give us cause to be angry, that is, our enemies. [LC I.186–87]

Meditation:
1. What is the aim of the Fifth Commandment? Why does God expect us to refrain from giving our neighbors what they deserve?
2. Why is it a common practice that no one is willing to suffer at the hands of another? Why should Christians be willing to do so?
3. What does it mean to commit to God the wrong that we suffer? What effect do we hope that this will have on our enemies?

Prayer:

Dear Jesus, to spare me from what I truly deserve, you suffered much wrong at the hands of your enemies. Help me to do likewise for the sake of others. Amen.

Week Seven – Wednesday

The Fifth Commandment

Thou shalt not kill.

What does this mean?—Answer. We should fear and love God that we may not hurt nor harm our neighbor in his body, but help and befriend him in every bodily need.

Therefore the entire sum of what it means not to kill is to be impressed most explicitly upon the simpleminded. In the first place, that we harm no one, first, with our hand or by deed. Then, that we do not employ our tongue to instigate or counsel thereto. Further, that we neither use nor assent to any kind of means or methods whereby anyone may be injured. And finally, that the heart be not ill disposed toward anyone, nor from anger and hatred wish him ill, so that body and soul may be innocent in regard to everyone, but especially those who wish you evil or inflict such upon you. For to do evil to one who wishes and does you good is not human, but diabolical.

Secondly, under this commandment not only he is guilty who does evil to his neighbor, but he also who can do him good, prevent, resist evil, defend and save him, so that no bodily harm or hurt happen to him, and yet does not do it. If, therefore, you send away one that is naked when you could clothe him, you have caused him to freeze to death; if you see one suffer hunger and do not give him food, you have caused him to starve. So also, if you see anyone innocently sentenced to death or in like distress, and do not save him, although you know ways and means to do so, you have killed him. And it will not avail you to make the pretext that you did not afford any help, counsel, or aid thereto, for you have withheld your love from him and deprived him of the benefit whereby his life would have been saved. [LC I.188–90]

Meditation:
1. What are some "sins of commission" that violate the Fifth Commandment? How can our tongues and hearts become deadly weapons?
2. What are some "sins of omission" that violate the Fifth Commandment? Why is it not enough simply to refrain from doing evil to our neighbors?
3. Why is it important for Christians to avoid anger, hatred, and ill will, and instead show kindness, toward those who desire or inflict our harm?

Prayer:

Father, forgive me for harming others, as well as failing to meet their needs when given the opportunity. Help me to love them as you love me. Amen.

Week Seven – Thursday

The Fifth Commandment

Thou shalt not kill.

What does this mean?—Answer. We should fear and love God that we may not hurt nor harm our neighbor in his body, but help and befriend him in every bodily need.

Therefore God also rightly calls all those murderers who do not afford counsel and help in distress and danger of body and life, and will pass a most terrible sentence upon them in the last day, as Christ himself has announced when he shall say, Matthew 25:42f: "I was hungry, and ye gave me no meat; I was thirsty, and ye gave me no drink; I was a stranger, and ye took me not in; naked, and ye clothed me not; sick and in prison, and ye visited me not." That is: You would have suffered me and mine to die of hunger, thirst, and cold, would have suffered the wild beasts to tear us to pieces, or left us to rot in prison or perish in distress. What else is that but to reproach them as murderers and bloodhounds? For although you have not actually done all this, you have nevertheless, so far as you were concerned, suffered him to pine and perish in misfortune.

It is just as if I saw someone navigating and laboring in deep water or one fallen into fire, and could extend to him the hand to pull him out and save him, and yet refused to do it. What else would I appear, even in the eyes of the world, than as a murderer and a criminal?

Therefore it is God's ultimate purpose that we suffer harm to befall no man, but show him all good and love; and, as we have said, it is specially directed toward those who are our enemies. For to do good to our friends is but an ordinary heathen virtue, as Christ says, Matthew 5:46. [LC I.191–94]

Meditation:

1. Why does God expect us to do what we can to look out for and take care of our fellow human beings?
2. What are some specific ways in which you can feed the hungry and thirsty? welcome the stranger? clothe the naked? visit the sick and imprisoned?
3. What kinds of people do you find it especially difficult to help in these ways? How can you show all good and love to them today?

Prayer:

Lord, you love and care for me despite my many faults. Help me to do likewise toward all whom you place along the path of my life's journey. Amen.

Week Seven – Friday

The Fifth Commandment

Thou shalt not kill.

What does this mean?—Answer. We should fear and love God that we may not hurt nor harm our neighbor in his body, but help and befriend him in every bodily need.

Here we have again the word of God whereby he would encourage and urge us to true noble and sublime works, as gentleness, patience, and, in short, love and kindness to our enemies, and would ever remind us to reflect upon the First Commandment, that he is our God, that is, that he will help, assist, and protect us, in order that he may thus quench the desire of revenge in us.

This we ought to practice and inculcate, and we would have our hands full doing good works. But this would not be preaching for monks; it would greatly detract from the religious estate, and infringe upon the sanctity of Carthusians, and would even be regarded as forbidding good works and clearing the convents. For in this wise the ordinary state of Christians would be considered just as worthy, and even worthier, and everybody would see how they mock and delude the world with a false, hypocritical show of holiness, because they have given this and other commandments to the winds, and have esteemed them unnecessary, as though they were not commandments, but mere counsels; and have at the same time shamelessly proclaimed and boasted their hypocritical estate and works as the most perfect life, in order that they might lead a pleasant, easy life, without the cross and without patience, for which reason, too, they have resorted to the cloisters, so that they might not be obliged to suffer any wrong from anyone or to do him any good. But know now that these are the true, holy, and godly works, in which, with all the angels, he rejoices, in comparison with which all human holiness is but stench and filth, and, besides, deserves nothing but wrath and damnation. [LC I.195–98]

Meditation:

1. What is the link between the Fifth Commandment and the fruits of the Spirit such as gentleness, patience, love, and kindness?
2. What is the link between the Fifth Commandment and the help, assistance, and protection that God provides to us and to our neighbors?
3. Why is the ordinary estate of Christians just as worthy as, and even worthier than, the religious estate of monks and nuns?

Prayer:

Gracious God, thank you for revealing in your commandments the kinds of good works that you have prepared in advance for us to do. Help us to do them. Amen.

Week Seven – Saturday

The Sixth Commandment

Thou shalt not commit adultery.

What does this mean?—Answer. We should fear and love God that we may lead a chaste and decent life in words and deeds, and each love and honor his spouse.

These commandments now are easily understood from the preceding; for they are all to the effect that we avoid doing any kind of injury to our neighbor. But they are arranged in fine order. In the first place, they treat of his own person. Then they proceed to the person nearest him, or the closest possession next after his body, namely, his wife, who is one flesh and blood with him, so that we cannot inflict a higher injury upon him in any good that is his. Therefore it is explicitly forbidden here to bring any disgrace upon him in respect to his wife. And it really aims at adultery, because among the Jews it was ordained and commanded that everyone must be married. Therefore also the young were early provided for, so that the virgin state was held in small esteem, neither were public prostitution and lewdness tolerated (as now). Therefore adultery was the most common form of unchastity among them.

But because among us there is such a shameful mess and the very dregs of all vice and lewdness, this commandment is directed also against all manner of unchastity, whatever it may be called; and not only is the external act forbidden, but also every kind of cause, incitement, and means, so that the heart, the lips, and the whole body may be chaste and afford no opportunity, help, or persuasion to unchastity. [LC I.200–3]

Meditation:
1. What is the significance of the fact that the Sixth Commandment immediately follows the Fifth Commandment?
2. What does it mean to live a chaste and decent life in words and deeds? Why is this no longer something that our culture values and encourages?
3. What do you perceive to be the most common form of unchastity among us today? How can we cultivate a mindset that cherishes purity instead?

Prayer:

Dear Lord, help those who are married to love and respect their spouses, and those who are not married to keep their hearts and bodies pure. Amen.

Week Eight – Sunday

The Sixth Commandment

Thou shalt not commit adultery.

What does this mean?—Answer. We should fear and love God that we may lead a chaste and decent life in words and deeds, and each love and honor his spouse.

And not only this, but that we also make resistance, afford protection and rescue wherever there is danger and need; and again, that we give help and counsel, so as to maintain our neighbor's honor. For whenever you omit this when you could make resistance, or connive at it as if it did not concern you, you are as truly guilty as the one perpetrating the deed. Thus, to state it in the briefest manner, there is required this much, that everyone both live chastely himself and help his neighbor do the same, so that God by this commandment wishes to hedge round about and protect every spouse that no one trespass against them.

But since this commandment is aimed directly at the state of matrimony and gives occasion to speak of the same, you must well understand and mark, first, how gloriously God honors and extols this estate, inasmuch as by his commandment he both sanctions and guards it. He has sanctioned it above in the Fourth Commandment: "Honor thy father and thy mother"; but here he has (as we said) hedged it about and protected it. Therefore he also wishes us to honor it, and to maintain and conduct it as a divine and blessed estate; because, in the first place, he has instituted it before all others, and therefore created man and woman separately (as is evident), not for lewdness, but that they should live together, be fruitful, beget children, and nourish and train them to the honor of God. [LC I.204–7]

Meditation:

1. What are some specific ways in which we can protect and rescue our neighbors, maintain their honor, and help them live chastely?
2. Why does God honor and extol the state of marriage? What is the connection between the Fourth and Sixth Commandments?
3. Why has God created man and woman separately? How and why does the world seek to overturn this arrangement?

Prayer:

Father, thank you for establishing marriage and sustaining the family. Help me to do my part to defend these institutions for the sake of my neighbors. Amen.

Week Eight – Monday

The Sixth Commandment

Thou shalt not commit adultery.

What does this mean?—Answer. We should fear and love God that we may lead a chaste and decent life in words and deeds, and each love and honor his spouse.

Therefore God has also most richly blessed this estate above all others, and, in addition, has bestowed on it and wrapped up in it everything in the world, to the end that this estate might be well and richly provided for. Married life is therefore no jest or presumption; but it is an excellent thing and a matter of divine seriousness. For it is of the highest importance to him that persons be raised who may serve the world and promote the knowledge of God, godly living, and all virtues, to fight against wickedness and the devil.

Therefore I have always taught that this estate should not be despised nor held in disrepute, as is done by the blind world and our false ecclesiastics, but that it be regarded according to God's word, by which it is adorned and sanctified, so that it is not only placed on an equality with other estates, but that it precedes and surpasses them all, whether they be that of emperor, princes, bishops, or whoever they please. For both ecclesiastical and civil estates must humble themselves and all be found in this estate, as we shall hear. Therefore it is not a peculiar estate, but the most common and noblest estate, which pervades all Christendom, yea which extends through all the world. [LC I.208–10]

Meditation:

1. What are some specific ways in which God well and richly provides for the estate of marriage? Why is it a matter of divine seriousness?
2. What are some specific ways in which the world despises marriage and holds it in disrepute? Why are such attitudes so common?
3. Is marriage peculiar to Christianity? What does the fact that it extends through all the world suggest about it?

Prayer:

Dear God, you established marriage from the beginning. Sanctify it through your word, and teach me to value it properly, whether I am married or not. Amen.

Week Eight – Tuesday

The Sixth Commandment

Thou shalt not commit adultery.

What does this mean?—Answer. We should fear and love God that we may lead a chaste and decent life in words and deeds, and each love and honor his spouse.

In the second place, you must know also that it is not only an honorable, but also a necessary state, and it is solemnly commanded by God that, in general, in all conditions, men and women, who were created for it, shall be found in this estate; yet with some exceptions (although few) whom God has especially excepted, so that they are not fit for the married estate, or whom he has released by a high, supernatural gift that they can maintain chastity without this estate. For where nature has its course, as it is implanted by God, it is not possible to remain chaste without marriage. For flesh and blood remain flesh and blood, and the natural inclination and excitement have their course without let or hindrance, as everybody sees and feels. In order, therefore, that it may be the more easy in some degree to avoid unchastity, God has commanded the estate of matrimony, that everyone may have his proper portion and be satisfied therewith; although God's grace besides is required in order that the heart also may be pure. [LC I.211–12]

Meditation:

1. Why is the estate of marriage not only honorable, but necessary? In what sense were men and women created for it?
2. Why is a supernatural gift necessary to maintain chastity without marriage? What tends to happen otherwise?
3. Why is God's grace required to keep the heart pure even within marriage? What kinds of temptations do husbands and wives still face?

Prayer:

Lord, guard my heart so that it remains pure. Forgive my unchaste thoughts and actions, and help me to be satisfied with what you have given me. Amen.

Week Eight – Wednesday

The Sixth Commandment

Thou shalt not commit adultery.

What does this mean?—Answer. We should fear and love God that we may lead a chaste and decent life in words and deeds, and each love and honor his spouse.

From this you see how this popish rabble, priests, monks, and nuns, resist God's order and commandment, inasmuch as they despise and forbid matrimony, and presume and vow to maintain perpetual chastity, and, besides, deceive the simpleminded with lying words and appearances. For no one has so little love and inclination to chastity as just those who because of great sanctity avoid marriage, and either indulge in open and shameless prostitution, or secretly do even worse, so that one dare not speak of it, as has, alas! been learned too fully. And, in short, even though they abstain from the act, their hearts are so full of unchaste thoughts and evil lusts that there is a continual burning and secret suffering, which can be avoided in the married life. Therefore all vows of chastity out of the married state are condemned by this commandment, and free permission is granted, yea, even the command is given, to all poor ensnared consciences which have been deceived by their monastic vows, to abandon the unchaste state and enter the married life, considering that even if the monastic life were godly, it would nevertheless not be in their power to maintain chastity, and if they remain in it, they must only sin more and more against this commandment. [LC I.213–16]

Meditation:

1. What is the difference between chastity and celibacy? Why is it problematic for religious orders to require the latter, rather than the former?
2. What tends to happen to those who intentionally avoid marriage? Why is it insufficient merely to abstain from the act?
3. Why is it not in anyone's power to maintain chastity apart from marriage? What are the implications of this for those who are single?

Prayer:

Heavenly Father, whether I am married or single, help me to live in chastity; not by my own power, but by your grace, which is sufficient for me. Amen.

Week Eight – Thursday

The Sixth Commandment

Thou shalt not commit adultery.

What does this mean?—Answer. We should fear and love God that we may lead a chaste and decent life in words and deeds, and each love and honor his spouse.

Now, I speak of this in order that the young may be so guided that they conceive a liking for the married estate, and know that it is a blessed estate and pleasing to God. For in this way we might in the course of time bring it about that married life be restored to honor, and that there might be less of the filthy, dissolute, disorderly doings which now run riot the world over in open prostitution and other shameful vices arising from disregard of married life. Therefore it is the duty of parents and the government to see to it that our youth be brought up to discipline and respectability, and when they have come to years of maturity, to provide for them in the fear of God and honorably; he would not fail to add his blessing and grace, so that men would have joy and happiness from the same.

Let me now say in conclusion that this commandment demands not only that everyone live chastely in thought, word, and deed in his condition, that is, especially in the estate of matrimony, but also that everyone love and esteem the spouse given him by God. For where conjugal chastity is to be maintained, man and wife must by all means live together in love and harmony, that one may cherish the other from the heart and with entire fidelity. For that is one of the principal points which enkindle love and desire of chastity, so that, where this is found, chastity will follow as a matter of course without any command. Therefore also St. Paul so diligently exhorts husband and wife to love and honor one another. Here you have again a precious, yea, many and great good works, of which you can joyfully boast, against all ecclesiastical estates, chosen without God's word and commandment. [LC I.217–21]

Meditation:
1. Why is it important for the young to be attracted to the estate of marriage? How can parents foster this in their children?
2. What is the connection between disregard of married life and declining public morality? How is this evident in our culture today?
3. Why are loving, esteeming, cherishing, and honoring one's spouse essential aspects of chastity for those who are married?

Prayer:

Lord God, help me appreciate your gift of marriage and do what I can to guard it from the assaults of the world. Teach all spouses to cherish one another. Amen.

Week Eight – Friday

The Seventh Commandment

Thou shalt not steal.

What does this mean?—Answer. We should fear and love God that we may not take our neighbor's money or property, nor get them by false ware or dealing, but help him to improve and protect his property and business.

After your person and spouse, temporal property comes next. That also God wishes to have protected, and he has commanded that no one shall subtract from, or curtail, his neighbor's possessions. For to steal is nothing else than to get possession of another's property wrongfully, which briefly comprehends all kinds of advantage in all sorts of trade to the disadvantage of our neighbor. Now, this is indeed quite a widespread and common vice, but so little regarded and observed that it exceeds all measure, so that if all who are thieves, and yet do not wish to be called such, were to be hanged on gallows, the world would soon be devastated, and there would be a lack both of executioners and gallows. For, as we have just said, to steal is to signify not only to empty our neighbor's coffer and pockets, but to be grasping in the market, in all stores, booths, wine- and beer-cellars, workshops, and, in short, wherever there is trading or taking and giving of money for merchandise or labor. [LC I.223–24]

Meditation:

1. What does the Seventh Commandment reveal about money and property? Why does God forbid stealing?
2. How does taking advantage of someone in a business transaction amount to stealing? What is the world's view of such behavior?
3. What are some other non-obvious ways in which we can subtract from, or curtail, our neighbor's possessions?

Prayer:

Father, forgive me for sometimes grasping that which is not mine, either overtly or covertly. Help me to respect my neighbors and their property instead. Amen.

Week Eight – Saturday

The Seventh Commandment

Thou shalt not steal.

What does this mean?—Answer. We should fear and love God that we may not take our neighbor's money or property, nor get them by false ware or dealing, but help him to improve and protect his property and business.

As, for instance, to explain this somewhat grossly for the common people, that it may be seen how godly we are: When a manservant or maidservant does not serve faithfully in the house, and does damage, or allows it to be done when it could be prevented, or otherwise ruins and neglects the goods entrusted to him, from indolence, idleness, or malice, to the spite and vexation of master and mistress, and in whatever way this can be done purposely (for I do not speak of what happens from oversight and against one's will), you can in a year abscond thirty, forty florins, which if another had taken secretly or carried away, he would be hanged with the rope. But here you may even bid defiance and become insolent, and no one dare call you a thief.

The same I say also of mechanics, workmen, and day laborers, who all follow their wanton notions, and never know enough ways to overcharge people, while they are lazy and unfaithful in their work. All these are far worse than sneak thieves, against whom we can guard with locks and bolts, or who, if apprehended, are treated in such a manner that they will not do the same again. But against these no one can guard, no one dare even look awry at them or accuse them of theft, so that one would ten times rather lose from his purse. For here are my neighbors, good friends, my own servants, from whom I expect good, who defraud me first of all. [LC I.225–26]

Meditation:

1. How does the Seventh Commandment apply to employees carrying out their work? Why is it important that we serve faithfully?
2. What are some subtle ways in which we can obtain money or things that we have not actually earned from our employers?
3. What is the connection between laziness and stealing? Why is laziness widely overlooked, rather than treated as stealing?

Prayer:

Almighty God, owner and giver of all things, forgive me for taking that which you have not granted to me. Help me to be content with your provision. Amen.

Week Nine – Sunday

The Seventh Commandment

Thou shalt not steal.

What does this mean?—Answer. We should fear and love God that we may not take our neighbor's money or property, nor get them by false ware or dealing, but help him to improve and protect his property and business.

Furthermore, in the market and in common trade likewise, this practice is in full swing and force to the greatest extent, where one openly defrauds another with bad merchandise, false measures, weights, coins, and by nimbleness and queer finances or dexterous tricks takes advantage of him; likewise, when one overcharges a person in a trade and wantonly drives a hard bargain, skins and distresses him. And who can recount or think of all these things? To sum up, this is the commonest craft and the largest guild on earth, and if we regard the world throughout all conditions of life, it is nothing else than a vast, wide stall, full of great thieves.

Therefore they are also called swivel-chair robbers, land and highway robbers, not picklocks and sneak thieves who snatch away the ready cash, but who sit on the chair and are styled great noblemen, and honorable, pious citizens, and yet rob and steal under a good pretext.

Yes, here we might be silent about the trifling individual thieves if we were to attack the great, powerful arch-thieves with whom lords and princes keep company, who daily plunder not only a city or two, but all Germany. Yea, where should we place the head and supreme protector of all thieves, the holy chair at Rome with all its retinue, which has grabbed by theft the wealth of all the world, and holds it to this day? [LC I.227–30]

Meditation:

1. Are the kinds of business practices described here any less common today than they were five hundred years ago? Why not?
2. What are some creative ways in which people steal from one another? Why is it important for us to be honest in our dealings with the world?
3. Why did Luther accuse the pope of theft? What are some current examples of people who use temporal or spiritual power to gain wealth improperly?

Prayer:

Dear Lord, forgive me for sometimes taking advantage of others in my dealings with them. Help me to be honest and fair in all my worldly transactions. Amen.

Week Nine – Monday

The Seventh Commandment

Thou shalt not steal.

What does this mean?—Answer. We should fear and love God that we may not take our neighbor's money or property, nor get them by false ware or dealing, but help him to improve and protect his property and business.

This is, in short, the course of the world: whoever can steal and rob openly goes free and secure, unmolested by anyone, and even demands that he be honored. Meanwhile the little sneak thieves, who have once trespassed, must bear the shame and punishment to render the former godly and honorable. But let them know that in the sight of God they are the greatest thieves, and that he will punish them as they are worthy and deserve.

Now, since this commandment is so far reaching, as just indicated, it is necessary to urge it well and to explain it to the common people, not to let them go on in their wantonness and security, but always to place before their eyes the wrath of God, and inculcate the same. For we have to preach this not to Christians, but chiefly to knaves and scoundrels, to whom it would be more fitting for judges, jailers, or Master Hannes [the executioner] to preach. Therefore let everyone know that it is his duty, at the risk of God's displeasure, not only to do no injury to his neighbor, nor to deprive him of gain, nor to perpetrate any act of unfaithfulness or malice in any bargain or trade, but faithfully to preserve his property for him, to secure and promote his advantage, especially when one accepts money, wages, and one's livelihood for such service. [LC I.231–33]

Meditation:

1. Why is it the course of the world to allow those who steal and rob openly to go free and secure, and even to demand that they be honored?
2. Why is it an even greater sin in the sight of God to steal in more subtle ways? How can we guard ourselves against this?
3. What does it mean to secure and promote our neighbor's advantage? How is this connected with what we do for a living?

Prayer:

Dear God, you desire that I not only avoid taking what is not mine, but also work for the advantage of others. Help me to do so faithfully and cheerfully. Amen.

Week Nine – Tuesday

The Seventh Commandment

Thou shalt not steal.

What does this mean?—Answer. We should fear and love God that we may not take our neighbor's money or property, nor get them by false ware or dealing, but help him to improve and protect his property and business.

He now who wantonly despises this may indeed pass along and escape the hangman, but he shall not escape the wrath and punishment of God; and when he has long practiced his defiance and arrogance, he shall yet remain a tramp and beggar, and, in addition, have all plagues and misfortune. Now you are going your way while you ought to preserve the property of your master and mistress, for which service you fill your crop and maw, take your wages like a thief, have people treat you as a nobleman; for there are many that are even insolent towards their masters and mistresses, and are unwilling to do them a favor or service by which to protect them from loss.

But reflect what you will gain when, having come into your own property and being set up in your home (to which God will help with all misfortunes), it will bob up again and come home to you, and you will find that where you have cheated or done injury to the value of one mite, you will have to pay thirty again. [LC I.234–36]

Meditation:
1. Why are people able to steal and yet escape worldly punishment? Does this mean that they escape worldly consequences?
2. Why do people tend to be insolent towards those who are over them? What attitude should we have instead toward them and their property?
3. If we attain positions of authority while breaking the Seventh Commandment, what can we expect from those under us?

Prayer:

Lord, help me to respect those who are in authority over me, as well as their property, and to be merciful toward those who are under my authority. Amen.

Week Nine – Wednesday

The Seventh Commandment

Thou shalt not steal.

What does this mean?—Answer. We should fear and love God that we may not take our neighbor's money or property, nor get them by false ware or dealing, but help him to improve and protect his property and business.

Such shall be the lot also of mechanics and day laborers of whom we are now obliged to hear and suffer such intolerable maliciousness, as though they were noblemen in another's possessions, and everyone were obliged to give them what they demand. Just let them continue practicing their exactions as long as they can; but God will not forget his commandment, and will reward them according as they have served, and will hang them, not upon a green gallows, but upon a dry one, so that all their life they shall neither prosper nor accumulate anything. And indeed, if there were a well-ordered government in the land, such wantonness might soon be checked and prevented, as was the custom in ancient times among the Romans, where such characters were promptly seized by the pate in a way that others took warning.

No more shall all the rest prosper who change the open free market into a carrion pit of extortion and a den of robbery, where the poor are daily overcharged, new burdens and high prices are imposed, and everyone uses the market according to his caprice, and is even defiant and brags as though it were his fair privilege and right to sell his goods for as high a price as he please, and no one had a right to say a word against it. We will indeed look on and let these people skin, pinch, and hoard, but we will trust in God—who will, however, do this of his own accord—that, after you have been skinning and scraping for a long time, he will pronounce such a blessing on your gains that your grain in the garner, your beer in the cellar, your cattle in the stalls shall perish; yea, where you have cheated and overcharged anyone to the amount of a florin, your entire pile shall be consumed with rust, so that you shall never enjoy it. [LC I.237–42]

Meditation:
1. Is it wrong to charge as high a price as possible for one's services or goods? Why or why not?
2. What role should the government play in regulating and intervening in the free market?
3. What are the risks of conducting business in accordance with the world's rules? How should Christians distinguish themselves in this regard?

Prayer:

Father, teach me to serve my neighbor in my worldly vocations, rather than working to enrich myself. Help me to trust in your daily provision. Amen.

Week Nine – Thursday

The Seventh Commandment

Thou shalt not steal.

What does this mean?—Answer. We should fear and love God that we may not take our neighbor's money or property, nor get them by false ware or dealing, but help him to improve and protect his property and business.

And indeed, we see and experience this being fulfilled daily before our eyes, that no stolen or dishonestly acquired possession thrives. How many there are who rake and scrape day and night, and yet grow not a farthing richer! And though they gather much, they must suffer so many plagues and misfortunes that they cannot relish it with cheerfulness nor transmit it to their children. But as no one minds it, and we go on as though it did not concern us, God must visit us in a different way and teach us manners by imposing one taxation after another, or billeting a troop of soldiers upon us, who in one hour empty our coffers and purses, and do not quit as long as we have a farthing left, and in addition, by way of thanks, burn and devastate house and home, and outrage and kill wife and children.

And, in short, if you steal much, depend upon it that again as much will be stolen from you; and he who robs and acquires with violence and wrong will submit to one who shall deal after the same fashion with him. For God is master of this art, that since everyone robs and steals from the other, he punishes one thief by means of another. Else where should we find enough gallows and ropes?

Now, whoever is willing to be instructed, let him know that this is the commandment of God, and that it must not be treated as a jest. For although you despise us, defraud, steal, and rob, we will indeed manage to endure your haughtiness, suffer, and, according to the Lord's Prayer, forgive and show pity; for we know that the godly shall nevertheless have enough, and you injure yourself more than another. [LC I.243–46]

Meditation:

1. Is it consistent with your own experience that no stolen or dishonestly acquired possession thrives? Why is this not always the outcome?
2. What risk are we taking when we resort to stealing, even if only covertly? How much truth is there in the saying, "you reap what you sow"?
3. How should we respond to those who steal from us? Why? In what sense do they harm themselves more than their victims?

Prayer:

Lord, help me to depend on you for everything, rather than relying on myself, and to forgive those who wrongly take from me what you have given me. Amen.

Week Nine – Friday

The Seventh Commandment

Thou shalt not steal.

What does this mean?—Answer. We should fear and love God that we may not take our neighbor's money or property, nor get them by false ware or dealing, but help him to improve and protect his property and business.

But beware of this: When the poor man comes to you (of whom there are so many now) who must buy with the penny of his daily wages and live upon it, and you are harsh to him, as though everyone lived by your favor, and you skin and scrape to the bone, and, besides, with pride and haughtiness turn him off to whom you ought to give for nothing, he will go away wretched and sorrowful, and since he can complain to no one, he will cry and call to heaven, then beware (I say again) as of the devil himself. For such groaning and calling will be no jest, but will have a weight that will prove too heavy for you and all the world. For it will reach him who takes care of the poor sorrowful hearts, and will not allow them to go unavenged. But if you despise this and become defiant, see whom you have brought upon you: if you succeed and prosper, you may before all the world call God and me a liar.

We have exhorted, warned, and protested enough; he who will not heed or believe it may go on until he learns this by experience. Yet it must be impressed upon the young that they may be careful not to follow the old lawless crowd, but keep their eyes fixed upon God's commandment, lest his wrath and punishment come upon them too. It behooves us to do no more than to instruct and reprove with God's word; but to check such open wantonness there is need of the princes and government, who themselves would have eyes and the courage to establish and maintain order in all manner of trade and commerce, lest the poor be burdened and oppressed nor they themselves be loaded with other men's sins. [LC I.247–49]

Meditation:
1. What are the implications of the Seventh Commandment for our attitude toward the poor and needy?
2. What do we risk when we refuse to give to the poor, or otherwise treat them harshly? Why?
3. What is the church's responsibility in this area? What is the government's responsibility?

Prayer:

Almighty God, forgive me when I fail or refuse to be your instrument in caring for poor sorrowful hearts. Help me to show your compassion instead. Amen.

Week Nine – Saturday

The Seventh Commandment

Thou shalt not steal.

What does this mean?—Answer. We should fear and love God that we may not take our neighbor's money or property, nor get them by false ware or dealing, but help him to improve and protect his property and business.

Let this suffice as an explanation of what stealing is, that it be not taken too narrowly, but made to extend as far as we have to do with our neighbors. And briefly, in a summary, as in the former commandments, it is herewith forbidden, in the first place, to do our neighbor any injury or wrong (in whatever manner supposable, by curtailing, forestalling, and withholding his possessions and property), or even to consent or allow such a thing, but to interpose and prevent it. And, on the other hand, it is commanded that we advance and improve his possessions, and in case he suffers want, that we help, communicate, and lend both to friends and foes.

Whoever now seeks and desires good works will find here more than enough such as are heartily acceptable and pleasing to God, and in addition are favored and crowned with excellent blessings, that we are to be richly compensated for all that we do for our neighbor's good and from friendship; as King Solomon also teaches, Proverbs 19:17: "He that hath pity upon the poor lendeth unto the Lord; and that which he hath given will he pay him again." Here, then, you have a rich Lord, who is certainly sufficient for you, and who will not suffer you to come short in anything or to want; thus you can with a joyful conscience enjoy a hundred times more than you could scrape together with unfaithfulness and wrong. Now, whoever does not desire the blessing will find wrath and misfortune enough. [LC I.250–53]

Meditation:

1. Why is it important not to take the Seventh Commandment, or any of the others, too narrowly?
2. How can we help not only our friends in this regard, but also our foes, especially when they suffer want?
3. What compensation does God promise to those who are generous to the poor? Have you found this to be true in your own life?

Prayer:

Lord, all that I have is yours. Help me to hold it with an open hand, that you may put in and take out in accordance with your good and gracious will. Amen.

Week Ten – Sunday

The Eighth Commandment

Thou shalt not bear false witness against thy neighbor.

What does this mean?—Answer. We should fear and love God that we may not deceitfully belie, betray, slander, or defame our neighbor, but defend him, speak well of him, and put the best construction on everything.

Over and above our own body, spouse, and temporal possessions, we have yet another treasure, namely, honor and good report, with which we cannot dispense. For it is intolerable to live among men in open shame and general contempt. Therefore God wishes the reputation, good name, and upright character of our neighbor to be taken away or diminished as little as his money and possessions, that everyone may stand in his integrity before wife, children, servants, and neighbors. And in the first place, we take the plainest meaning of this commandment according to the words, as pertaining to the public courts of justice, where a poor innocent man is accused and oppressed by false witnesses in order to be punished in his body, property, or honor.

Now, this appears as if it were of little concern to us at present; but with the Jews it was quite a common and ordinary matter. For the people were organized under an excellent and regular government; and where there is still such a government, instances of this sin will not be wanting. The cause of it is that where judges, burgomasters, princes, or others in authority sit in judgment, things never fail to go according to the course of the world; namely, men do not like to offend anybody, flatter, and speak to gain favor, money, prospects, or friendship; and in consequence a poor man and his cause must be oppressed, denounced as wrong, and suffer punishment. And it is a common calamity in the world that in courts of justice there seldom preside godly men. [LC I.255–58]

Meditation:

1. What treasure that each person possesses is the Eighth Commandment intended to protect?
2. Why is it important to maintain a good reputation? What are some potential consequences for a person who does not?
3. In what context does the Eighth Commandment most directly apply? Why is telling the truth so important in the public courts of justice?

Prayer:

Father, you desire that my testimony always be truthful, whether in a court of law or the court of public opinion. Help me to live and speak accordingly. Amen.

Week Ten – Monday

The Eighth Commandment

Thou shalt not bear false witness against thy neighbor.

What does this mean?—Answer. We should fear and love God that we may not deceitfully belie, betray, slander, or defame our neighbor, but defend him, speak well of him, and put the best construction on everything.

For to be a judge requires above all things a godly man, and not only a godly, but also a wise, modest, yea, a brave and bold man; likewise, to be a witness requires a fearless and especially a godly man. For a person who is to judge all matters rightly and carry them through with his decision will often offend good friends, relatives, neighbors, and the rich and powerful, who can greatly serve or injure him. Therefore he must be quite blind, have his eyes and ears closed, neither see nor hear, but go straight forward in everything that comes before him, and decide accordingly.

Therefore this commandment is given first of all that everyone shall help his neighbor to secure his rights, and not allow them to be hindered or twisted, but shall promote and strictly maintain them, no matter whether he be judge or witness, and let it pertain to whatsoever it will. And especially is a goal set up here for our jurists that they be careful to deal truly and uprightly with every case, allowing right to remain right, and, on the other hand, not perverting anything, nor glossing it over or keeping silent concerning it, irrespective of a person's money, possessions, honor, or power. This is one part and the plainest sense of this commandment concerning all that takes place in court. [LC I.259–61]

Meditation:
1. What five characteristics does a good judge need to have? Why is each of them important for carrying out that role?
2. What kinds of risks might a judge have to take by deciding matters with genuine impartiality?
3. Why is it important for all of us to help our neighbors secure their rights, no matter what their station in life might be?

Prayer:

Dear Lord, grant wisdom, modesty, bravery, boldness, and (above all) godliness to those who serve as judges. Help me look out for my neighbors' rights. Amen.

Week Ten – Tuesday

The Eighth Commandment

Thou shalt not bear false witness against thy neighbor.

What does this mean?—Answer. We should fear and love God that we may not deceitfully belie, betray, slander, or defame our neighbor, but defend him, speak well of him, and put the best construction on everything.

Next, it extends very much further, if we are to apply it to spiritual jurisdiction or administration; here it is a common occurrence that everyone bears false witness against his neighbor. For wherever there are godly preachers and Christians, they must bear the sentence before the world that they are called heretics, apostates, yea, seditious and desperately wicked miscreants. Besides, the word of God must suffer in the most shameful and malicious manner, being persecuted, blasphemed, contradicted, perverted, and falsely cited and interpreted. But let this pass; for it is the way of the blind world that she condemns and persecutes the truth and the children of God, and yet esteems it no sin.

In the third place, what concerns us all, this commandment forbids all sins of the tongue whereby we may injure or approach too closely to our neighbor. For to bear false witness is nothing else than a work of the tongue. Now, whatever is done with the tongue against a fellow man God would have prohibited, whether it be false preachers with their doctrine and blasphemy, false judges and witnesses with their verdict, or outside of court by lying and evil-speaking. Here belongs particularly the detestable, shameful vice of speaking behind a person's back and slandering, to which the devil spurs us on, and of which there would be much to be said. For it is a common evil plague that everyone prefers hearing evil to hearing good of his neighbor; and although we ourselves are so bad that we cannot suffer that anyone should say anything bad about us, but everyone would much rather that all the world should speak of him in terms of gold, yet we cannot bear that the best is spoken about others. [LC I.262–64]

Meditation:

1. Why is it the way of the blind world to condemn and persecute the truth and the children of God? How have you witnessed this firsthand?
2. What are some specific ways in which we can injure our neighbors with the tongue? How have you suffered from someone else's words?
3. Why does everyone prefer hearing evil to hearing good about their neighbors? How do you react when the best is spoken about others?

Prayer:

Almighty God, forgive me for falling into the ways of the world by harming my neighbors with my tongue. Help me to build them up with it instead. Amen.

Week Ten – Wednesday

The Eighth Commandment

Thou shalt not bear false witness against thy neighbor.

What does this mean?—Answer. We should fear and love God that we may not deceitfully belie, betray, slander, or defame our neighbor, but defend him, speak well of him, and put the best construction on everything.

Therefore, to avoid this vice we should note that no one is allowed publicly to judge and reprove his neighbor, although he may see him sin, unless he have a command to judge and to reprove. For there is a great difference between these two things, judging sin and knowing sin. You may indeed know it, but you are not to judge it. I can indeed see and hear that my neighbor sins, but I have no command to report it to others. Now, if I rush in, judging and passing sentence, I fall into a sin which is greater than his. But if you know it, do nothing else than turn your ears into a grave and cover it, until you are appointed to be judge and to punish by virtue of your office.

Those, then, are called slanderers who are not content with knowing a thing, but proceed to assume jurisdiction, and when they know a slight offense of another, carry it into every corner, and are delighted and tickled that they can stir up another's displeasure, as swine roll themselves in the dirt and root in it with the snout. This is nothing else than meddling with the judgment and office of God, and pronouncing sentence and punishment with the most severe verdict. For no judge can punish to a higher degree nor go farther than to say: "He is a thief, a murderer, a traitor," etc. Therefore, whoever presumes to say the same of his neighbor goes just as far as the emperor and all governments. For although you do not wield the sword, you employ your poisonous tongue to the shame and hurt of your neighbor. [LC I.265-68]

Meditation:

1. What is the prerequisite for publicly judging and reproving another person? For whom (if anyone) do you have such a specific command and office?
2. What is the difference between judging sin and knowing sin? Why are we tempted to judge and report the sins of others that we know?
3. Why is it wrong to assume jurisdiction by gossiping about the slight offenses of others? What should we do for them instead?

Prayer:

Father, there are certain roles that you have given me, and others that you have not given me. Help me to recognize the difference and act accordingly. Amen.

Week Ten – Thursday

The Eighth Commandment

Thou shalt not bear false witness against thy neighbor.

What does this mean?—Answer. We should fear and love God that we may not deceitfully belie, betray, slander, or defame our neighbor, but defend him, speak well of him, and put the best construction on everything.

God therefore would have it prohibited that anyone speak evil of another even though he be guilty, and the latter know it right well; much less if he do not know it, and have it only from hearsay. But you say: "Shall I not say it if it be the truth?" Answer: "Why do you not make accusation to regular judges?" "Ah, I cannot prove it publicly, and hence I might be silenced and turned away in a harsh manner." "Ah, indeed, do you smell the roast?" If you do not trust yourself to stand before the proper authorities and to make answer, then hold your tongue. But if you know it, know it for yourself and not for another. For if you tell it to others, although it be true, you will appear as a liar, because you cannot prove it, and you are, besides, acting like a knave. For we ought never to deprive anyone of his honor or good name unless it be first taken away from him publicly.

False witness, then, is everything which cannot be properly proved. Therefore, what is not manifest upon sufficient evidence no one shall make public or declare for truth; and, in short, whatever is secret should be allowed to remain secret, or, at any rate, should be secretly reproved, as we shall hear. Therefore, if you encounter an idle tongue which betrays and slanders someone, contradict such a one promptly to his face, that he may blush; thus many a one will hold his tongue who else would bring some poor man into bad repute, from which he would not easily extricate himself. For honor and a good name are easily taken away, but not easily restored. [LC I.269–73]

Meditation:

1. Why does God prohibit speaking evil of another, even if that person is truly guilty and knows it? What is God's desire for that person?
2. What is the proper course of action when we know that someone else has done something wrong? What questions should we ask ourselves?
3. Why is it easy to take away someone's honor and good name, but difficult to restore them? Do you have any personal experience with this?

Prayer:

Lord God, forgive me for readily speaking evil of others. Help me instead to do whatever I can to help them maintain their honor and good name. Amen.

Week Ten – Friday

The Eighth Commandment

Thou shalt not bear false witness against thy neighbor.

What does this mean?—Answer. We should fear and love God that we may not deceitfully belie, betray, slander, or defame our neighbor, but defend him, speak well of him, and put the best construction on everything.

Thus you see that it is summarily forbidden to speak any evil of our neighbor, however, the civil government, preachers, father and mother excepted, on the understanding that this commandment does not allow evil to go unpunished. Now, as according to the Fifth Commandment no one is to be injured in body, and yet the executioner is excepted, who by virtue of his office does his neighbor no good, but only evil and harm, and nevertheless does not sin against God's commandment, because God has on his own account instituted that office; for he has reserved punishment for his own good pleasure, as he threatens in the First Commandment—just so also, although no one has a right in his own person to judge and condemn anybody, yet if they to whose office it belongs fail to do it, they sin as well as he who would do so of his own accord, without such office. For here necessity requires one to speak of the evil, to prefer charges, to investigate and testify; and it is not different from the case of a physician who is sometimes compelled to examine and handle the patient whom he is to cure in secret parts. Just so governments, father and mother, brothers and sisters, and other good friends are under obligation to each other to reprove evil wherever it is needful and profitable. [LC I.274-75]

Meditation:
1. What are four specific offices that God has established with the authority to speak about other people's behavior? For what purpose?
2. Why is it sinful when those who hold these offices fail to judge and condemn when they should? What long-term effects could this have?
3. Why is the executioner excepted from the Fifth Commandment? How should this inform our understanding of the other commandments?

Prayer:

Dear God, you have called me to various offices in my relationships with others. Help me to carry out each one in accordance with your will. Amen.

Week Ten – Saturday

The Eighth Commandment

Thou shalt not bear false witness against thy neighbor.

What does this mean?—Answer. We should fear and love God that we may not deceitfully belie, betray, slander, or defame our neighbor, but defend him, speak well of him, and put the best construction on everything.

But the true way in this matter would be to observe the order according to the gospel, Matthew 18:15, where Christ says: "If thy brother shall trespass against thee, go and tell him his fault between thee and him alone." Here you have a precious and excellent teaching for governing well the tongue, which is to be carefully observed against this detestable misuse. Let this, then, be your rule, that you do not too readily spread evil concerning your neighbor and slander him to others, but admonish him privately that he may amend. Likewise, also, if someone report to you what this or that one has done, teach him, too, to go and admonish him personally, if he have seen it himself; but if not, that he hold his tongue.

The same you can learn also from the daily government of the household. For when the master of the house sees that the servant does not do what he ought, he admonishes him personally. But if he were so foolish as to let the servant sit at home, and went on the streets to complain of him to his neighbors, he would no doubt be told: "You fool, what does that concern us? Why do you not tell it to him?" Behold, that would be acting quite brotherly, so that the evil would be stayed, and your neighbor would retain his honor. As Christ also says in the same place: "If he hear thee, thou hast gained thy brother." Then you have done a great and excellent work; for do you think it is a little matter to gain a brother? Let all monks and holy orders step forth, with all their works melted together into one mass, and see if they can boast that they have gained a brother. [LC I.276-78]

Meditation:

1. What did Jesus say to do when someone sins against you? What is the desired outcome when admonishing someone privately?
2. What should you do if one person reports to you what another has done? Why does it depend on whether the behavior was observed firsthand?
3. What are the benefits of private admonition? Why is it a significant matter to gain a brother or sister?

Prayer:

Father, help me to show love to those who sin against me by forgiving them and admonishing them privately, that I may gain them as brothers and sisters. Amen.

Week Eleven – Sunday

The Eighth Commandment

Thou shalt not bear false witness against thy neighbor.

What does this mean?—Answer. We should fear and love God that we may not deceitfully belie, betray, slander, or defame our neighbor, but defend him, speak well of him, and put the best construction on everything.

Further, Christ teaches: "But if he will not hear thee, then take with thee one or two more, that in the mouth of two or three witnesses every word may be established." So he whom it concerns is always to be treated with personally, and not to be spoken of without his knowledge. But if that do not avail, then bring it publicly before the community, whether before the civil or the ecclesiastical tribunal. For then you do not stand alone, but you have those witnesses with you by whom you can convict the guilty one, relying on whom the judge can pronounce sentence and punish. This is the right and regular course for checking and reforming a wicked person. But if we gossip about another in all corners, and stir the filth, no one will be reformed, and afterwards when we are to stand up and bear witness, we deny having said so. Therefore it would serve such tongues right if their itch for slander were severely punished, as a warning to others. If you were acting for your neighbor's reformation or from love of the truth, you would not sneak about secretly nor shun the day and the light. [LC I.279–83]

Meditation:
1. What is the next step if someone will not listen when confronted privately? Why is it important to establish the matter with multiple witnesses?
2. What should happen if the person still will not listen? Why does society have people who are specifically designated to hear and judge cases?
3. What should be our goal when we see a neighbor doing something wrong? Why is gossiping about it ineffective in accomplishing this?

Prayer:

Dear Lord, forgive me for talking *about* people who do wrong, rather than talking *to* them. Help me to seek their reformation and love the truth. Amen.

Week Eleven – Monday

The Eighth Commandment

Thou shalt not bear false witness against thy neighbor.

What does this mean?—Answer. We should fear and love God that we may not deceitfully belie, betray, slander, or defame our neighbor, but defend him, speak well of him, and put the best construction on everything.

All this has been said regarding secret sins. But where the sin is quite public so that the judge and everybody know it, you can without any sin avoid him and let him go, because he has brought himself into disgrace, and you may also publicly testify concerning him. For when a matter is public in the light of day, there can be no slandering or false judging or testifying; as, when we now reprove the pope with his doctrine, which is publicly set forth in books and proclaimed in all the world. For where the sin is public, the reproof also must be public, that everyone may learn to guard against it.

Thus we have now the sum and general understanding of this commandment, to wit, that no one do any injury with the tongue to his neighbor, whether friend or foe, nor speak evil of him, no matter whether it be true or false, unless it be done by commandment or for his reformation, but that everyone employ his tongue and make it serve for the best of everyone else, to cover up his neighbor's sins and infirmities, excuse them, palliate and garnish them with his own reputation. The chief reason for this should be the one which Christ alleges in the gospel, in which he comprehends all commandments respecting our neighbor, Matthew 7:12: "Whatsoever ye would that men should do to you, do ye even so to them." [LC I.284–86]

Meditation:

1. What is the difference between secret sins and public sins? How should we behave toward someone who has sinned publicly?
2. What specific example of public sin is given here? Why is it important to reprove false doctrine publicly?
3. What is the chief reason for obeying the Eighth Commandment and all other commandments respecting our neighbor?

Prayer:

Lord God, grant me the wisdom to discern when the sins of others are private or public, as well as the courage to reprove them accordingly. Amen.

Week Eleven – Tuesday

The Eighth Commandment

Thou shalt not bear false witness against thy neighbor.

What does this mean?—Answer. We should fear and love God that we may not deceitfully belie, betray, slander, or defame our neighbor, but defend him, speak well of him, and put the best construction on everything.

Even nature teaches the same thing in our own bodies, as St. Paul says, 1 Corinthians 12:22: "Much more, those members of the body which seem to be more feeble are necessary; and those members of the body which we think to be less honorable, upon these we bestow more abundant honor; and our uncomely parts have more abundant comeliness." No one covers his face, eyes, nose, and mouth, for they, being in themselves the most honorable members which we have, do not require it. But the most infirm members, of which we are ashamed, we cover with all diligence; hands, eyes, and the whole body must help to cover and conceal them. Thus also among ourselves should we adorn whatever blemishes and infirmities we find in our neighbor, and serve and help him to promote his honor to the best of our ability, and, on the other hand, prevent whatever may be discreditable to him. And it is especially an excellent and noble virtue for one always to explain advantageously and put the best construction upon all he may hear of his neighbor (if it be not notoriously evil), or at any rate to condone it over and against the poisonous tongues that are busy wherever they can pry out and discover something to blame in a neighbor, and that explain and pervert it in the worst way; as is done now especially with the precious word of God and its preachers.

There are comprehended therefore in this commandment quite a multitude of good works which please God most highly, and bring abundant good and blessing, if only the blind world and the false saints would recognize them. For there is nothing on or in entire man which can do both greater and more extensive good or harm in spiritual and in temporal matters than the tongue, though it is the least and feeblest member. [LC I.287-91]

Meditation:

1. Why do we cover certain parts of our bodies, but not others? How does this analogy apply to obeying the Eighth Commandment?
2. What does it mean to put the best construction on everything that we hear or read? What makes this especially difficult in our day and age?
3. What are some examples of the great and extensive good that the tongue can do? of the great and extensive harm that it can do?

Prayer:

Father, you have given me the ability to use words to build up and to tear down. Help me always to exercise that power in love and according to your will. Amen.

Week Eleven – Wednesday

The Ninth Commandment

Thou shalt not covet thy neighbor's house.

What does this mean?—Answer. We should fear and love God that we may not craftily seek to get our neighbor's inheritance or house, and obtain it by a show of right, etc., but help and be of service to him in keeping it.

The Tenth Commandment

Thou shalt not covet thy neighbor's wife, nor his manservant, nor his maidservant, nor his cattle, nor anything that is his.

What does this mean?—Answer. We should fear and love God that we may not estrange, force, or entice away our neighbor's wife, servants, or cattle, but urge them to stay and do their duty.

These two commandments are given quite exclusively to the Jews; nevertheless, in part they also concern us. For they do not interpret them as referring to unchastity or theft, because these are sufficiently forbidden above. They also thought that they had kept all those when they had done or not done the external act. Therefore God has added these two commandments in order that it be esteemed as sin and forbidden to desire or in any way to aim at getting our neighbor's wife or possessions; and especially because under the Jewish government, manservants and maidservants were not free as now to serve for wages as long as they pleased, but were their master's property with their body and all they had, as cattle and other possessions. Moreover, every man had power over his wife to put her away publicly by giving her a bill of divorce, and to take another. Therefore they were in constant danger among each other that if one took a fancy to another's wife, he might allege any reason both to dismiss his own wife and to estrange the other's wife from him, that he might obtain her under pretext of right. That was not considered a sin nor disgrace with them; as little as now with hired help, when a proprietor dismisses his manservant or maidservant, or takes another's servants from him in any way. [LC I.293–95]

Meditation:

1. What is the key difference between the Sixth and Seventh Commandments on the one hand, and the Ninth and Tenth Commandments on the other?
2. Why does God forbid not only taking our neighbor's wife or possessions, but even desiring or aiming to do so?
3. How is our culture's view of marriage similar to that of the Jews as described here? What temptations are fostered by such an attitude?

Prayer:

Dear God, I am a sinner not only in my words and actions, but also in my thoughts, desires, and intentions. Please forgive me and help me. Amen.

Week Eleven – Thursday

The Ninth Commandment

Thou shalt not covet thy neighbor's house.

What does this mean?—Answer. We should fear and love God that we may not craftily seek to get our neighbor's inheritance or house, and obtain it by a show of right, etc., but help and be of service to him in keeping it.

Therefore (I say) they thus interpreted these commandments, and that rightly (although their scope reaches somewhat farther and higher), that no one think or purpose to obtain what belongs to another, such as his wife, servants, house and estate, land, meadows, cattle, even with a show of right or by a subterfuge, yet with injury to his neighbor. For above, in the Seventh Commandment, the vice is forbidden where one wrests to himself the possessions of others, or withholds them from his neighbor, which he cannot do by right. But here it is also forbidden to alienate anything from your neighbor, even though you could do so with honor in the eyes of the world, so that no one could accuse or blame you as though you had obtained it wrongfully.

For we are so inclined by nature that no one desires to see another have as much as himself, and each one acquires as much as he can; the other may fare as best he can. And yet we pretend to be godly, know how to adorn ourselves most finely and conceal our rascality, resort to and invent adroit devices and deceitful artifices (such as now are daily most ingeniously contrived) as though they were derived from the law codes; yea, we even dare impertinently to refer to it, and boast of it, and will not have it called rascality, but shrewdness and caution. In this lawyers and jurists assist, who twist and stretch the law to suit it to their cause, stress words and use them for a subterfuge, irrespective of equity or their neighbor's necessity. And, in short, whoever is the most expert and cunning in these affairs finds most help in law, as they themselves say: "The laws favor the watchful." [LC I.296–99]

Meditation:
1. Why is it wrong to think or purpose to obtain what belongs to another? Who gave it to that person? Who gave you what you already have?
2. Why does no one desire to see another have as much as himself? Why does each one acquire as much as he can?
3. Why should Christians hold themselves to a higher standard than mere compliance with civil laws?

Prayer:

Lord, forgive me for resenting the success and wealth of others. Help me to be content with what you have given me, rather than always seeking more. Amen.

Week Eleven – Friday

The Ninth Commandment

Thou shalt not covet thy neighbor's house.

What does this mean?—Answer. We should fear and love God that we may not craftily seek to get our neighbor's inheritance or house, and obtain it by a show of right, etc., but help and be of service to him in keeping it.

This last commandment therefore is given not for rogues in the eyes of the world, but just for the most pious, who wish to be praised and be called honest and upright people, since they have not offended against the former commandments, as especially the Jews claimed to be, and even now many great noblemen, gentlemen, and princes. For the other common masses belong yet farther down, under the Seventh Commandment, as those who are not much concerned whether they acquire their possessions with honor and right.

Now, this occurs most frequently in cases that are brought into court, where it is the purpose to get something from our neighbor and to force him out of his own. As (to give examples), when people quarrel and wrangle about a large inheritance, real estate, etc., they avail themselves of, and resort to, whatever has the appearance of right, so dressing and adorning everything that the law must favor their side, and they keep the property with such title that no one can make complaint or lay claim thereto. In like manner, if anyone desire to have a castle, city, duchy, or any other great thing, he practices so much financiering through relationships, and by any means he can, that the other is judicially deprived of it, and it is adjudicated to him, and confirmed with deed and seal and declared to have been acquired by princely title and honestly. [LC I.300–2]

Meditation:

1. In what sense are the Ninth and Tenth Commandments given for honest and upright people, rather than rogues in the eyes of the world?
2. How does the prohibition against coveting help us to avoid the mistake of thinking that we have truly kept all the commandments?
3. Is it wrong to pursue our genuine legal rights in court? Under what circumstances should we be willing to give them up?

Prayer:

Father, even when I am perceived by the world as honest and upright, you know what is in my heart. Forgive me and cleanse me by your Holy Spirit. Amen.

Week Eleven – Saturday

The Ninth Commandment

Thou shalt not covet thy neighbor's house.

What does this mean?—Answer. We should fear and love God that we may not craftily seek to get our neighbor's inheritance or house, and obtain it by a show of right, etc., but help and be of service to him in keeping it.

Likewise also in common trade where one dexterously slips something out of another's hand, so that he must look after it, or surprises and defrauds him in a matter in which he sees advantage and benefit for himself, so that the latter, perhaps on account of distress or debt, cannot regain or redeem it without injury, and the former gains the half or even more; and yet this must not be considered as acquired by fraud or stolen, but honestly bought. Here they say: "First come, first served, and everyone must look to his own interest, let another get what he can." And who can be so smart as to think of all the ways in which one can get many things into his possession by such specious pretexts? This the world does not consider wrong, and will not see that the neighbor is thereby placed at a disadvantage, and must sacrifice what he cannot spare without injury. Yet there is no one who wishes this to be done to him; from which we can easily perceive that such devices and pretexts are false. [LC I.303–4]

Meditation:

1. What are some ways in which one person can legally take advantage of another? Why does God forbid us to do this?
2. Why does the world urge everyone to look to his own interest? What does the apostle Paul urge instead (Phil. 2:4)?
3. Why is the world not concerned about placing others at a disadvantage? How does the Golden Rule (Matt. 7:12) foster the opposite attitude?

Prayer:

Lord God, help me to look not only to my own interests, but also to the interests of others, and to do unto others as I would have them do unto me. Amen.

Week Twelve – Sunday

The Tenth Commandment

Thou shalt not covet thy neighbor's wife, nor his manservant, nor his maidservant, nor his cattle, nor anything that is his.

What does this mean?—Answer. We should fear and love God that we may not estrange, force, or entice away our neighbor's wife, servants, or cattle, but urge them to stay and do their duty.

Thus it was done formerly also with respect to wives: they knew such devices that if one were pleased with another woman, he personally or through others (as there were many ways and means to be invented) caused her husband to conceive a displeasure toward her, or had her resist him and so conduct herself that he was obliged to dismiss her and leave her to the other. That sort of thing undoubtedly prevailed much under the law, as also we read in the gospel of King Herod that he took his brother's wife while he was yet living, and yet wished to be thought an honorable, pious man, as St. Mark also testifies of him. But such an example, I trust, will not occur among us, because in the New Testament those who are married are forbidden to be divorced, except in such a case where one by some stratagem takes away a rich bride from another. But it is not a rare thing with us that one estranges or alienates another's manservant or maidservant, or entices them away by flattering words. [LC I.305–6]

Meditation:

1. Why do you suppose that there are two distinct commandments against coveting? What is the key difference between them?
2. Why are those who are married forbidden to be divorced? Why has our culture largely abandoned this New Testament teaching?
3. How does the Tenth Commandment also apply to the employer-employee relationship? Why is loyalty important in that context?

Prayer:

Heavenly Father, help me to be content with and faithful to all the relationships that you have given to me and others, at home and in the world. Amen.

Week Twelve – Monday

The Tenth Commandment

Thou shalt not covet thy neighbor's wife, nor his manservant, nor his maidservant, nor his cattle, nor anything that is his.

What does this mean?—Answer. We should fear and love God that we may not estrange, force, or entice away our neighbor's wife, servants, or cattle, but urge them to stay and do their duty.

In whatever way such things happen, we must know that God does not wish that you deprive your neighbor of anything that belongs to him, so that he suffer the loss and you gratify your avarice with it, even if you could keep it honorably before the world; for it is a secret and insidious imposition practiced under the hat, as we say, that it may not be observed. For although you go your way as if you had done no one any wrong, you have nevertheless injured your neighbor; and if it is not called stealing and cheating, yet it is called coveting your neighbor's property, that is, aiming at possession of it, enticing it away from him without his will, and being unwilling to see him enjoy what God has granted him. And although the judge and everyone must leave you in possession of it, yet God will not leave you therein: for he sees the deceitful heart and the malice of the world, which is sure to take an ell in addition wherever you yield to her a finger's breadth, and at length public wrong and violence follow.

Therefore we allow these commandments to remain in their ordinary meaning, that it is commanded, first, that we do not desire our neighbor's damage, nor even assist, nor give occasion for it, but gladly wish and leave him what he has, and, besides, advance and preserve for him what may be for his profit and service, as we should wish to be treated. Thus these commandments are especially directed against envy and miserable avarice, God wishing to remove all causes and sources whence arises everything by which we do injury to our neighbor, and therefore he expresses it in plain words. For he would especially have the heart pure, although we shall never attain to that as long as we live here; so that this commandment will remain, like all the rest, one that will constantly accuse us and show how godly we are in the sight of God! [LC I.307–10]

Meditation:

1. What is the difference between the basis on which the world judges us and the basis on which God judges us? Which judgment is more accurate?
2. What attitude toward our neighbors does keeping the Ninth and Tenth Commandments foster? How does this help us also keep the others?
3. Why do all God's commandments constantly accuse us? What is God's purpose in using them that way?

Prayer:

Almighty God, your commandments constantly accuse me, thus showing me my need for you. Thank you for giving your Son so that I may be forgiven. Amen.

Week Twelve – Tuesday

The Close of the Commandments

What does God say of all these commandments?—Answer.
He says thus: I the Lord, thy God, am a jealous God,
visiting the iniquity of the fathers upon the children
unto the third and fourth generation of them that hate me,
and showing mercy unto thousands of them
that love me and keep my commandments.

In order that it may be seen that God will not have [the First Commandment] thrown to the winds, but will most strictly enforce it, he has attached to it first a terrible threat, and then a beautiful, comforting promise which is also to be urged and impressed upon young people, that they may take it to heart and retain it. . . .

Although these words relate to all the commandments (as we shall hereafter learn), yet they are joined to this chief commandment because it is of first importance that men have a right head; for where the head is right, the whole life must be right, and vice versa. Learn, therefore, from these words how angry God is with those who trust in anything but him, and again, how good and gracious he is to those who trust and believe in him alone with the whole heart; so that his anger does not cease until the fourth generation, while, on the other hand, his blessing and goodness extend to many thousands, lest you live in such security and commit yourself to chance, as men of brutal heart, who think that it makes no great difference. He is a God who will not leave it unavenged if men turn from him, and will not cease to be angry until the fourth generation, even until they are utterly exterminated. Therefore he is to be feared, and not to be despised. [LC I.29, 31–34]

Meditation:

1. What terrible threat has God attached to the Ten Commandments? What beautiful, comforting promise has he also attached to them?
2. What does it mean in this context to have a right head? In what sense does this cause a person's whole life to be right?
3. For how many generations does God's anger persist? For how many generations does his mercy persist? What does this indicate about him?

Prayer:

Dear Lord, give me a right head and a right life by helping me to love you and keep your commandments. Thank you for your abundant mercy. Amen.

Week Twelve – Wednesday

The Close of the Commandments

What does God say of all these commandments?—Answer.

He says thus: I the Lord, thy God, am a jealous God,
visiting the iniquity of the fathers upon the children
unto the third and fourth generation of them that hate me,
and showing mercy unto thousands of them
that love me and keep my commandments.

He has also demonstrated this in all history, as the Scriptures abundantly show and daily experience still teaches. For from the beginning he has utterly extirpated all idolatry, and, on account of it, both heathen and Jews; even as at the present day he overthrows all false worship, so that all who remain therein must finally perish. Therefore, although proud, powerful, and rich worldlings are now to be found, who boast defiantly of their mammon, with utter disregard whether God is angry at or smiles on them, and dare to withstand his wrath, yet they shall not succeed, but before they are aware, they shall be wrecked, with all in which they trusted; as all others have perished who have thought themselves more secure or powerful.

And just because of such hardened heads who imagine because God connives and allows them to rest in security, that he either is entirely ignorant or cares nothing about such matters, he must deal a smashing blow and punish them, so that he cannot forget it unto children's children; so that everyone may take note and see that this is no joke to him. [LC I.35–37]

Meditation:
1. How has God demonstrated in history that his threats and promises are not to be taken lightly? How does your daily experience teach this?
2. What are some current examples of rich worldlings who boast defiantly of their mammon? What makes them successful in the world's eyes?
3. Why does God allow such people to rest in security, at least for a time? What kinds of consequences are suffered by subsequent generations?

Prayer:

Father, help me always to keep in mind that my actions and attitudes do not affect only me, but also those around me and those who come after me. Amen.

Week Twelve – Thursday

The Close of the Commandments

What does God say of all these commandments?—Answer.
He says thus: I the Lord, thy God, am a jealous God,
visiting the iniquity of the fathers upon the children
unto the third and fourth generation of them that hate me,
and showing mercy unto thousands of them
that love me and keep my commandments.

For they are those whom he means when he says: "Who hate me," i.e., those who persist in their defiance and pride; whatever is preached or said to them, they will not listen; when they are reproved, in order that they may learn to know themselves and amend before the punishment begins, they become mad and foolish so as to fairly merit wrath, as now we see daily in bishops and princes.

But terrible as are these threatenings, so much the more powerful is the consolation in the promise, that those who cling to God alone should be sure that he will show them mercy, that is, show them pure goodness and blessing, not only for themselves, but also to their children and children's children, even to the thousandth generation and beyond that. This ought certainly to move and impel us to risk our hearts in all confidence with God, if we wish all temporal and eternal good, since the Supreme Majesty makes such sublime offers and presents such cordial inducements and such rich promises.

Therefore let everyone seriously take this to heart, lest it be regarded as though a man had spoken it. For to you it is a question either of eternal blessing, happiness, and salvation, or of eternal wrath, misery, and woe. What more would you have or desire than that he so kindly promises to be yours with every blessing, and to protect and help you in all need? [LC I.38–41]

Meditation:

1. Why do some people hate God, and thus persist in their defiance and pride? How do they typically respond to being reproved?
2. Why is God's promise to show mercy to those who cling to him alone a powerful source of consolation? How should we respond to it?
3. What are the two possible destinies that lie ahead of every person? Why is there no middle ground? What are the implications of this?

Prayer:

Dear God, I deserve eternal wrath for my failure to keep your commandments, but in your mercy, you grant me eternal blessing instead. Thank you. Amen.

Week Twelve – Friday

The Close of the Commandments

What does God say of all these commandments?—Answer.
He says thus: I the Lord, thy God, am a jealous God,
visiting the iniquity of the fathers upon the children
unto the third and fourth generation of them that hate me,
and showing mercy unto thousands of them
that love me and keep my commandments.

But, alas! here is the failure, that the world believes nothing of this, nor regards it as God's word because it sees that those who trust in God and not in mammon suffer care and want, and the devil opposes and resists them, that they have neither money, favor, nor honor, and, besides, can scarcely support life; while, on the other hand, those who serve mammon have power, favor, honor, possessions, and every comfort in the eyes of the world. For this reason, these words must be grasped as being directed against such appearances; and we must consider that they do not lie or deceive, but must come true.

Reflect for yourself or make inquiry and tell me: Those who have employed all their care and diligence to accumulate great possessions and wealth, what have they finally attained? You will find that they have wasted their toil and labor, or even though they have amassed great treasures, they have been dispersed and scattered, so that they themselves have never found happiness in their wealth, and afterwards it never reached the third generation.

Instances of this you will find a plenty in all histories, also in the memory of aged and experienced people. Only observe and ponder them. [LC I.42–44]

Meditation:

1. Why does the world not believe God's threats and promises? Do you sometimes struggle to believe them, too?
2. What do those who serve mammon tend to have in the eyes of the world? Why should we believe God's word rather than such appearances?
3. What do those who accumulate great possessions and wealth finally attain? What examples come to mind from history and your own experience?

Prayer:

Gracious Lord, help me to cling to your word, both law and gospel, especially when I am tempted to see things through the eyes of the world instead. Amen.

Week Twelve – Saturday

The Close of the Commandments

What does this mean?—Answer. God threatens to punish all that transgress these commandments. Therefore we should dread his wrath and not act contrary to these commandments. But he promises grace and every blessing to all that keep these commandments. Therefore we should also love and trust in him, and gladly do according to his commandments.

Let this be sufficient concerning the first part of the common Christian doctrine, both for teaching and urging what is necessary. In conclusion, however, we must repeat the text which belongs here, of which we have treated already in the First Commandment, in order that we may learn what pains God requires to the end we may learn to inculcate and practice the Ten Commandments. . . .

Although (as we have heard above) this appendix was primarily attached to the First Commandment, it was nevertheless laid down for the sake of all the commandments, as all of them are to be referred and directed to it. Therefore I have said that this, too, should be presented to and inculcated upon the young, that they may learn and remember it, in order to see what is to urge and compel us to keep these Ten Commandments. And it is to be regarded as though this part were specially added to each, so that it inheres in, and pervades, them all.

Now, there is comprehended in these words (as said before) both an angry word of threatening and a friendly promise to terrify and warn us, and, moreover, to induce and encourage us to receive and highly esteem his word as a matter of divine earnestness, because he himself declares how much he is concerned about it, and how rigidly he will enforce it, namely, that he will horribly and terribly punish all who despise and transgress his commandments; and again, how richly he will reward, bless, and do all good to those who hold them in high esteem, and gladly do and live according to them. [LC I.319, 321–23a]

Meditation:

1. What effect should fearing God's wrath have on our behavior? What effect should loving and trusting in God have on our behavior?
2. What is the key difference between these two responses to the Ten Commandments? How is this reflected in Luther's explanation of each one?
3. Why is God so concerned that we receive and highly esteem his word? What is the role of the Ten Commandments in Christian living?

Prayer:

Heavenly Father, help me to fear, love, and trust in you so that I think, speak, and act according to your word, including the Ten Commandments. Amen.

Week Thirteen – Sunday

The Close of the Commandments

What does this mean?—Answer. God threatens to punish all that transgress these commandments. Therefore we should dread his wrath and not act contrary to these commandments. But he promises grace and every blessing to all that keep these commandments. Therefore we should also love and trust in him, and gladly do according to his commandments.

Thus he demands that all our works proceed from a heart which fears and regards God alone, and from such fear avoids everything that is contrary to his will, lest it should move him to wrath; and, on the other hand, also trusts in him alone and from love to him does all he wishes, because he speaks to us as friendly as a father, and offers us all grace and every good.

Just this is also the meaning and true interpretation of the first and chief commandment, from which all the others must flow and proceed, so that this word: "Thou shalt have no other gods before me," in its simplest meaning states nothing else than this demand: "Thou shalt fear, love, and trust in me as thine only true God." For where there is a heart thus disposed towards God, the same has fulfilled this and all the other commandments. On the other hand, whoever fears and loves anything else in heaven and upon earth will keep neither this nor any. Thus the entire Scriptures have everywhere preached and inculcated this commandment, aiming always at these two things: fear of God and trust in him. And especially the prophet David throughout the Psalms, as when he says: "The Lord taketh pleasure in them that fear him, in those that hope in his mercy." As if the entire commandment were explained by one verse, as much as to say: "The Lord taketh pleasure in those who have no other gods." [LC I.323b–25]

Meditation:

1. How are law and gospel summarized in the Close of the Commandments? What distinction does it make between them? Why is this important?
2. In what sense is the Close of the Commandments a restatement of the first one? How does having a heart disposed towards God fulfill all of them?
3. How does fearing God reflect having no other gods? How does hoping in God's mercy reflect having no other gods?

Prayer:

Almighty God, thank you for revealing your law and gospel. Teach me to fear you alone and to hope in your mercy rather than relying on anything else. Amen.

Week Thirteen – Monday

The Close of the Commandments

What does this mean?—Answer. God threatens to punish all that transgress these commandments. Therefore we should dread his wrath and not act contrary to these commandments. But he promises grace and every blessing to all that keep these commandments. Therefore we should also love and trust in him, and gladly do according to his commandments.

Thus the First Commandment is to shine and impart its splendor to all the others. Therefore you must let this declaration run through all the commandments, like a hoop in a wreath, joining the end to the beginning and holding them all together, that it be continually repeated and not forgotten; as, namely, in the Second Commandment, that we fear God and do not take his name in vain for cursing, lying, deceiving, and other modes of leading men astray, or rascality, but make proper and good use of it by calling upon him in prayer, praise, and thanksgiving, derived from love and trust according to the First Commandment. In like manner such fear, love, and trust is to urge and force us not to despise his word, but gladly to learn, hear, and esteem it holy, and honor it.

Thus continuing through all the following commandments towards our neighbor likewise, everything is to proceed by virtue of the First Commandment, to wit, that we honor father and mother, masters, and all in authority, and be subject and obedient to them, not on their own account, but for God's sake. For you are not to regard or fear father or mother, or from love of them do or omit anything. But see to that which God would have you do, and what he will quite surely demand of you; if you omit that, you have an angry Judge, but in the contrary case a gracious Father. [LC I.326–27]

Meditation:

1. How do the threat and promise attached to the Ten Commandments run through all of them? Why is it important always to keep them in mind?
2. How does keeping the Second and Third Commandments demonstrate proper fear, love, and trust toward God?
3. For whose sake are we to keep the Fourth Commandment? What mistake might we make if we honor parents or authorities on their own account?

Prayer:

Gracious Lord, help me to remember your threats and promises at all times, to recognize your authority above all others, and to live accordingly. Amen.

Week Thirteen – Tuesday

The Close of the Commandments

What does this mean?—Answer. God threatens to punish all that transgress these commandments. Therefore we should dread his wrath and not act contrary to these commandments. But he promises grace and every blessing to all that keep these commandments. Therefore we should also love and trust in him, and gladly do according to his commandments.

Again, that you do your neighbor no harm, injury, or violence, nor in any wise encroach upon him as touching his body, wife, property, honor, or rights, as all these things are commanded in their order, even though you have opportunity and cause to do so and no man would reprove you; but that you do good to all men, help them, and promote their interest, howsoever and wherever you can, purely from love of God and in order to please him, in the confidence that he will abundantly reward you for everything. Thus you see how the First Commandment is the chief source and fountainhead which flows into all the rest, and again, all return to that and depend upon it, so that beginning and end are fastened and bound to each other.

This (I say) it is profitable and necessary always to teach to the young people, to admonish them and to remind them of it, that they may be brought up not only with blows and compulsion, like cattle, but in the fear and reverence of God. For where this is considered and laid to heart that these things are not human trifles, but the commandments of the Divine Majesty, who insists upon them with such earnestness, is angry with and punishes those who despise them, and, on the other hand, abundantly rewards those who keep them, there will be a spontaneous impulse and a desire gladly to do the will of God. [LC I.328–30]

Meditation:

1. How does keeping the Fifth through Tenth Commandments demonstrate proper fear, love, and trust toward God?
2. Why does God desire that we do good to all, help them, and promote their interest, even when we have opportunity and cause to do otherwise?
3. What does it mean to admonish someone? What effect will it typically have? Why is this preferable to compulsion?

Prayer:

Heavenly Father, you discipline your children, whom you love. Thank you for admonishing me with your word so that I desire gladly to do your will. Amen.

Week Thirteen – Wednesday

The Close of the Commandments

What does this mean?—Answer. God threatens to punish all that transgress these commandments. Therefore we should dread his wrath and not act contrary to these commandments. But he promises grace and every blessing to all that keep these commandments. Therefore we should also love and trust in him, and gladly do according to his commandments.

Therefore it is not in vain that it is commanded in the Old Testament to write the Ten Commandments on all walls and corners, yes, even on the garments, not for the sake of merely having them written in these places and making a show of them, as did the Jews, but that we might have our eyes constantly fixed upon them, and have them always in our memory, and that we might practice them in all our actions and ways, and everyone make them his daily exercise in all cases, in every business and transaction, as though they were written in every place wherever he would look, yea, wherever he walks or stands. Thus there would be occasion enough, both at home in our own house and abroad with our neighbors, to practice the Ten Commandments, that no one need run far from them.

From this it again appears how highly these Ten Commandments are to be exalted and extolled above all estates, commandments, and works which are taught and practiced aside from them. For here we can boast and say: Let all the wise and saints step forth and produce, if they can, a work like these commandments, upon which God insists with such earnestness, and which he enjoins with his greatest wrath and punishment, and, besides, adds such glorious promises that he will pour out upon us all good things and blessings. Therefore they should be taught above all others, and be esteemed precious and dear, as the highest treasure given by God. [LC I.331–33]

Meditation:

1. What did the Old Testament require the Jews to do with the Ten Commandments? Why?
2. What are some specific ways in which you can have your eyes constantly fixed upon them? How might this help you practice them?
3. What should our attitude be toward the Ten Commandments and God's law in general? Why are we often tempted to view them otherwise?

Prayer:

Lord, thank you for giving me your Ten Commandments. Keep them always before me. Help me to love and treasure them so that I also practice them. Amen.

Week Thirteen – Thursday

The Apostles' Creed

I believe in God the Father Almighty,
Maker of heaven and earth.
And in Jesus Christ, his only Son, our Lord;
who was conceived by the Holy Ghost,
born of the Virgin Mary;
suffered under Pontius Pilate,
was crucified, dead, and buried;
he descended into hell;
the third day he rose again from the dead;
he ascended into heaven,
and sitteth on the right hand of God the Father Almighty;
from thence he shall come to judge the quick and the dead.
I believe in the Holy Ghost;
one holy Christian church, the communion of saints;
the forgiveness of sins; the resurrection of the body;
and the life everlasting. Amen.

Thus far we have heard the first part of Christian doctrine, in which we have seen all that God wishes us to do or to leave undone. Now, there properly follows the Creed, which sets forth to us everything that we must expect and receive from God, and, to state it quite briefly, teaches us to know him fully. And this is intended to help us do that which according to the Ten Commandments we ought to do. For (as said above) they are set so high that all human ability is far too feeble and weak to keep them. Therefore it is as necessary to learn this part as the former in order that we may know how to attain thereto, whence and whereby to obtain such power. For if we could by our own powers keep the Ten Commandments as they are to be kept, we would need nothing further, neither the Creed nor the Lord's Prayer. But before we explain this advantage and necessity of the Creed, it is sufficient at first for the simpleminded that they learn to comprehend and understand the Creed itself. [LC II.1–4]

Meditation:

1. What is the first part of Christian doctrine, which we have just finished reviewing at length? What does it reveal to us about God?
2. What properly follows next? What does it reveal to us about God? Why is this sequence important?
3. Do we have the ability to keep the Ten Commandments by our own powers? Why not? What has God done for us to address this?

Prayer:

God, thank you for giving me the law to teach me your will and the gospel to show me all that you have done to make up for my failure to obey it. Amen.

Week Thirteen – Friday

The Apostles' Creed

I believe in God the Father Almighty,
Maker of heaven and earth.
And in Jesus Christ, his only Son, our Lord;
who was conceived by the Holy Ghost,
born of the Virgin Mary;
suffered under Pontius Pilate,
was crucified, dead, and buried;
he descended into hell;
the third day he rose again from the dead;
he ascended into heaven,
and sitteth on the right hand of God the Father Almighty;
from thence he shall come to judge the quick and the dead.
I believe in the Holy Ghost;
one holy Christian church, the communion of saints;
the forgiveness of sins; the resurrection of the body;
and the life everlasting. Amen.

In the first place, the Creed has hitherto been divided into twelve articles, although, if all points which are written in the Scriptures and which belong to the Creed were to be distinctly set forth, there would be far more articles, nor could they all be clearly expressed in so few words. But that it may be most easily and clearly understood as it is to be taught to children, we shall briefly sum up the entire Creed in three chief articles, according to the three persons in the Godhead, to whom everything that we believe is related, so that the First Article, of God the Father, explains creation; the Second Article, of the Son, redemption; and the Third, of the Holy Ghost, sanctification. Just as though the Creed were briefly comprehended in so many words: I believe in God the Father, who has created me; I believe in God the Son, who has redeemed me; I believe in the Holy Ghost, who sanctifies me. One God and one faith, but three persons, therefore also three articles or confessions. Let us briefly run over the words. [LC II.5–8]

Meditation:
1. Why do you suppose that the Apostles' Creed was traditionally divided into twelve articles prior to Luther's time?
2. Into how many articles did Luther divide the Creed instead? Why? What heading did he assign to each article?
3. What is the significance of the doctrine of the Trinity, that the one true God has revealed himself as eternally three persons?

Prayer:

God the Father, thank you for creating me. God the Son, thank you for redeeming me. God the Holy Spirit, thank you for sanctifying me. Amen.

Week Thirteen – Saturday

The First Article: Of Creation

I believe in God the Father Almighty,
Maker of heaven and earth.

This portrays and sets forth most briefly what is the essence, will, activity, and work of God the Father. For since the Ten Commandments have taught that we are to have not more than one God, the question might be asked, "What kind of a person is God? What does he do? How can we praise, or portray and describe him, that he may be known?" Now, that is taught in this and in the following article, so that the Creed is nothing else than the answer and confession of Christians arranged with respect to the First Commandment. As if you were to ask a little child: "My dear, what sort of a God have you? What do you know of him?" he could say: "This is my God: first, the Father, who has created heaven and earth; besides this only One I regard nothing else as God; for there is no one else who could create heaven and earth."

But for the learned, and those who are somewhat advanced, these three articles may all be expanded and divided into as many parts as there are words. But now for young scholars let it suffice to indicate the most necessary points, namely, as we have said, that this article refers to the creation: that we emphasize the words: "Creator of heaven and earth." [LC II.10–12]

Meditation:

1. How does the First Article summarize what kind of person God is? Why do we call him Father? Almighty? Creator?
2. How is the First Article connected with the First Commandment? Why is it important to know something about God before we begin to worship him?
3. What is the significance of recognizing that God created both heaven and earth? Is anything excluded, other than God himself?

Prayer:

Father Almighty, I praise and worship you as creator of all things. Thank you for revealing yourself so that I may know you and introduce others to you. Amen.

Week Fourteen – Sunday

The First Article: Of Creation

What does this mean?—Answer.I believe that God has made me and all creatures; that he has given me my body and soul, eyes, ears, and all my limbs, my reason, and all my senses, and still preserves them; in addition thereto, clothing and shoes, meat and drink, house and homestead, wife and children, fields, cattle, and all my goods; that he provides me richly and daily with all that I need to support this body and life, protects me from all danger, and guards me and preserves me from all evil; and all this out of pure, fatherly, divine goodness and mercy, without any merit or worthiness in me; for all which I owe it to him to thank, praise, serve, and obey him. This is most certainly true.

But what is the force of this, or what do you mean by these words? Answer: This is what I mean and believe, that I am a creature of God; that is, that he has given and constantly preserves to me my body, soul, and life, members great and small, all my senses, reason, and understanding, and so on, food and drink, clothing and support, wife and children, domestics, house and home, etc. Besides, he causes all creatures to serve for the uses and necessities of life: sun, moon, and stars in the firmament, day and night, air, fire, water, earth, and whatever it bears and produces, birds and fishes, beasts, grain, and all kinds of produce, and whatever else there is of bodily and temporal goods, good government, peace, security. Thus we learn from this article that none of us has of himself, nor can preserve, his life nor anything that is here enumerated or can be enumerated, however small and unimportant a thing it might be, for all is comprehended in the word *Creator*.

Moreover, we also confess that God the Father has not only given us all that we have and see before our eyes, but daily preserves and defends us against all evil and misfortune, averts all sorts of danger and calamity; and that he does all this out of pure love and goodness, without our merit, as a benevolent Father, who cares for us that no evil befall us. But to speak more of this belongs in the other two parts of this article, where we say, "Father Almighty." [LC II.13-18]

Meditation:
1. What does it mean to be a creature of God? Why does the world resist the truth that God has made each of us and everything else?
2. What can you add to the list of things that God has given and constantly preserves to you? Why do we need to recognize that it all comes from him?
3. From what kinds of evil, misfortune, danger, and calamity does God defend us daily? Why? Who seeks to bring these things upon us? Why?

Prayer:

Lord God, thank you for giving me my life and all that I have. Remind me to acknowledge this at all times, and protect me against the evil one. Amen.

Week Fourteen – Monday

The First Article: Of Creation

What does this mean?—Answer. I believe that God has made me and all creatures; that he has given me my body and soul, eyes, ears, and all my limbs, my reason, and all my senses, and still preserves them; in addition thereto, clothing and shoes, meat and drink, house and homestead, wife and children, fields, cattle, and all my goods; that he provides me richly and daily with all that I need to support this body and life, protects me from all danger, and guards me and preserves me from all evil; and all this out of pure, fatherly, divine goodness and mercy, without any merit or worthiness in me; for all which I owe it to him to thank, praise, serve, and obey him. This is most certainly true.

Now, since all that we possess, and, moreover, whatever, in addition, is in heaven and upon the earth, is daily given, preserved, and kept for us by God, it is readily inferred and concluded that it is our duty to love, praise, and thank him for it without ceasing, and, in short, to serve him with all these things, as he demands and has enjoined in the Ten Commandments.

Here we could say much if we were to expatiate, how few there are that believe this article. For we all pass over it, hear it and say it, but neither see nor consider what the words teach us. For if we believed it with the heart, we would also act accordingly, and not stalk about proudly, act defiantly, and boast as though we had life, riches, power, and honor, etc., of ourselves, so that others must fear and serve us, as is the practice of the wretched, perverse world, which is drowned in blindness, and abuses all the good things and gifts of God only for its own pride, avarice, lust, and luxury, and never once regards God, so as to thank him or acknowledge him as Lord and Creator. [LC II.19–21]

Meditation:

1. What duty is readily inferred and concluded from all that God gives, preserves, and keeps for us?
2. What is the connection between the First Article and the Ten Commandments? How is God's law evident in God's creation?
3. What attitude does the world typically adopt toward life, riches, power, and honor? Why? What kinds of behavior tend to result from this?

Prayer:

Heavenly Father, I love, praise, and thank you for all that you give, preserve, and keep for me. Empower me to serve you with all these things gladly. Amen.

Week Fourteen – Tuesday

The First Article: Of Creation

What does this mean?—Answer. I believe that God has made me and all creatures; that he has given me my body and soul, eyes, ears, and all my limbs, my reason, and all my senses, and still preserves them; in addition thereto, clothing and shoes, meat and drink, house and homestead, wife and children, fields, cattle, and all my goods; that he provides me richly and daily with all that I need to support this body and life, protects me from all danger, and guards me and preserves me from all evil; and all this out of pure, fatherly, divine goodness and mercy, without any merit or worthiness in me; for all which I owe it to him to thank, praise, serve, and obey him. This is most certainly true.

Therefore, this article ought to humble and terrify us all, if we believed it. For we sin daily with eyes, ears, hands, body and soul, money and possessions, and with everything we have, especially those who even fight against the word of God. Yet Christians have this advantage, that they acknowledge themselves in duty bound to serve God for all these things, and to be obedient to him.

We ought, therefore, daily to practice this article, impress it upon our mind, and to remember it in all that meets our eyes, and in all good that falls to our lot, and wherever we escape from calamity or danger, that it is God who gives and does all these things, that therein we sense and see his paternal heart and his transcendent love toward us. Thereby the heart would be warmed and kindled to be thankful, and to employ all such good things to the honor and praise of God.

Thus we have most briefly presented the meaning of this article, as much as is at first necessary for the most simple to learn, both as to what we have and receive from God, and what we owe in return, which is a most excellent knowledge, but a far greater treasure. For here we see how the Father has given himself to us, together with all creatures, and has most richly provided for us in this life, besides that he has overwhelmed us with unspeakable, eternal treasures by his Son and the Holy Ghost, as we shall hear. [LC II.22-24]

Meditation:

1. Despite all that God does for us, what do we daily do with his gifts? Why? What advantage do Christians have in dealing with this reality?
2. What should we do whenever we experience something good or avoid something bad during the course of our lives?
3. What are some specific ways in which you can employ all the good things that you have received from God to his honor and praise today?

Prayer:

Dear God, forgive me for often taking your gifts for granted, and even misusing them. Teach me to recognize your hand on my life and be grateful for it. Amen.

Week Fourteen – Wednesday

The Second Article: Of Redemption

I believe in God the Father Almighty,
Maker of heaven and earth.
And in Jesus Christ, his only Son, our Lord;
who was conceived by the Holy Ghost,
born of the Virgin Mary;
suffered under Pontius Pilate,
was crucified, dead, and buried;
he descended into hell;
the third day he rose again from the dead;
he ascended into heaven,
and sitteth on the right hand of God the Father Almighty;
from thence he shall come to judge the quick and the dead.
I believe in the Holy Ghost;
one holy Christian church, the communion of saints;
the forgiveness of sins; the resurrection of the body;
and the life everlasting. Amen.

Here we learn to know the Second Person of the Godhead, so that we see what we have from God over and above the temporal goods aforementioned; namely, how he has completely poured forth himself and withheld nothing from us that he has not given us. Now, this article is very rich and broad; but in order to expound it also briefly and in a childlike way we shall take up one word and sum up in that the entire article, namely (as we have said), that we may here learn how we have been redeemed; and we shall base this on these words: "In Jesus Christ, our Lord."

If now you are asked, "What do you believe in the Second Article of Jesus Christ?" answer briefly: "I believe that Jesus Christ, true Son of God, has become my Lord." But what is it to become Lord? It is this, that he has redeemed me from sin, from the devil, from death, and from all evil. For before I had no Lord nor King, but was captive under the power of the devil, condemned to death, enmeshed in sin and blindness. [LC II.26–27]

Meditation:

1. Why is it important to recognize that God has done far more for us than just providing temporal goods?
2. What does it mean to be redeemed? From what has God redeemed us? What was the price that he paid to do so?
3. What does it mean to confess that Jesus Christ is your Lord? What is the only alternative? How is the world's captivity to the devil evident?

Prayer:

Dear Jesus, thank you for delivering me from sin, from the devil, from death, and from all evil. I bow before you as my Lord. Help me to live accordingly. Amen.

Week Fourteen – Thursday

The Second Article: Of Redemption

What does this mean?—Answer. I believe that Jesus Christ, true God, begotten of the Father from eternity, and also true man, born of the Virgin Mary, is my Lord, who has redeemed me, a lost and condemned creature, purchased and won me from all sins, from death, and from the power of the devil, not with gold or silver, but with his holy, precious blood and with his innocent suffering and death, in order that I may be his own, and live under him in his kingdom, and serve him in everlasting righteousness, innocence, and blessedness, even as he is risen from the dead, lives and reigns to all eternity. This is most certainly true.

For when we had been created by God the Father, and had received from him all manner of good, the devil came and led us into disobedience, sin, death, and all evil, so that we fell under his wrath and displeasure and were doomed to eternal damnation, as we had merited and deserved. There was no counsel, help, or comfort until this only and eternal Son of God in his unfathomable goodness had compassion upon our misery and wretchedness, and came from heaven to help us. Those tyrants and jailers, then, are all expelled now, and in their place has come Jesus Christ, Lord of life, righteousness, every blessing, and salvation, and has delivered us poor lost men from the jaws of hell, has won us, made us free, and brought us again into the favor and grace of the Father, and has taken us as his own property under his shelter and protection, that he may govern us by his righteousness, wisdom, power, life, and blessedness.

Let this, then, be the sum of this article that the little word *Lord* signifies simply as much as *Redeemer*, i.e., he who has brought us from Satan to God, from death to life, from sin to righteousness, and who preserves us in the same. But all the points which follow in order in this article serve no other end than to explain and express this redemption, how and whereby it was accomplished, that is, how much it cost him, and what he spent and risked that he might win us and bring us under his dominion . . . [LC II.28–31a]

Meditation:

1. What did the devil do soon after God created the first humans? Did Adam and Eve sin willingly or unwillingly? Are we any different?
2. What have you merited and deserved from God because of your sin? Why are the consequences so severe? What is our only counsel, help, or comfort?
3. Why did the Son of God have compassion upon our misery and wretchedness? What did he do for us as a result?

Prayer:

Lord Jesus, I deserve nothing but your wrath, displeasure, and damnation, yet you came from heaven to help me. I thank and praise you for your mercy. Amen.

Week Fourteen – Friday

The Second Article: Of Redemption

What does this mean?—Answer. I believe that Jesus Christ, true God, begotten of the Father from eternity, and also true man, born of the Virgin Mary, is my Lord, who has redeemed me, a lost and condemned creature, purchased and won me from all sins, from death, and from the power of the devil, not with gold or silver, but with his holy, precious blood and with his innocent suffering and death, in order that I may be his own, and live under him in his kingdom, and serve him in everlasting righteousness, innocence, and blessedness, even as he is risen from the dead, lives and reigns to all eternity. This is most certainly true.

... namely, that he became man, conceived and born without sin, of the Holy Ghost and of the Virgin Mary, that he might overcome sin; moreover, that he suffered, died, and was buried, that he might make satisfaction for me and pay what I owe, not with silver nor gold, but with his own precious blood. And all this, in order to become my Lord; for he did none of these for himself, nor had he any need of it. And after that he rose again from the dead, swallowed up and devoured death, and finally ascended into heaven and assumed the government at the Father's right hand, so that the devil and all powers must be subject to him and lie at his feet, until finally, at the last day, he will completely part and separate us from the wicked world, the devil, death, sin, etc.

But to explain all these single points separately belongs not to brief sermons for children, but rather to the ampler sermons that extend throughout the entire year, especially at those times which are appointed for the purpose of treating at length of each article—of the birth, sufferings, resurrection, ascension of Christ, etc.

Ay, the entire gospel which we preach is based on this, that we properly understand this article as that upon which our salvation and all our happiness rest, and which is so rich and comprehensive that we never can learn it fully. [LC II.31b–33]

Meditation:

1. Why is it important that Jesus was conceived and born without sin? What did this enable him to do? For whose sake did he suffer and die?
2. To whom did Jesus make satisfaction? What did we owe that he paid? What was the price? What did his resurrection and ascension demonstrate?
3. Why did Luther not attempt to explain this article in further detail? How does observing the church year serve that purpose instead?

Prayer:

Son of God, I can never thank you enough for obeying the law perfectly and enduring its punishment, both in my place. You are my Savior and Lord. Amen.

Week Fourteen – Saturday

The Third Article: Of Sanctification

I believe in the Holy Ghost;
one holy Christian church, the communion of saints;
the forgiveness of sins; the resurrection of the body;
and the life everlasting. Amen.

This article (as I have said) I cannot relate better than to sanctification, that through the same the Holy Ghost, with his office, is declared and depicted, namely, that he makes holy. Therefore we must take our stand upon the word "Holy Ghost," because it is so precise and comprehensive that we cannot find another. For there are, besides, many kinds of spirits mentioned in the Holy Scriptures, as, the spirit of man, heavenly spirits, and evil spirits. But the Spirit of God alone is called Holy Ghost, that is, he who has sanctified and still sanctifies us. For as the Father is called Creator, the Son Redeemer, so the Holy Ghost, from his work, must be called Sanctifier, or One that makes holy. But how is such sanctifying done? Answer: Just as the Son obtains dominion, whereby he wins us, through his birth, death, resurrection, etc., so also the Holy Ghost effects our sanctification by the following parts, namely, by the communion of saints or the Christian church, the forgiveness of sins, the resurrection of the body, and the life everlasting; that is, he first leads us into his holy congregation, and places us in the bosom of the church, whereby he preaches to us and brings us to Christ. [LC II.35–37]

Meditation:

1. What is sanctification? What does it mean to make something holy? In what sense does the Holy Spirit set Christians apart from other people?
2. What other kinds of spirits are mentioned in the Bible? What distinguishes the Holy Spirit from all of these?
3. What does it mean to be part of the church, the communion of saints? What does the Holy Spirit do there for us and through us?

Prayer:

Holy Spirit, thank you for sanctifying me so that I may share in the communion of saints. Please continue to sanctify me through word and sacrament. Amen.

Week Fifteen – Sunday

The Third Article: Of Sanctification

I believe in the Holy Ghost;
one holy Christian church, the communion of saints;
the forgiveness of sins; the resurrection of the body;
and the life everlasting. Amen.

For neither you nor I could ever know anything of Christ, or believe on him, and obtain him for our Lord, unless it were offered to us and granted to our hearts by the Holy Ghost through the preaching of the gospel. The work is done and accomplished; for Christ has acquired and gained the treasure for us by his suffering, death, resurrection, etc. But if the work remained concealed so that no one knew of it, then it would be in vain and lost. That this treasure, therefore, might not lie buried, but be appropriated and enjoyed, God has caused the word to go forth and be proclaimed, in which he gives the Holy Ghost to bring this treasure home and appropriate it to us. Therefore sanctifying is nothing else than bringing us to Christ to receive this good, to which we could not attain of ourselves.

Learn, then, to understand this article most clearly. If you are asked: What do you mean by the words: "I believe in the Holy Ghost"? you can answer: "I believe that the Holy Ghost makes me holy, as his name implies." But whereby does he accomplish this, or what are his method and means to this end? Answer: By the Christian church, the forgiveness of sins, the resurrection of the body, and the life everlasting. For, in the first place, he has a peculiar congregation in the world, which is the mother that begets and bears every Christian through the word of God, which he reveals and preaches, he illumines and enkindles hearts, that they understand, accept it, cling to it, and persevere in it. [LC II.38–42]

Meditation:

1. When did Christ accomplish his work of redemption for us? What was its scope? What does this mean for our proclamation of the gospel?
2. What is the primary means by which God delivers salvation to people? How can his word do such great things?
3. In what sense is the church the mother of every child of God? What role can you play in bringing the word of God to others?

Prayer:

Lord, thank you for doing all that was necessary for my salvation, including its revelation to me by the Holy Spirit. Help me to share your saving word. Amen.

Week Fifteen – Monday

The Third Article: Of Sanctification

I believe in the Holy Ghost;
one holy Christian church, the communion of saints;
the forgiveness of sins; the resurrection of the body;
and the life everlasting. Amen.

For where he does not cause [the word of God] to be preached and made alive in the heart, so that it is understood, it is lost, as was the case under the papacy, where faith was entirely put under the bench, and no one recognized Christ as his Lord or the Holy Ghost as his Sanctifier, that is, no one believed that Christ is our Lord in the sense that he has acquired this treasure for us, without our works and merit, and made us acceptable to the Father. What, then, was lacking? This, that the Holy Ghost was not there to reveal it and cause it to be preached; but men and evil spirits were there, who taught us to obtain grace and be saved by our works. Therefore it is not a Christian church either; for where Christ is not preached, there is no Holy Ghost who creates, calls, and gathers the Christian church, without which no one can come to Christ the Lord. Let this suffice concerning the sum of this article. But because the parts which are here enumerated are not quite clear to the simple, we shall run over them also. [LC II.43–46]

Meditation:

1. What happens when the word of God is improperly taught or otherwise misused? Who alone can make it alive in the heart so that it is understood?
2. In what sense does the Holy Spirit cause us to believe that Christ is our Lord? Why is it important that we recognize this truth?
3. What false belief commonly arises when Christ is not preached? Why are we so easily tempted to think that we are saved by our works?

Prayer:

Dear God, thank you for all those who proclaimed to me what you have done for me. Guard me from the danger of thinking that I am saved by what I do. Amen.

Week Fifteen – Tuesday

The Third Article: Of Sanctification

I believe in the Holy Ghost;
one holy Christian church, the communion of saints;
the forgiveness of sins; the resurrection of the body;
and the life everlasting. Amen.

The Creed denominates the holy Christian church a "communion of saints"; for both expressions, taken together, are identical. But formerly the one expression was not there, and it has been poorly and unintelligibly translated into German. If it is to be rendered plainly, it must be expressed quite differently in the German idiom; for the word *ecclesia* properly means in German an assembly. But we are accustomed to the word *church*, by which the simple do not understand an assembled multitude, but the consecrated house or building, although the house ought not to be called a church, except only for the reason that the multitude assembles there. For we who assemble there make and choose for ourselves a particular place, and give a name to the house according to the assembly.

Thus the word *church* means really nothing else than a common assembly, and is not German by idiom, but Greek (as is also the word *ecclesia*); for in their own language they call it *kyria*, as in Latin it is called *curia*. Therefore in genuine German, in our mother tongue, it ought to be called "a Christian congregation or assembly," or, best of all and most clearly, "holy Christendom."

So also the word *communio*, which is added, ought not to be rendered *communion*, but *congregation*. And it is nothing else than an interpretation or explanation by which someone meant to explain what the Christian church is. This our people, who understood neither Latin nor German, have rendered "communion of saints," although no German language speaks thus, nor understands it thus. But to speak correct German, it ought to be a "congregation of saints," that is, a congregation made up purely of saints, or, to speak yet more plainly, a "holy congregation." I say this in order that the words "communion of saints" may be understood, because the expression has become so established by custom that it cannot well be eradicated, and it is

The Lutheran Catechism

treated almost as heresy if one should attempt to change a word. [LC II.47–50]

Meditation:
1. What are the different definitions of the word "church"? Which of these meanings is applicable within the context of the Third Article?
2. Why is it important for Christians to come together in an assembly? Is it necessary for them to have a specific building where they do so?
3. In what sense does a local assembly of Christians constitute a holy congregation? How is it connected with the rest of holy Christendom?

Prayer:

Lord, thank you for gathering your saints into local congregations. Help me to participate actively, for my own edification and the benefit of others. Amen.

Week Fifteen – Wednesday

The Third Article: Of Sanctification

What does this mean?—Answer. I believe that I cannot by my own reason or strength believe in Jesus Christ, my Lord, or come to him; but the Holy Ghost has called me by the gospel, enlightened me with his gifts, sanctified and kept me in the true faith; even as he calls, gathers, enlightens, and sanctifies the whole Christian church on earth, and keeps it with Jesus Christ in the one true faith; in which Christian church he forgives daily and richly all sins to me and all believers, and at the last day will raise up me and all the dead, and will give to me and to all believers in Christ everlasting life. This is most certainly true.

But this is the meaning and substance of this addition: "I believe that there is upon earth a little holy group and congregation of pure saints, under one head, even Christ, called together by the Holy Ghost in one faith, one mind, and one understanding, with manifold gifts, yet agreeing in love, without sects or schisms. I am also a part and member of the same, a sharer and joint owner of all the goods it possesses, brought to it and incorporated into it by the Holy Ghost by having heard and continuing to hear the word of God, which is the beginning of entering it." For formerly, before we had attained to this, we were altogether of the devil, knowing nothing of God and of Christ. Thus, until the last day, the Holy Ghost abides with the holy congregation or Christendom, by means of which he fetches us to Christ and which he employs to teach and preach to us the word, whereby he works and promotes sanctification, causing it daily to grow and become strong in the faith and its fruits which he produces. [LC II.51–53]

Meditation:
1. Who is the one head of the congregation of pure saints? In what sense do its members share one faith, one mind, and one understanding?
2. How did you become a member of this little holy group? What benefits do you receive? What was your previous condition?
3. What does the Holy Spirit do for us by means of the holy congregation, until the last day? What are the results? How is this evident in our lives?

Prayer:

Holy Spirit, thank you for granting and strengthening my faith through the proclamation of the word of God. Help me daily to grow and be fruitful. Amen.

Week Fifteen – Thursday

The Third Article: Of Sanctification

What does this mean?—Answer. I believe that I cannot by my own reason or strength believe in Jesus Christ, my Lord, or come to him; but the Holy Ghost has called me by the gospel, enlightened me with his gifts, sanctified and kept me in the true faith; even as he calls, gathers, enlightens, and sanctifies the whole Christian church on earth, and keeps it with Jesus Christ in the one true faith; in which Christian church he forgives daily and richly all sins to me and all believers, and at the last day will raise up me and all the dead, and will give to me and to all believers in Christ everlasting life. This is most certainly true.

We further believe that in this Christian church we have forgiveness of sin, which is wrought through the holy sacraments and absolution, moreover, through all manner of consolatory promises of the entire gospel. Therefore, whatever is to be preached concerning the sacraments belongs here, and, in short, the whole gospel and all the offices of Christianity, which also must be preached and taught without ceasing. For although the grace of God is secured through Christ, and sanctification is wrought by the Holy Ghost through the word of God in the unity of the Christian church, yet on account of our flesh which we bear about with us we are never without sin.

Everything, therefore, in the Christian church is ordered to the end that we shall daily obtain there nothing but the forgiveness of sin through the word and signs, to comfort and encourage our consciences as long as we live here. Thus, although we have sins, the Holy Ghost does not allow them to injure us, because we are in the Christian church, where there is nothing but forgiveness of sin, both in that God forgives us, and in that we forgive, bear with, and help each other. [LC II.54–55]

Meditation:
1. What is the most important thing that we have as members of the Christian church? Why? How does God convey his forgiveness of sin to us?
2. Does God's forgiveness mean that we can be completely without sin in this life? Why not? What are the implications of this for the church on earth?
3. What effect does receiving God's forgiveness have on our consciences? What effect should it have on our relationships with others?

Prayer:

Merciful God, I confess that I am a poor, miserable sinner. Please forgive me, comfort and encourage my conscience, and help me to forgive others. Amen.

Week Fifteen – Friday

The Third Article: Of Sanctification

What does this mean?—Answer. I believe that I cannot by my own reason or strength believe in Jesus Christ, my Lord, or come to him; but the Holy Ghost has called me by the gospel, enlightened me with his gifts, sanctified and kept me in the true faith; even as he calls, gathers, enlightens, and sanctifies the whole Christian church on earth, and keeps it with Jesus Christ in the one true faith; in which Christian church he forgives daily and richly all sins to me and all believers, and at the last day will raise up me and all the dead, and will give to me and to all believers in Christ everlasting life. This is most certainly true.

But outside of this Christian church, where the gospel is not, there is no forgiveness, as also there can be no holiness. Therefore all who seek and wish to merit holiness, not through the gospel and forgiveness of sin, but by their works, have expelled and severed themselves.

Meanwhile, however, while sanctification has begun and is growing daily, we expect that our flesh will be destroyed and buried with all its uncleanness, and will come forth gloriously, and arise to entire and perfect holiness in a new eternal life. For now we are only half pure and holy, so that the Holy Ghost has ever to continue his work in us through the word, and daily to dispense forgiveness, until we attain to that life where there will be no more forgiveness, but only perfectly pure and holy people, full of godliness and righteousness, removed and free from sin, death, and all evil, in a new, immortal, and glorified body.

Behold, all this is to be the office and work of the Holy Ghost, that he begin and daily increase holiness upon earth by means of these two things, the Christian church and the forgiveness of sin. But in our dissolution he will accomplish it altogether in an instant, and will forever preserve us therein by the last two parts. [LC II.56–59]

Meditation:

1. Why is there neither forgiveness nor holiness outside of the Christian church? What is the fundamental nature of every other religion?
2. Why do we continue to need forgiveness throughout our lives here on earth? How does the Holy Spirit dispense it to us? How often?
3. In what sense is our sanctification growing daily? When will it finally be completed, such that we are perfectly pure and holy people?

Prayer:

Dear Lord, forgive me for seeking and wishing to merit holiness by my works. Help me to rely entirely on your works of redemption and sanctification. Amen.

Week Fifteen – Saturday

The Third Article: Of Sanctification

What does this mean?—Answer. I believe that I cannot by my own reason or strength believe in Jesus Christ, my Lord, or come to him; but the Holy Ghost has called me by the gospel, enlightened me with his gifts, sanctified and kept me in the true faith; even as he calls, gathers, enlightens, and sanctifies the whole Christian church on earth, and keeps it with Jesus Christ in the one true faith; in which Christian church he forgives daily and richly all sins to me and all believers, and at the last day will raise up me and all the dead, and will give to me and to all believers in Christ everlasting life. This is most certainly true.

But the term "resurrection of the flesh" here employed is not according to good German idiom. For when we Germans hear the word "flesh," we think no farther than of the shambles [meat market]. But in good German idiom we would say "resurrection of the body." However, it is not a matter of much moment, if we only understand the words aright.

This, now, is the article which must ever be and remain in operation. For creation we have received; redemption, too, is finished. But the Holy Ghost carries on his work without ceasing to the last day. And for that purpose he has appointed a congregation upon earth by which he speaks and does everything. For he has not yet brought together all his Christian church nor dispensed forgiveness. Therefore we believe in him who through the word daily brings us into the fellowship of this Christian church, and through the same word and the forgiveness of sins bestows, increases, and strengthens faith, in order that when he has accomplished it all, and we abide therein, and die to the world and to all evil, he may finally make us perfectly and forever holy; which now we expect in faith through the word.

Behold, here you have the entire divine essence, will, and work depicted most exquisitely in quite short and yet rich words, wherein consists all our wisdom, which surpasses and exceeds the wisdom, mind, and reason of all men. [LC II.60–63a]

Meditation:

1. What comes to mind when you hear the word "flesh"? Why is it significant that there will be a resurrection of the body? What will be different about it?
2. What is different about the work of the Holy Spirit in comparison with creation and redemption? Why is his work not yet finished?
3. What must happen for us to become perfectly and forever holy? What does the Holy Spirit do for us in the meantime?

Prayer:

Holy Spirit, please bestow, increase, and strengthen my faith through the word and the forgiveness of sins in the fellowship of the Christian church. Amen.

Week Sixteen – Sunday

The Third Article: Of Sanctification

What does this mean?—Answer. I believe that I cannot by my own reason or strength believe in Jesus Christ, my Lord, or come to him; but the Holy Ghost has called me by the gospel, enlightened me with his gifts, sanctified and kept me in the true faith; even as he calls, gathers, enlightens, and sanctifies the whole Christian church on earth, and keeps it with Jesus Christ in the one true faith; in which Christian church he forgives daily and richly all sins to me and all believers, and at the last day will raise up me and all the dead, and will give to me and to all believers in Christ everlasting life. This is most certainly true.

For although the whole world with all diligence has endeavored to ascertain what God is, what he has in mind and does, yet has she never been able to attain to any of these things. But here we have everything in richest measure; for here in all three articles he has himself revealed and opened the deepest abyss of his paternal heart and of his pure unutterable love. For he has created us for this very object, that he might redeem and sanctify us; and in addition to giving and imparting to us everything in heaven and upon earth, he has given to us even his Son and the Holy Ghost, by whom to bring us to himself. For (as explained above) we could never attain to the knowledge of the grace and favor of the Father except through the Lord Christ, who is a mirror of the paternal heart, outside of whom we see nothing but an angry and terrible Judge. But of Christ we could know nothing either, unless it had been revealed by the Holy Ghost.

These articles of the Creed, therefore, divide and separate us Christians from all other people upon earth. For all outside of Christianity, whether heathen, Turks, Jews, or false Christians and hypocrites, although they believe in, and worship, only one true God, yet know not what his mind towards them is, and cannot expect any love or blessing from him; therefore they abide in eternal wrath and damnation. For they have not the Lord Christ, and, besides, are not illumined and favored by any gifts of the Holy Ghost. [LC II.63b–66]

Meditation:

1. Why is the whole world unable to ascertain what God is, what he has in mind and does, apart from his revelation?
2. For what reason has God created us? What has he given to us toward this end? Who reveals the Father to us? Who reveals the Lord Christ to us?
3. Why is it insufficient for salvation to believe in, and worship, only one true God? What do Christians know about God that non-Christians do not?

Prayer:

Lord God, thank you for revealing yourself as Father, Son, and Holy Spirit, as well as your grace, favor, love, and blessing by bringing me to yourself. Amen.

Week Sixteen – Monday

The Third Article: Of Sanctification

What does this mean?—Answer. I believe that I cannot by my own reason or strength believe in Jesus Christ, my Lord, or come to him; but the Holy Ghost has called me by the gospel, enlightened me with his gifts, sanctified and kept me in the true faith; even as he calls, gathers, enlightens, and sanctifies the whole Christian church on earth, and keeps it with Jesus Christ in the one true faith; in which Christian church he forgives daily and richly all sins to me and all believers, and at the last day will raise up me and all the dead, and will give to me and to all believers in Christ everlasting life. This is most certainly true.

From this you perceive that the Creed is a doctrine quite different from the Ten Commandments; for the latter teaches indeed what we ought to do, but the former tells what God does for us and gives to us. Moreover, apart from this, the Ten Commandments are written in the hearts of all men; the Creed, however, no human wisdom can comprehend, but it must be taught by the Holy Ghost alone. The latter doctrine, therefore, makes no Christian, for the wrath and displeasure of God abide upon us still, because we cannot keep what God demands of us; but this brings pure grace, and makes us godly and acceptable to God. For by this knowledge we obtain love and delight in all the commandments of God, because here we see that God gives himself entire to us, with all that he has and is able to do, to aid and direct us in keeping the Ten Commandments—the Father, all creatures; the Son, his entire work; and the Holy Ghost, all his gifts.

Let this suffice concerning the Creed to lay a foundation for the simple, that they may not be burdened, so that, if they understand the substance of it, they themselves may afterwards strive to acquire more, and to refer to these parts whatever they learn in the Scriptures, and may ever grow and increase in richer understanding. For as long as we live here, we shall daily have enough to do to preach and to learn this. [LC II.67–70]

Meditation:

1. In what sense are the Ten Commandments written in the hearts of all men? Why is it impossible for human wisdom to comprehend the Apostles' Creed?
2. Why is the law unable to make anyone a Christian? What does the gospel bring to us and do for us? How does this change our view of the law?
3. How does learning the Creed lay a foundation for us? How can referring back to it help us grow and increase in richer understanding?

Prayer:

Gracious Lord, thank you for your law and gospel. Continue using them to convict me of sin, assure me of forgiveness, and show me how to live. Amen.

Week Sixteen – Tuesday

The Lord's Prayer

Our Father who art in heaven
hallowed be thy name.
Thy kingdom come.
Thy will be done on earth as it is in heaven.
Give us this day our daily bread,
and forgive us our trespasses
as we forgive those who trespass against us.
And lead us not into temptation,
but deliver us from evil. Amen.

We have now heard what we must do and believe, in which things the best and happiest life consists. Now follows the third part, how we ought to pray. For since we are so situated that no man can perfectly keep the Ten Commandments, even though he have begun to believe, and since the devil with all his power, together with the world and our own flesh, resists our endeavors, nothing is so necessary as that we should continually resort to the ear of God, call upon him, and pray to him, that he would give, preserve, and increase in us faith and the fulfilment of the Ten Commandments, and that he would remove everything that is in our way and opposes us therein. But that we might know what and how to pray, our Lord Christ has himself taught us both the mode and the words, as we shall see.

But before we explain the Lord's Prayer part by part, it is most necessary first to exhort and incite people to prayer, as Christ and the apostles also have done. And the first matter is to know that it is our duty to pray because of God's commandment. For thus we heard in the Second Commandment: "Thou shalt not take the name of the Lord, thy God, in vain," that we are there required to praise that holy name, and call upon it in every need, or to pray. For to call upon the name of God is nothing else than to pray. [LC III.1–5]

Meditation:

1. Which part of the catechism tells us what we must do? Which tells what we must believe? Why does the best and happiest life consist in these things?
2. Why is prayer an essential aspect of Christian discipleship? What three enemies continuously resist our endeavors? Why?
3. What is the connection between the Lord's Prayer and the Second Commandment? What does it mean to call upon the name of God?

Prayer:

God, I call upon your name this day. Help me to obey your commands and trust your promises despite the resistance of the devil, the world, and my flesh. Amen.

Week Sixteen – Wednesday

The Lord's Prayer

Our Father who art in heaven
hallowed be thy name.
Thy kingdom come.
Thy will be done on earth as it is in heaven.
Give us this day our daily bread,
and forgive us our trespasses
as we forgive those who trespass against us.
And lead us not into temptation,
but deliver us from evil. Amen.

Prayer is therefore as strictly and earnestly commanded as all other commandments: to have no other god, not to kill, not to steal, etc. Let no one think that it is all the same whether he pray or not, as vulgar people do, who grope in such delusion and ask, "Why should I pray? Who knows whether God heeds or will hear my prayer? If I do not pray, someone else will." And thus they fall into the habit of never praying, and frame a pretext, as though we taught that there is no duty or need of prayer, because we reject false and hypocritical prayers.

But this is true indeed that such prayers as have been offered hitherto when men were babbling and bawling in the churches were no prayers. For such external matters, when they are properly observed, may be a good exercise for young children, scholars, and simple persons, and may be called singing or reading, but not really praying. But praying, as the Second Commandment teaches, is to call upon God in every need. This he requires of us, and has not left it to our choice. But it is our duty and obligation to pray if we would be Christians, as much as it is our duty and obligation to obey our parents and the government; for by calling upon it and praying, the name of God is honored and profitably employed. This you must note above all things, that thereby you may silence and repel such thoughts as would keep and deter us from prayer. [LC III.6–8]

Meditation:

1. Why might someone think that it is all the same whether he pray or not? How can we be assured that God will hear our prayers?
2. What are some examples of false and hypocritical prayers? Why is saying them not really praying, and thus to be rejected?
3. Why do you suppose that God requires us to pray? How does prayer honor the name of God? What keeps and deters you from prayer?

Prayer:

Dear God, thank you for desiring my prayers and promising to hear them. Help me to overcome anything that might otherwise hinder me from praying. Amen.

Week Sixteen – Thursday

The Lord's Prayer

Our Father who art in heaven
hallowed be thy name.
Thy kingdom come.
Thy will be done on earth as it is in heaven.
Give us this day our daily bread,
and forgive us our trespasses
as we forgive those who trespass against us.
And lead us not into temptation,
but deliver us from evil. Amen.

For just as it would be idle for a son to say to his father, "Of what advantage is my obedience? I will go and do what I can; it is all the same"; but there stands the commandment, "Thou shalt and must do it"; so also here it is not left to my will to do it or leave it undone, but prayer shall and must be offered at the risk of God's wrath and displeasure.

This is therefore to be understood and noted before everything else, in order that thereby we may silence and repel the thoughts which would keep and deter us from praying, as though it were not of much consequence if we do not pray, or as though it were commanded those who are holier and in better favor with God than we; as, indeed, the human heart is by nature so despondent that it always flees from God and imagines that he does not wish or desire our prayer, because we are sinners and have merited nothing but wrath. Against such thoughts (I say) we should regard this commandment and turn to God, that we may not by such disobedience excite his anger still more. For by this commandment he gives us plainly to understand that he will not cast us from him nor chase us away, although we are sinners, but rather draw us to himself, so that we might humble ourselves before him, bewail this misery and plight of ours, and pray for grace and help. Therefore we read in the Scriptures that he is angry also with those who were smitten for their sin, because they did not return to him and by their prayers assuage his wrath and seek his grace. [LC III.9–11]

Meditation:

1. What kind of attitude is evident in a son who refuses to obey his father? How does this apply to a Christian who refuses to pray?
2. Why is it tempting to doubt that it matters whether we pray, or that we are holy enough to pray? What mistake are we making when we think that way?
3. What assurances does God offer to those who come to him in prayer? What kind of attitude should we adopt when we pray?

Prayer:

Father, thank you for the wonderful privilege of prayer. Give me your grace and help so that I come before you humbly, yet confident that you hear me. Amen.

Week Sixteen – Friday

The Lord's Prayer

Our Father who art in heaven
hallowed be thy name.
Thy kingdom come.
Thy will be done on earth as it is in heaven.
Give us this day our daily bread,
and forgive us our trespasses
as we forgive those who trespass against us.
And lead us not into temptation,
but deliver us from evil. Amen.

Now, from the fact that it is so solemnly commanded to pray, you are to conclude and think that no one should by any means despise his prayer, but rather set great store by it, and always seek an illustration from the other commandments. A child should by no means despise his obedience to father and mother, but should always think: "This work is a work of obedience, and what I do I do with no other intention than that I may walk in the obedience and commandment of God, on which I can settle and stand firm, and esteem it a great thing, not on account of my worthiness, but on account of the commandment." So here also, what and for what we pray we should regard as demanded by God and done in obedience to him, and should reflect thus: "On my account it would amount to nothing; but it shall avail, for the reason that God has commanded it." Therefore everybody, no matter what he has to say in prayer, should always come before God in obedience to this commandment. [LC III.12–13]

Meditation:

1. Why might someone be tempted to despise his own prayer? What is wrong with that way of thinking?
2. How can reflecting on the other commandments help us to recognize the necessity of obeying the Second Commandment by praying?
3. Are any of us truly worthy to come before God in prayer? Why does God insist that we do so anyway?

Prayer:

Lord, forgive me for sometimes being reluctant to pray. Help me to do so in obedience to your commandment and in faith that you will gladly hear me. Amen.

Week Sixteen – Saturday

The Lord's Prayer

Our Father who art in heaven
hallowed be thy name.
Thy kingdom come.
Thy will be done on earth as it is in heaven.
Give us this day our daily bread,
and forgive us our trespasses
as we forgive those who trespass against us.
And lead us not into temptation,
but deliver us from evil. Amen.

We pray, therefore, and exhort everyone most diligently to take this to heart and by no means to despise our prayer. For hitherto it has been taught thus in the devil's name that no one regarded these things, and men supposed it to be sufficient to have done the work, whether God would hear it or not. But that is staking prayer on a risk, and murmuring it at a venture; and therefore it is a lost prayer. For we allow such thoughts as these to lead us astray and deter us: "I am not holy or worthy enough; if I were as godly and holy as St. Peter or St. Paul, then I would pray." But put such thoughts far away, for just the same commandment which applied to St. Paul applies also to me; and the Second Commandment is given as much on my account as on his account, so that he can boast of no better or holier commandment.

Therefore you should say: "My prayer is as precious, holy, and pleasing to God as that of St. Paul or of the most holy saints. This is the reason: For I will gladly grant that he is holier in his person, but not on account of the commandment; since God does not regard prayer on account of the person, but on account of his word and obedience thereto. For on the commandment on which all the saints rest their prayer I, too, rest mine. Moreover, I pray for the same thing for which they all pray and ever have prayed; besides, I have just as great a need of it as those great saints, yea, even a greater one than they." [LC III.14–16]

Meditation:

1. Is it sufficient merely to have done the work of praying, regardless of whether one believes that God would hear it? Why not?
2. Why is it tempting to assume that we are not holy or worthy enough to pray? How can we overcome such thoughts?
3. Why are our prayers as precious, holy, and pleasing to God as those of St. Paul or of the most holy saints? On what basis does God regard prayer?

Prayer:

Dear God, help me always to recognize my great need to pray. Thank you for regarding this prayer and all my prayers on account of your word. Amen.

Week Seventeen – Sunday

The Introduction

Our Father who art in heaven.

What does this mean?—Answer. God would thereby tenderly urge us to believe that he is our true Father, and that we are his true children, so that we may ask him confidently with all assurance, as dear children ask their dear father.

Let this be the first and most important point, that all our prayers must be based and rest upon obedience to God, irrespective of our person, whether we be sinners or saints, worthy or unworthy. And we must know that God will not have it treated as a jest, but be angry, and punish all who do not pray, as surely as he punishes all other disobedience; next, that he will not suffer our prayers to be in vain or lost. For if he did not intend to answer your prayer, he would not bid you pray and add such a severe commandment to it.

In the second place, we should be the more urged and incited to pray because God has also added a promise, and declared that it shall surely be done to us as we pray, as he says, Psalm 50:15: "Call upon me in the day of trouble: I will deliver thee." And Christ in the Gospel of St. Matthew 7:7: "Ask, and it shall be given you. For everyone that asketh receiveth." Such promises ought certainly to encourage and kindle our hearts to pray with pleasure and delight, since he testifies with his word that our prayer is heartily pleasing to him, moreover, that it shall assuredly be heard and granted, in order that we may not despise it or think lightly of it, and pray at a venture.

This you can hold up to him and say: "Here I come, dear Father, and pray, not of my own purpose nor upon my own worthiness, but at thy commandment and promise, which cannot fail or deceive me." Whoever, therefore, does not believe this promise must know again that he excites God to anger as a person who most highly dishonors him and reproaches him with falsehood. [LC III.17–21]

Meditation:

1. How does God invite us to address him in prayer? What does speaking to God as our Father imply about what and how we can pray?
2. What assurance should it give us that God has commanded us to pray? What promise has he added that should encourage us all the more?
3. Whose purpose should we have in mind when we pray? Whose worthiness obtains for us the privilege of prayer?

Prayer:

Heavenly Father, I come to you in prayer as you have commanded, trusting your promise to hear and answer me. Thank you for your tender invitation. Amen.

Week Seventeen – Monday

The Introduction

Our Father who art in heaven.

What does this mean?—Answer. God would thereby tenderly urge us to believe that he is our true Father, and that we are his true children, so that we may ask him confidently with all assurance, as dear children ask their dear father.

Besides this, we should be incited and drawn to prayer because in addition to this commandment and promise God anticipates us, and himself arranges the words and form of prayer for us, and places them upon our lips as to how and what we should pray, that we may see how heartily he pities us in our distress, and may never doubt that such prayer is pleasing to him and shall certainly be answered; which is a great advantage indeed over all other prayers that we might compose ourselves. For in them the conscience would ever be in doubt and say: "I have prayed, but who knows how it pleases him, or whether I have hit upon the right proportions and form?" Hence there is no nobler prayer to be found upon earth than the Lord's Prayer which we daily pray, because it has this excellent testimony, that God loves to hear it, which we ought not to surrender for all the riches of the world.

And it has been prescribed also for this reason, that we should see and consider the distress which ought to urge and compel us to pray without ceasing. For whoever would pray must have something to present, state, and name which he desires; if not, it cannot be called a prayer.

Therefore we have rightly rejected the prayers of monks and priests, who howl and growl day and night like fiends; but none of them think of praying for a hair's breadth of anything. And if we would assemble all the churches, together with all ecclesiastics, they would be obliged to confess that they have never from the heart prayed for even a drop of wine. For none of them has ever purposed to pray from obedience to God and faith in his promise, nor has anyone regarded any distress, but (when they had done their best) they thought no further than this, to do a good work, whereby they might repay God, as being unwilling

The Lutheran Catechism

to take anything from him, but wishing only to give him something. [LC III.22–25]

Meditation:
1. What has God given us, besides his commandment and promise, to facilitate our prayers? What does this indicate about the Lord's Prayer?
2. Why does God desire that we pray without ceasing? What does this mean from a practical standpoint?
3. What was wrong with the typical prayers of monks and priests? Why is wishing to give something to God the wrong attitude for prayer?

Prayer:

Lord, thank you for giving me not only your commandment and promise, but also the words for how and what I should pray. Teach me to ask in faith. Amen.

Week Seventeen – Tuesday

The Introduction

Our Father who art in heaven.

What does this mean?—Answer. God would thereby tenderly urge us to believe that he is our true Father, and that we are his true children, so that we may ask him confidently with all assurance, as dear children ask their dear father.

But where there is to be a true prayer, there must be earnestness. Men must feel their distress, and such distress as presses them and compels them to call and cry out; then prayer will be made spontaneously, as it ought to be, and men will require no teaching how to prepare for it and to attain to the proper devotion. But the distress which ought to concern us most, both as regards ourselves and everyone, you will find abundantly set forth in the Lord's Prayer. Therefore it is to serve also to remind us of the same, that we contemplate it and lay it to heart, lest we become remiss in prayer. For we all have enough that we lack, but the great want is that we do not feel nor see it. Therefore God also requires that you lament and plead such necessities and wants, not because he does not know them, but that you may kindle your heart to stronger and greater desires, and make wide and open your cloak to receive much.

Therefore, every one of us should accustom himself from his youth daily to pray for all his wants, whenever he is sensible of anything affecting his interests or that of other people among whom he may live, as for preachers, the government, neighbors, domestics, and always (as we have said) to hold up to God his commandment and promise, knowing that he will not have them disregarded. This I say because I would like to see these things brought home again to the people that they might learn to pray truly, and not go about coldly and indifferently, whereby they become daily more unfit for prayer; which is just what the devil desires, and for what he works with all his powers. For he is well aware what damage and harm it does him when prayer is in proper practice. [LC III.26–29]

Meditation:

1. What does it mean to be earnest in prayer? What kinds of distress do you feel, such that you are pressed and compelled to call and cry out?
2. How does the daily discipline of prayer remind us of our need for God? Does he learn anything from our prayers? What can we learn from them?
3. Why does God desire that we pray for others, and not just ourselves? Why does the devil desire that we refrain from praying at all?

Prayer:

God, help me to feel my own distress and that of my neighbors, so that I am pressed and compelled to pray daily for myself and others, as you desire. Amen.

Week Seventeen – Wednesday

The Introduction

Our Father who art in heaven.

What does this mean?—Answer. God would thereby tenderly urge us to believe that he is our true Father, and that we are his true children, so that we may ask him confidently with all assurance, as dear children ask their dear father.

For this we must know, that all our shelter and protection rest in prayer alone. For we are far too feeble to cope with the devil and all his power and adherents that set themselves against us, and they might easily crush us under their feet. Therefore we must consider and take up those weapons with which Christians must be armed in order to stand against the devil. For what do you think has hitherto accomplished such great things, has checked or quelled the counsels, purposes, murder, and riot of our enemies, whereby the devil thought to crush us, together with the gospel, except that the prayer of a few godly men intervened like a wall of iron on our side? They should else have witnessed a far different tragedy, namely, how the devil would have destroyed all Germany in its own blood. But now they may confidently deride it and make a mock of it; however, we shall nevertheless be a match both for themselves and the devil by prayer alone, if we only persevere diligently and not become slack. For whenever a godly Christian prays: "Dear Father, let thy will be done," God speaks from on high and says: "Yes, dear child, it shall be so, in spite of the devil and all the world."

Let this be said as an exhortation, that men may learn, first of all, to esteem prayer as something great and precious, and to make a proper distinction between babbling and praying for something. For we by no means reject prayer, but the bare, useless howling and murmuring we reject, as Christ himself also rejects and prohibits long palavers. Now we shall most briefly and clearly treat of the Lord's Prayer. Here there is comprehended in seven successive articles, or petitions, every need which never ceases to relate to us, and each so great that it ought to constrain us to keep praying it all our lives. [LC III.30–34]

Meditation:
1. In what sense do all our shelter and protection rest in prayer alone? Why? How does prayer enable us to cope with the devil and all his power?
2. What can the prayers of godly men and women accomplish? When have you observed this, either as one who prayed or as one for whom others prayed?
3. Do you esteem prayer as something great and precious? Why or why not? What is the difference between babbling and praying for something?

Prayer:

Jesus, help me to recognize the power of prayer and thus esteem it as something great and precious. Teach me to pray as you taught your disciples. Amen.

Week Seventeen – Thursday

The First Petition

Hallowed be thy name.

What does this mean?—Answer. God's name is indeed holy in itself; but we pray in this petition that it may become holy among us also.

This is, indeed, somewhat obscure, and not expressed in good German, for in our mother tongue we would say: "Heavenly Father, help that by all means thy name may be holy." But what is it to pray that his name may be holy? Is it not holy already? Answer: Yes, it is always holy in its nature, but in our use it is not holy. For God's name was given us when we became Christians and were baptized, so that we are called children of God and have the sacraments, by which he so incorporates us in himself that everything which is God's must serve for our use.

Here now the great need exists for which we ought to be most concerned, that this name have its proper honor, be esteemed holy and sublime as the greatest treasure and sanctuary that we have; and that as godly children we pray that the name of God, which is already holy in heaven, may also be and remain holy with us upon earth and in all the world. [LC III.36–38]

Meditation:
1. Are our prayers necessary for God's name to be holy? Why, then, does God desire that we pray for this?
2. What are some ways in which we use God's name that are not holy? Why does it properly deserve honor and esteem instead?
3. What is the connection between God's name and our baptism? How does the behavior of children reflect on their parents, whose name they bear?

Prayer:

Dear God, help me to recognize and proclaim the holiness of your name, not only with my words, but also with my actions as your child who bears it. Amen.

Week Seventeen – Friday

The First Petition

Hallowed be thy name.

How is this done?—Answer. When the word of God is taught in its truth and purity, and we as the children of God also lead holy lives in accordance with it. To this end help us, dear Father in heaven. But he that teaches and lives otherwise than God's word teaches profanes the name of God among us. From this preserve us, heavenly Father.

But how does it become holy among us? Answer, as plainly as it can be said: When both our doctrine and life are godly and Christian. For since in this prayer we call God our Father, it is our duty always to deport and demean ourselves as godly children, that he may not receive shame, but honor and praise from us.

Now the name of God is profaned by us either in words or in works. (For whatever we do upon the earth must be either words or works, speech or act.) In the first place, then, it is profaned when men preach, teach, and speak in the name of God what is false and misleading, so that his name must serve to adorn and to find a market for falsehood. That is, indeed, the greatest profanation and dishonor of the divine name. Furthermore, also when men, by swearing, cursing, conjuring, etc., grossly abuse the holy name as a cloak for their shame. In the second place, also by an openly wicked life and works, when those who are called Christians and the people of God are adulterers, drunkards, misers, envious, and slanderers. Here again must the name of God come to shame and be profaned because of us. For just as it is a shame and disgrace to a natural father to have a bad, perverse child that opposes him in words and deeds, so that on its account he suffers contempt and reproach, so also it brings dishonor upon God if we who are called by his name and have all manner of goods from him teach, speak, and live in any other manner except as godly and heavenly children, so that people say of us that we must be not God's, but the devil's children. [LC III.39–44]

Meditation:

1. How does teaching only true and pure doctrine uphold the holiness of God's name? How does living a godly life do so?
2. How is God's name profaned by our words? Why does false teaching dishonor it? What other kinds of speech should we avoid?
3. How is God's name profaned by our works? Why does wicked living dishonor it? What specific kinds of acts should we avoid?

Prayer:

Father, forgive me for dishonoring your name, which you have given me. Guard my words and my works, so that they proclaim and exhibit your holiness. Amen.

Week Seventeen – Saturday

The First Petition

Hallowed be thy name.

How is this done?—Answer. When the word of God is taught in its truth and purity, and we as the children of God also lead holy lives in accordance with it. To this end help us, dear Father in heaven. But he that teaches and lives otherwise than God's word teaches profanes the name of God among us. From this preserve us, heavenly Father.

Thus you see that in this petition we pray just for that which God demands in the Second Commandment; namely, that his name be not taken in vain to swear, curse, lie, deceive, etc., but be usefully employed to the praise and honor of God. For whoever employs the name of God for any sort of wrong profanes and desecrates this holy name, as aforetime a church was considered desecrated when a murder or any other crime had been committed in it, or when a pyx or relic was desecrated, as being holy in themselves, yet become unholy in use. Thus this point is easy and clear if only the language is understood, that to hallow is the same as in our idiom to praise, magnify, and honor both in word and deed.

Here, now, learn how great need there is of such prayer. For because we see how full the world is of sects and false teachers, who all wear the holy name as a cover and sham for their doctrines of devils, we ought by all means to pray without ceasing, and to cry and call upon God against all such as preach and believe falsely and whatever opposes and persecutes our gospel and pure doctrine, and would suppress it, as bishops, tyrants, enthusiasts, etc. Likewise also for ourselves who have the word of God, but are not thankful for it, nor live as we ought according to the same. If now you pray for this with your heart, you can be sure that it pleases God; for he will not hear anything more dear to him than that his honor and praise is exalted above everything else, and his word is taught in its purity and is esteemed precious and dear. [LC III.45–48]

Meditation:

1. What is the connection between the First Petition and the Second Commandment? Why does God's name require such reverence?
2. What are some specific ways in which you have observed the name of God employed for any sort of wrong? How have you done so yourself?
3. Why is it important to pray against false teaching and belief? Why does God desire that his word be taught in purity, and esteemed precious and dear?

Prayer:

Dear Lord, forgive me for often taking your name and word for granted. Help me steadfastly to maintain your truth by my own words and actions. Amen.

Week Eighteen – Sunday

The Second Petition

Thy kingdom come.

What does this mean?—Answer. The kingdom of God comes indeed without our prayer, of itself; but we pray in this petition that it may come unto us also.

As we prayed in the First Petition concerning the honor and name of God that he would prevent the world from adorning its lies and wickedness with it, but cause it to be esteemed sublime and holy both in doctrine and life, so that he may be praised and magnified in us, so here we pray that his kingdom also may come. But just as the name of God is in itself holy, and we pray nevertheless that it be holy among us, so also his kingdom comes of itself, without our prayer, yet we pray nevertheless that it may come to us, that is, prevail among us and with us, so that we may be a part of those among whom his name is hallowed and his kingdom prospers.

But what is the kingdom of God? Answer: Nothing else than what we learned in the Creed, that God sent his Son Jesus Christ, our Lord, into the world to redeem and deliver us from the power of the devil, and to bring us to himself, and to govern us as a king of righteousness, life, and salvation against sin, death, and an evil conscience, for which end he has also bestowed his Holy Ghost, who is to bring these things home to us by his holy word, and to illumine and strengthen us in the faith by his power.

Therefore we pray here in the first place that this may become effective with us, and that his name be so praised through the holy word of God and a Christian life that both we who have accepted it may abide and daily grow therein, and that it may gain approbation and adherence among other people and proceed with power throughout the world, that many may find entrance into the kingdom of grace, be made partakers of redemption, being led thereto by the Holy Ghost, in order that thus we may all together remain forever in the one kingdom now begun. [LC III.49–52]

Meditation:

1. Are our prayers necessary for God's kingdom to come? Why, then, does God desire that we pray for this?
2. What is the connection between the Second Petition and the Second and Third Articles? Who reigns in God's kingdom? Who makes us his subjects?
3. What is the intent of this petition with respect to us who already belong to God's kingdom? What is its intent with respect to other people?

Prayer:

God, thank you for making me a member of your kingdom. Help me to abide and daily grow in that citizenship, so that others are drawn to faith in you. Amen.

Week Eighteen – Monday

The Second Petition

Thy kingdom come.

How is this done?—Answer. When our heavenly Father gives us his Holy Spirit, so that by his grace we believe his holy word and lead a godly life here in time and yonder in eternity.

For the coming of God's kingdom to us occurs in two ways; first, here in time through the word and faith; and secondly, in eternity forever through revelation. Now we pray for both these things, that it may come to those who are not yet in it, and, by daily increase, to us who have received the same, and hereafter in eternal life. All this is nothing else than saying: "Dear Father, we pray, give us first thy word, that the gospel be preached properly throughout the world; and secondly, that it be received in faith, and work and live in us, so that through the word and the power of the Holy Ghost thy kingdom may prevail among us, and the kingdom of the devil be put down, that he may have no right or power over us, until at last it shall be utterly destroyed, and sin, death, and hell shall be exterminated, that we may live forever in perfect righteousness and blessedness."

From this you perceive that we pray here not for a crust of bread or a temporal, perishable good, but for an eternal inestimable treasure and everything that God himself possesses; which is far too great for any human heart to think of desiring if he had not himself commanded us to pray for the same. But because he is God, he also claims the honor of giving much more and more abundantly than anyone can comprehend—like an eternal, unfailing fountain, which, the more it pours forth and overflows, the more it continues to give—and he desires nothing more earnestly of us than that we ask much and great things of him, and again is angry if we do not ask and pray confidently. [LC III.53–56]

Meditation:

1. In what two ways does the coming of God's kingdom to us occur? What is the connection between them? Why do we pray for both of them?
2. Whose kingdom opposes the kingdom of God? By what means is that other kingdom put down? When will it finally be defeated and destroyed?
3. What is the value of that for which we pray in the Second Petition? Why does God grant us this and more? How should this inform all of our prayers?

Prayer:

Heavenly Father, thank you for giving us faith now and life forever. Help us to recognize the value of these gifts and seek to share them with others. Amen.

Week Eighteen – Tuesday

The Second Petition

Thy kingdom come.

How is this done?—Answer. When our heavenly Father gives us his Holy Spirit, so that by his grace we believe his holy word and lead a godly life here in time and yonder in eternity.

For just as when the richest and most mighty emperor would bid a poor beggar ask whatever he might desire, and were ready to give great imperial presents, and the fool would beg only for a dish of gruel, he would be rightly considered a rogue and a scoundrel, who treated the command of his imperial majesty as a jest and sport, and was not worthy of coming into his presence: so also it is a great reproach and dishonor to God if we, to whom he offers and pledges so many unspeakable treasures, despise the same, or have not the confidence to receive them, but scarcely venture to pray for a piece of bread.

All this is the fault of the shameful unbelief which does not look to God for as much good as will satisfy the stomach, much less expects without doubt such eternal treasures of God. Therefore we must strengthen ourselves against it, and let this be our first prayer; then, indeed, we shall have all else in abundance, as Christ teaches: "Seek ye first the kingdom of God and his righteousness, and all these things shall be added unto you." For how could he allow us to suffer want and to be straitened in temporal things when he promises that which is eternal and imperishable? [LC III.57–58]

Meditation:

1. Why would it be foolish for a poor beggar to ask only for a dish of gruel from a rich and mighty emperor? What might cause him to do so?
2. What hinders you from asking God for the great blessings that he is eager to give you? What should enable us to be bold in our prayers?
3. What does it mean to seek God's kingdom first? How would doing so manifest itself in your prayers? How would it be evident in your lifestyle?

Prayer:

Lord, I believe; help my unbelief! Teach me to seek your kingdom first, boldly ask for everything else that I need, and trust that you will provide it. Amen.

Week Eighteen – Wednesday

The Third Petition

Thy will be done on earth as it is in heaven.

What does this mean?—Answer. The good and gracious will of God is done indeed without our prayer; but we pray in this petition that it may be done among us also.

Thus far we have prayed that God's name be honored by us, and that his kingdom prevail among us; in which two points is comprehended all that pertains to the honor of God and to our salvation, that we receive as our own God and all his riches. But now a need just as great arises, namely, that we firmly keep them, and do not suffer ourselves to be torn therefrom. For as in a good government it is not only necessary that there be those who build and govern well, but also those who make defense, afford protection, and maintain it firmly, so here likewise, although we have prayed for the greatest need, for the gospel, faith, and the Holy Ghost, that he may govern us and redeem us from the power of the devil, we must also pray that his will be done. For there will be happenings quite strange if we are to abide therein, as we shall have to suffer many thrusts and blows on that account from everything that ventures to oppose and prevent the fulfilment of the two petitions that precede.

For no one believes how the devil opposes and resists them, and cannot suffer that anyone teach or believe aright. And it hurts him beyond measure to suffer his lies and abominations, that have been honored under the most specious pretexts of the divine name, to be exposed, and to be disgraced himself, and, besides, be driven out of the heart, and suffer such a breach to be made in his kingdom. Therefore he chafes and rages as a fierce enemy with all his power and might, and marshals all his subjects, and, in addition, enlists the world and our own flesh as his allies. [LC III.60–62]

Meditation:

1. Are our prayers necessary for God's will to be done? Why, then, does God desire that we pray for this?
2. What is God's will regarding his name and kingdom? Why do we need his help in order to fulfill the First and Second Petitions?
3. Why does the devil oppose and resist both God and us? What does he enlist as his allies in this fight? Who alone is capable of overcoming them?

Prayer:

God, forgive me for often seeking that my own will be done, rather than yours. Help me to recognize that your will for me and for others is far better. Amen.

Week Eighteen – Thursday

The Third Petition

Thy will be done on earth as it is in heaven.

How is this done?—Answer. When God breaks and hinders every evil counsel and will which would not let us hallow the name of God nor let his kingdom come, such as the will of the devil, the world, and our flesh; but strengthens and keeps us steadfast in his word and in faith unto our end. This is his gracious and good will.

For our flesh is in itself indolent and inclined to evil, even though we have accepted and believe the word of God. The world, however, is perverse and wicked; this [the devil] incites against us, fans and stirs the fire, that he may hinder and drive us back, cause us to fall, and again bring us under his power. Such is all his will, mind, and thought, for which he strives day and night, and never rests a moment, employing all arts, wiles, ways, and means whichever he can invent.

If we would be Christians, therefore, we must surely expect and reckon upon having the devil with all his angels and the world as our enemies who will bring every possible misfortune and grief upon us. For where the word of God is preached, accepted, or believed, and produces fruit, there the holy cross cannot be wanting. And let no one think that he shall have peace; but he must risk whatever he has upon earth—possessions, honor, house and estate, wife and children, body and life. Now, this hurts our flesh and the old Adam; for the test is to be steadfast and to suffer with patience in whatever way we are assailed, and to let go whatever is taken from us.

Hence there is just as great need, as in all the others, that we pray without ceasing: "Dear Father, thy will be done, not the will of the devil and of our enemies, nor of anything that would persecute and suppress thy holy word or hinder thy kingdom; and grant that we may bear with patience and overcome whatever is to be endured on that account, lest our poor flesh yield or fall away from weakness or sluggishness." [LC III.63–67]

Meditation:

1. What are some specific ways in which the devil, the world, and our flesh each attempt to prevent fulfillment of the First and Second Petitions?
2. What kind of reaction should a faithful Christian expect from the world? Why? How have you observed this in your own experience?
3. What is the connection between following Christ and taking up one's cross daily (Luke 9:23–24)? With this in mind, how should we pray?

Prayer:

Dear Jesus, you warn us that in the world we will have tribulation, but you also assure us that you have overcome the world (John 16:33). Thank you. Amen.

Week Eighteen – Friday

The Third Petition

Thy will be done on earth as it is in heaven.

How is this done?—Answer. When God breaks and hinders every evil counsel and will which would not let us hallow the name of God nor let his kingdom come, such as the will of the devil, the world, and our flesh; but strengthens and keeps us steadfast in his word and in faith unto our end. This is his gracious and good will.

Behold, thus we have in these three petitions, in the simplest manner, the need which relates to God himself, yet all for our sakes. For whatever we pray concerns only us, namely, as we have said, that what must be done anyway without us, may also be done in us. For as his name must be hallowed and his kingdom come without our prayer, so also his will must be done and succeed, although the devil with all his adherents raise a great tumult, are angry and rage against it, and undertake to exterminate the gospel utterly. But for our own sakes we must pray that even against their fury his will be done without hindrance also among us, that they may not be able to accomplish anything and we remain firm against all violence and persecution, and submit to such will of God.

Such prayer, then, is to be our protection and defense now, is to repel and put down all that the devil, pope, bishops, tyrants, and heretics can do against our gospel. Let them all rage and attempt their utmost, and deliberate and resolve how they may suppress and exterminate us, that their will and counsel may prevail: over and against this one or two Christians with this petition alone shall be our wall against which they shall run and dash themselves to pieces. This consolation and confidence we have, that the will and purpose of the devil and of all our enemies shall and must fail and come to naught, however proud, secure, and powerful they know themselves to be. For if their will were not broken and hindered, the kingdom of God could not abide on earth nor his name be hallowed. [LC III.68–70]

Meditation:

1. What do the first three petitions of the Lord's Prayer have in common? What do they remind us about God?
2. How does remaining steadfast in God's word strengthen our faith? What are some specific ways in which God helps you to do this?
3. What is the basis for our confidence that the will and purpose of the devil and our enemies must fail? How should this affect our prayers?

Prayer:

Lord, thank you for the assurance that your good and gracious will for me will prevail over everything that opposes it. Keep me steadfast in your word. Amen.

Week Eighteen – Saturday

The Fourth Petition

Give us this day our daily bread.

What does this mean?—Answer. God gives daily bread, even without our prayer, to all wicked men; but we pray in this petition that he would lead us to know it, and to receive our daily bread with thanksgiving.

Here, now, we consider the poor bread basket, the necessaries of our body and of the temporal life. It is a brief and simple word, but it has a very wide scope. For when you mention and pray for daily bread, you pray for everything that is necessary in order to have and enjoy daily bread and, on the other hand, against everything which interferes with it. Therefore you must open wide and extend your thoughts not only to the oven or the flour bin, but to the distant field and the entire land, which bears and brings to us daily bread and every sort of sustenance. For if God did not cause it to grow, and bless and preserve it in the field, we could never take bread from the oven or have any to set upon the table.

To comprise it briefly, this petition includes everything that belongs to our entire life in the world, because on that account alone do we need daily bread. Now for our life it is not only necessary that our body have food and covering and other necessaries, but also that we spend our days in peace and quiet among the people with whom we live and have intercourse in daily business and conversation and all sorts of doings, in short, whatever pertains both to the domestic and to the neighborly or civil relation and government. For where these two things are hindered that they do not prosper as they ought, the necessaries of life also are impeded, so that ultimately life cannot be maintained. [LC III.72–73]

Meditation:

1. Are our prayers necessary for us to receive daily sustenance from God? Why, then, does he desire that we pray for this?
2. What all must happen for you to have food every day? How many people are involved? What does this indicate about the importance of vocations?
3. What all is necessary for you to spend your days in peace and quiet among family, friends, and so forth? Why do we tend to take this for granted?

Prayer:

Father, thank you for not only creating me, but sustaining me, and for the people who faithfully carry out their daily vocations to provide for my needs. Amen.

Week Nineteen – Sunday

The Fourth Petition

Give us this day our daily bread.

What does this mean?—Answer. God gives daily bread, even without our prayer, to all wicked men; but we pray in this petition that he would lead us to know it, and to receive our daily bread with thanksgiving.

And there is, indeed, the greatest need to pray for temporal authority and government, as that by which most of all God preserves to us our daily bread and all the comforts of this life. For though we have received of God all good things in abundance, we are not able to retain any of them or use them in security and happiness, if he did not give us a permanent and peaceful government. For where there are dissension, strife, and war, there the daily bread is already taken away, or at least checked.

Therefore it would be very proper to place in the coat of arms of every pious prince a loaf of bread instead of a lion, or a wreath of rue, or to stamp it upon the coin, to remind both them and their subjects that by their office we have protection and peace, and that without them we could not eat and retain our daily bread. Therefore they are also worthy of all honor, that we give to them for their office what we ought and can, as to those through whom we enjoy in peace and quietness what we have, because otherwise we would not keep a farthing; and that, in addition, we also pray for them that through them God may bestow on us the more blessing and good. [LC III.74–75]

Meditation:

1. What is the role of temporal authority and government in God's provision of our daily needs? Why is it important that we pray for them?
2. What kinds of symbols typically represent governments? What alternative does Luther suggest here? Why would it be fitting?
3. What is the connection between the Fourth Petition and the Fourth Commandment? How can we show honor to temporal authorities?

Prayer:

Almighty God, thank you for providing governments to maintain peace so that we may enjoy the comforts of this life. Please continue to preserve them. Amen.

The Lutheran Catechism

Week Nineteen – Monday

The Fourth Petition

Give us this day our daily bread.

What is meant by daily bread?—Answer. Everything that belongs to the support and wants of the body, such as meat, drink, clothing, shoes, house, homestead, field, cattle, money, goods, a pious spouse, pious children, pious servants, pious and faithful magistrates, good government, good weather, peace, health, discipline, honor, good friends, faithful neighbors, and the like.

Let this be a very brief explanation and sketch, showing how far this petition extends through all conditions on earth. Of this anyone might indeed make a long prayer, and with many words enumerate all the things that are included therein, as that we pray God to give us food and drink, clothing, house, and home, and health of body; also that he cause the grain and fruits of the field to grow and mature well; furthermore, that he help us at home towards good housekeeping, that he give and preserve to us a godly wife, children, and servants, that he cause our work, trade, or whatever we are engaged in to prosper and succeed, favor us with faithful neighbors and good friends, etc. Likewise, that he give to emperors, kings, and all estates, and especially to the rulers of our country and to all counselors, magistrates, and officers, wisdom, strength, and success that they may govern well and vanquish the Turks and all enemies; to subjects and the common people, obedience, peace, and harmony in their life with one another; and on the other hand, that he would preserve us from all sorts of calamity to body and livelihood, as lightning, hail, fire, flood, poison, pestilence, cattle plague, war and bloodshed, famine, destructive beasts, wicked men, etc. All this it is well to impress upon the simple, namely, that these things come from God, and must be prayed for by us. [LC III.76–79]

Meditation:
1. What all is included when we ask God for our daily bread? Can you think of other items that you should add to your own list?
2. What is the significance of praying for all these things daily? Can we change the past? Should we worry about the future? Why not?
3. Is there anything that we have or need that does not come from God? How should this affect our attitude toward all such things?

Prayer:

Lord, thank you for this day and for all that you have already provided to see me through it. Help me to depend on you each day for everything that I need. Amen.

Week Nineteen – Tuesday

The Fourth Petition

Give us this day our daily bread.

What is meant by daily bread?—Answer. Everything that belongs to the support and wants of the body, such as meat, drink, clothing, shoes, house, homestead, field, cattle, money, goods, a pious spouse, pious children, pious servants, pious and faithful magistrates, good government, good weather, peace, health, discipline, honor, good friends, faithful neighbors, and the like.

But this petition is especially directed also against our chief enemy, the devil. For all his thought and desire is to deprive us of all that we have from God, or to hinder it; and he is not satisfied to obstruct and destroy spiritual government in leading souls astray by his lies and bringing them under his power, but he also prevents and hinders the stability of all government and honorable, peaceable relations on earth. There he causes so much contention, murder, sedition, and war, also lightning and hail to destroy grain and cattle, to poison the air, etc. In short, he is sorry that anyone has a morsel of bread from God and eats it in peace; and if it were in his power, and our prayer (next to God) did not prevent him, we would not keep a straw in the field, a farthing in the house, yea, not even our life for an hour, especially those who have the word of God and would like to be Christians.

Behold, thus God wishes to indicate to us how he cares for us in all our need, and faithfully provides also for our temporal support. And although he abundantly grants and preserves these things even to the wicked and knaves, yet he wishes that we pray for them, in order that we may recognize that we receive them from his hand, and may feel his paternal goodness toward us therein. For when he withdraws his hand, nothing can prosper nor be maintained in the end, as, indeed, we daily see and experience. How much trouble there is now in the world only on account of bad coin, yea, on account of daily oppression and raising of prices in common trade, bargaining and labor on the part of those who wantonly oppress the poor and deprive them of their daily bread! This we must suffer indeed; but let them take care that they do not lose the common intercession, and beware lest this petition in the Lord's Prayer be against them. [LC III.80–84]

Meditation:
1. Who is our chief enemy? Why does he relentlessly seek to deprive us of all that we have from God?
2. What are some specific ways in which the devil opposes us? How does this affect your understanding of world events?
3. How has God cared for you in all your need, and faithfully provided also for your temporal support? What does this suggest about the future?

Prayer:

Father, thank you for caring and providing for me despite the devil's efforts to deprive and hinder me. Preserve and protect me always by your grace. Amen.

Week Nineteen – Wednesday

The Fifth Petition

And forgive us our trespasses,

as we forgive those who trespass against us.

What does this mean?—Answer. We pray in this petition that our Father in heaven would not look upon our sins, nor deny such petitions on account of them; for we are worthy of none of the things for which we pray, neither have we deserved them; but that he would grant them all to us by grace; for we daily sin much, and indeed deserve nothing but punishment. So will we verily, on our part, also heartily forgive and also readily do good to those who sin against us.

This part now relates to our poor miserable life, which, although we have and believe the word of God, and do and submit to his will, and are supported by his gifts and blessings, is nevertheless not without sin. For we still stumble daily and transgress because we live in the world among men who do us much harm and give us cause for impatience, anger, revenge, etc. Besides, we have Satan at our back, who sets upon us on every side, and fights (as we have heard) against all the foregoing petitions, so that it is not possible always to stand firm in such a persistent conflict.

Therefore there is here again great need to call upon God and to pray: "Dear Father, forgive us our trespasses." Not as though he did not forgive sin without and even before our prayer (for he has given us the gospel, in which is pure forgiveness before we prayed or ever thought about it). But this is to the intent that we may recognize and accept such forgiveness. For since the flesh in which we daily live is of such a nature that it neither trusts nor believes God, and is ever active in evil lusts and devices, so that we sin daily in word and deed, by commission and omission, by which the conscience is thrown into unrest, so that it is afraid of the wrath and displeasure of God, and thus loses the comfort and confidence derived from the gospel; therefore it is ceaselessly necessary that we run hither and obtain consolation to comfort the conscience again. [LC III.86–89]

Meditation:

1. Why are we unworthy and undeserving of anything for which we pray? Why does God want us to ask him anyway? What does this indicate about him?
2. How often do we sin? Why? How often should we ask God for forgiveness? Why can we be confident that he has already granted it?
3. What can hinder us from recognizing and accepting the forgiveness that God offers? How is confessing to and receiving absolution from a pastor helpful?

Prayer:

Gracious God, thank you for already forgiving all my sins through the death of your Son, Jesus Christ. Help me to cling daily to that forgiveness in faith. Amen.

Week Nineteen – Thursday

The Fifth Petition

And forgive us our trespasses,

as we forgive those who trespass against us.

What does this mean?—Answer. We pray in this petition that our Father in heaven would not look upon our sins, nor deny such petitions on account of them; for we are worthy of none of the things for which we pray, neither have we deserved them; but that he would grant them all to us by grace; for we daily sin much, and indeed deserve nothing but punishment. So will we verily, on our part, also heartily forgive and also readily do good to those who sin against us.

But this should serve God's purpose of breaking our pride and keeping us humble. For in case anyone should boast of his godliness and despise others, God has reserved this prerogative to himself, that the person is to consider himself and place this prayer before his eyes, and he will find that he is no better than others, and that in the presence of God all must lower their plumes, and be glad that they can attain forgiveness. And let no one think that as long as we live here he can reach such a position that he will not need such forgiveness. In short, if God does not forgive without ceasing, we are lost.

It is therefore the intent of this petition that God would not regard our sins and hold up to us what we daily deserve, but would deal graciously with us, and forgive, as he has promised, and thus grant us a joyful and confident conscience to stand before him in prayer. For where the heart is not in right relation towards God, nor can take such confidence, it will nevermore venture to pray. But such a confident and joyful heart can spring from nothing else than the knowledge of the forgiveness of sin.

But there is here attached a necessary, yet consolatory addition: "As we forgive." He has promised that we shall be sure that everything is forgiven and pardoned, yet in the manner that we also forgive our neighbor. For just as we daily sin much against God, and yet he forgives everything through grace, so we, too, must ever forgive our neighbor who does us injury, violence, and wrong, shows malice toward us, etc. [LC III.90–94]

Meditation:
1. Why does God seek to break our pride and keep us humble? How does frequently praying the Fifth Petition serve this purpose?
2. Are some Christians better than others? Why not? Are Christians better than non-Christians? Why not? What effect should this have on our prayers?
3. Why is it impossible in this life not to need God's constant forgiveness? What effect should this have on our relationships with our neighbors?

Prayer:

Lord, I confess that I sin daily and need your constant forgiveness. Cleanse my heart so that it may be confident, joyful, and likewise forgiving of others. Amen.

Week Nineteen – Friday

The Fifth Petition

And forgive us our trespasses, as we forgive those who trespass against us.

What does this mean?—Answer. We pray in this petition that our Father in heaven would not look upon our sins, nor deny such petitions on account of them; for we are worthy of none of the things for which we pray, neither have we deserved them; but that he would grant them all to us by grace; for we daily sin much, and indeed deserve nothing but punishment. So will we verily, on our part, also heartily forgive and also readily do good to those who sin against us.

If, therefore, you do not forgive, then do not think that God forgives you; but if you forgive, you have this consolation and assurance, that you are forgiven in heaven, not on account of your forgiving, for God forgives freely and without condition, out of pure grace, because he has so promised, as the gospel teaches, but in order that he may set this up for our confirmation and assurance for a sign alongside of the promise which accords with this prayer, Luke 6:37: "Forgive, and ye shall be forgiven." Therefore Christ also repeats it soon after the Lord's Prayer, and says, Matthew 6:14: "For if ye forgive men their trespasses, your heavenly Father will also forgive you," etc.

This sign is therefore attached to this petition, that, when we pray, we remember the promise and reflect thus: "Dear Father, for this reason I come and pray thee to forgive me, not that I can make satisfaction, or can merit anything by my works, but because thou hast promised and attached the seal thereto that I should be as sure as though I had absolution pronounced by thyself." For as much as baptism and the Lord's Supper, appointed as external signs, effect, so much also this sign can effect to confirm our consciences and cause them to rejoice. And it is especially given for this purpose, that we might use and practice it every hour, as a thing that we have with us at all times. [LC III.95–98]

Meditation:
1. Should we expect God's forgiveness if we do not forgive others? Why not? Does this mean that forgiving others is what *causes* God to forgive us?
2. How does forgiving others give us confirmation and assurance of our own forgiveness from God? What effect will this have on our relationships?
3. How is the Fifth Petition similar to the sacraments? How is it different? How often is it available to us? Why is this important?

Prayer:

Father, forgive me for not always forgiving others as I should. Help me to cling to your forgiveness at all times and extend it to my earthly relationships. Amen.

Week Nineteen – Saturday

The Sixth Petition

And lead us not into temptation.

What does this mean?—Answer. God, indeed, tempts no one; but we pray in this petition that God would guard and keep us, so that the devil, the world, and our flesh may not deceive us, nor seduce us into misbelief, despair, and other great shame and vice; and though we be assailed by them, that still we may finally overcome and gain the victory.

We have now heard enough what toil and labor is required to retain all that for which we pray, and to persevere therein, which, however, is not achieved without infirmities and stumbling. Besides, although we have received forgiveness and a good conscience and are entirely acquitted, yet is our life of such a nature that one stands today and tomorrow falls. Therefore, even though we be godly now and stand before God with a good conscience, we must pray again that he would not suffer us to relapse and yield to trials and temptations.

Temptation, however, or (as our Saxons in olden times used to call it) *Bekoerunge*, is of three kinds, namely, of the flesh, of the world, and of the devil. For in the flesh we dwell and carry the old Adam about our neck, who exerts himself and incites us daily to unchastity, laziness, gluttony and drunkenness, avarice and deception, to defraud our neighbor and to overcharge him, and, in short, to all manner of evil lusts which cleave to us by nature, and to which we are incited by the society, example, and what we hear and see of other people, which often wound and inflame even an innocent heart.

Next comes the world, which offends us in word and deed, and impels us to anger and impatience. In short, there is nothing but hatred and envy, enmity, violence and wrong, unfaithfulness, vengeance, cursing, raillery, slander, pride and haughtiness, with superfluous finery, honor, fame, and power, where no one is willing to be the least, but everyone desires to sit at the head and to be seen before all. [LC III.100–3]

Meditation:

1. If God indeed tempts no one, why do we pray the Sixth Petition? What are the three sources of temptation? How often do they assail us?
2. Why does our own flesh tempt us? What are some examples of temptations that you face because of it? How might you avoid or escape them today?
3. Why does the world tempt us? What are some examples of temptations that you face because of it? How might you avoid or escape them today?

Prayer:

God, help me to recognize and flee or resist temptation, regardless of its source. Thank you for the assurance that you always provide a way of escape. Amen.

Week Twenty – Sunday

The Sixth Petition

And lead us not into temptation.

What does this mean?—Answer. God, indeed, tempts no one; but we pray in this petition that God would guard and keep us, so that the devil, the world, and our flesh may not deceive us, nor seduce us into misbelief, despair, and other great shame and vice; and though we be assailed by them, that still we may finally overcome and gain the victory.

Then comes the devil, inciting and provoking in all directions, but especially agitating matters that concern the conscience and spiritual affairs, namely, to induce us to despise and disregard both the word and works of God, to tear us away from faith, hope, and love, and bring us into misbelief, false security, and obduracy, or, on the other hand, to despair, denial of God, blasphemy, and innumerable other shocking things. These are indeed snares and nets, yea, real fiery darts which are shot most venomously into the heart, not by flesh and blood, but by the devil.

Great and grievous, indeed, are these dangers and temptations which every Christian must bear, even though each one were alone by himself, so that every hour that we are in this vile life where we are attacked on all sides, chased and hunted down, we are moved to cry out and to pray that God would not suffer us to become weary and faint and to relapse into sin, shame, and unbelief. For otherwise it is impossible to overcome even the least temptation.

This, then, is leading us not into temptation, to wit, when he gives us power and strength to resist; the temptation, however, not being taken away or removed. For while we live in the flesh and have the devil about us, no one can escape temptation and allurements; and it cannot be otherwise than that we must endure trials, yea, be engulfed in them; but we pray for this, that we may not fall and be drowned in them. [LC III.104–6]

Meditation:

1. Why does the devil tempt us? What are some examples of temptations that you face because of him? How might you avoid or escape them today?
2. Why does the devil especially desire that we fall into misbelief and despair? What has God given us to protect and defend against his constant attacks?
3. Why is temptation unavoidable in this life? In what sense is spiritual warfare an integral aspect of genuine discipleship?

Prayer:

Lord, guard me against the assaults of the devil, as well as the world and my own sinful flesh. Give me the spiritual armor and weapons to withstand them. Amen.

The Lutheran Catechism

Week Twenty – Monday

The Sixth Petition

And lead us not into temptation.

What does this mean?—Answer. God, indeed, tempts no one; but we pray in this petition that God would guard and keep us, so that the devil, the world, and our flesh may not deceive us, nor seduce us into misbelief, despair, and other great shame and vice; and though we be assailed by them, that still we may finally overcome and gain the victory.

To feel temptation is therefore a far different thing from consenting or yielding to it. We must all feel it, although not all in the same manner, but some in a greater degree and more severely than others; as, the young suffer especially from the flesh, afterwards, they that attain to middle life and old age, from the world, but others who are occupied with spiritual matters, that is, strong Christians, from the devil. But such feeling, as long as it is against our will and we would rather be rid of it, can harm no one. For if we did not feel it, it could not be called a temptation. But to consent thereto is when we give it the reins and do not resist or pray against it.

Therefore we Christians must be armed and daily expect to be incessantly attacked, in order that no one may go on in security and heedlessly, as though the devil were far from us, but at all times expect and parry his blows. For though I am now chaste, patient, kind, and in firm faith, the devil will this very hour send such an arrow into my heart that I can scarcely stand. For he is an enemy that never desists nor becomes tired, so that when one temptation ceases, there always arise others and fresh ones.

Accordingly, there is no help or comfort except to run hither and to take hold of the Lord's Prayer, and thus speak to God from the heart: "Dear Father, thou hast bidden me pray; let me not relapse because of temptations." Then you will see that they must desist, and finally acknowledge themselves conquered. Else if you venture to help yourself by your own thoughts and counsel, you will only make the matter worse and give the devil more space. For he has a serpent's head, which if it gain an opening into which he can slip, the whole body will follow without check. But prayer can prevent him and drive him back. [LC III.107–11]

Meditation:

1. What is the difference between feeling temptation and consenting or yielding to it? Can we avoid the former in this life? What about the latter?
2. Why are young people especially tempted by the flesh? older people by the world? strong Christians by the devil? With which do you struggle most?
3. Can we conquer temptations by our own thoughts and counsel? Why not? What should we do instead?

Prayer:

Father, I am weak, but your power is made perfect in my weakness. Give me that power today and every day, that I may resist temptation and do your will. Amen.

Week Twenty – Tuesday

The Seventh Petition

But deliver us from evil.

What does this mean?—Answer. We pray in this petition, as in a summary, that our Father in heaven would deliver us from all manner of evil, of body and soul, property and honor, and at last, when our last hour shall come, grant us a blessed end, and graciously take us from this vale of tears to himself into heaven.

In the Greek text this petition reads thus: "Deliver or preserve us from the Evil One, or the malicious one"; and it looks as if he were speaking of the devil, as though he would comprehend everything in one, so that the entire substance of all our prayer is directed against our chief enemy. For it is he who hinders among us everything that we pray for: the name or honor of God, God's kingdom and will, our daily bread, a cheerful good conscience, etc.

Therefore we finally sum it all up and say: "Dear Father, pray, help that we be rid of all these calamities." But there is nevertheless also included whatever evil may happen to us under the devil's kingdom—poverty, shame, death, and, in short, all the agonizing misery and heartache of which there is such an unnumbered multitude on the earth. [LC III.113–15a]

Meditation:

1. What is evil? What are some examples of evils of the body? of the soul? of property? of honor? How do these things make this life into a vale of tears?
2. Against whom is the Seventh Petition primarily directed? In what sense does this make it a summary of the Lord's Prayer in its entirety?
3. What is the blessed end for which we pray? How do we experience the gracious presence of God until then?

Prayer:

Dear Jesus, in the midst of misery and heartache in this vale of tears, help me cling to your promise that you are with me always, to the end of the age. Amen.

Week Twenty – Wednesday

The Seventh Petition

But deliver us from evil.

What does this mean?—Answer. We pray in this petition, as in a summary, that our Father in heaven would deliver us from all manner of evil, of body and soul, property and honor, and at last, when our last hour shall come, grant us a blessed end, and graciously take us from this vale of tears to himself into heaven.

For since the devil is not only a liar, but also a murderer, he constantly seeks our life, and wreaks his anger whenever he can afflict our bodies with misfortune and harm. Hence it comes that he often breaks men's necks or drives them to insanity, drowns some, and incites many to commit suicide, and to many other terrible calamities. Therefore there is nothing for us to do upon earth but to pray against this archenemy without ceasing. For unless God preserved us, we would not be safe from him even for an hour.

Hence you see again how God wishes us to pray to him also for all the things which affect our bodily interests, so that we seek and expect help nowhere else except in him. But this matter he has put last; for if we are to be preserved and delivered from all evil, the name of God must first be hallowed in us, his kingdom must be with us, and his will be done. After that he will finally preserve us from sin and shame, and, besides, from everything that may hurt or injure us. [LC III.115b–18]

Meditation:

1. What kind of being is the devil? Why are lies, murder, and anger characteristic of him? Why does he desire our misfortune and harm?
2. How have you seen the devil at work in your own life? in other people's lives? What is our only hope for resisting and defeating him?
3. Why does God care about our bodily interests? How are they connected with our spiritual interests? Why does the Seventh Petition come last?

Prayer:

Lord God, help me to hallow your name, live in your kingdom, and do your will. Preserve me from sin, shame, and everything that may hurt or injure me. Amen.

Week Twenty – Thursday

The Conclusion

Amen.

What does this mean?—Answer. That I should be certain

that these petitions are acceptable to our Father in heaven and heard; for he himself has commanded us so to pray, and has promised that he will hear us. Amen, amen; that is, "Yea, yea, it shall be so."

Thus God has briefly placed before us all the distress which may ever come upon us, so that we might have no excuse whatever for not praying. But all depends upon this, that we learn also to say Amen, that is, that we do not doubt that our prayer is surely heard, and shall be done. For this is nothing else than the word of undoubting faith, which does not pray at a venture, but knows that God does not lie to him, since he has promised to grant it. Therefore, where there is no such faith, there cannot be true prayer either.

It is, therefore, a pernicious delusion of those who pray in such a manner that they dare not from the heart say yea and positively conclude that God hears them, but remain in doubt and say, "How should I be so bold as to boast that God hears my prayer? For I am but a poor sinner," etc.

The reason for this is, they regard not the promise of God, but their own work and worthiness, whereby they despise God and reproach him with lying, and therefore they receive nothing. As St. James 1:6 says: "But let him ask in faith, nothing wavering; for he that wavereth is like a wave of the sea, driven with the wind and tossed. For let not that man think that he shall receive anything of the Lord." Behold, such importance God attaches to the fact that we are sure we do not pray in vain, and that we do not in any way despise our prayer. [LC III.119–24]

Meditation:

1. Why can we be certain that God hears and accepts what we request in the Lord's Prayer? Why is it so important to cling to his command and promise?
2. What are some excuses that you have given for not praying? Were any of them truly valid? Why should you never hesitate to pray boldly?
3. Why is it dangerous to downplay God's willingness to hear and answer our prayers? How can you be more intentional in your daily prayer life?

Prayer:

Father in heaven, thank you for both your command to pray and your promise always to hear me. Help me to stay in constant communication with you. Amen.

Week Twenty – Friday

The Sacrament of Holy Baptism

First: What is baptism?—Answer. Baptism is not simple water only, but it is the water comprehended in God's command and connected with God's word.

Which is that word of God?—Answer. Christ, our Lord, says in the last chapter of Matthew: "Go ye into all the world and teach all nations, baptizing them in the name of the Father, and of the Son, and of the Holy Ghost."

We have now finished the three chief parts of the common Christian doctrine. Besides these we have yet to speak of our two sacraments instituted by Christ, of which also every Christian ought to have at least an ordinary, brief instruction, because without them there can be no Christian; although, alas! hitherto no instruction concerning them has been given. But, in the first place, we take up baptism, by which we are first received into the Christian church. However, in order that it may be readily understood, we will treat of it in an orderly manner, and keep only to that which it is necessary for us to know. For how it is to be maintained and defended against heretics and sects we will commend to the learned.

In the first place, we must above all things know well the words upon which baptism is founded, and to which everything refers that is to be said on the subject, namely, where the Lord Christ speaks in Matthew 28:19 . . . .

In these words you must note, in the first place, that here stand God's commandment and institution, lest we doubt that baptism is divine, not devised nor invented by men. For as truly as I can say, "No man has spun the Ten Commandments, the Creed, and the Lord's Prayer out of his head, but they are revealed and given by God himself," so also I can boast that baptism is no human trifle, but instituted by God himself; moreover, that it is most solemnly and strictly commanded that we must be baptized or we cannot be saved, lest anyone regard it as a trifling matter, like putting on a new red coat. [LC IV.1–3, 6]

Meditation:

1. What are the three chief parts of the common Christian doctrine? Who has revealed and given them to us? Why is this important to recognize?
2. What are the two sacraments instituted by Christ? What does this entail about them? What are the purpose and importance of baptism, in particular?
3. Why is it wrong to regard baptism as a trifling matter? What are some specific ways in which people do so?

Prayer:

Jesus, thank you for instituting baptism as the means by which you first received me into your church. Help me to uphold this sacrament accordingly. Amen.

Week Twenty – Saturday

The Sacrament of Holy Baptism

First: What is baptism?—Answer. Baptism is not simple water only, but it is the water comprehended in God's command and connected with God's word.

Which is that word of God?—Answer. Christ, our Lord, says in the last chapter of Matthew: "Go ye into all the world and teach all nations, baptizing them in the name of the Father, and of the Son, and of the Holy Ghost."

For it is of the greatest importance that we esteem baptism excellent, glorious, and exalted, for which we contend and fight chiefly, because the world is now so full of sects clamoring that baptism is an external thing, and that external things are of no benefit. But let it be ever so much an external thing, here stand God's word and command which institute, establish, and confirm baptism. But what God institutes and commands cannot be a vain, but must be a most precious thing, though in appearance it were of less value than a straw. If hitherto people could consider it a great thing when the pope with his letters and bulls dispensed indulgences and confirmed altars and churches, solely because of the letters and seals, we ought to esteem baptism much more highly and more precious, because God has commanded it, and, besides, it is performed in his name. For these are the words, "Go ye, baptize; however, not in your name, but in the name of God."

For to be baptized in the name of God is to be baptized not by men, but by God himself. Therefore, although it is performed by human hands, it is nevertheless truly God's own work. From this fact everyone may himself readily infer that it is a far higher work than any work performed by a man or a saint. For what work greater than the work of God can we do? [LC IV.7–10]

Meditation:

1. Why might some Christians think that external things like baptism are of no benefit? What is wrong with taking such a position?
2. What does it indicate about God that he institutes and commands an external thing like baptism? What does your own baptism mean to you?
3. What is the significance of doing something in another's name? Who really performs the work in baptism? Why is this important?

Prayer:

God, I praise you for using the external things that you have created to work in my life. Help me to be your instrument to work in others' lives, as well. Amen.

Week Twenty-one – Sunday

The Sacrament of Holy Baptism

First: What is baptism?—Answer. Baptism is not simple water only, but it is the water comprehended in God's command and connected with God's word.

Which is that word of God?—Answer. Christ, our Lord, says in the last chapter of Matthew: "Go ye into all the world and teach all nations, baptizing them in the name of the Father, and of the Son, and of the Holy Ghost."

But here the devil is busy to delude us with false appearances, and lead us away from the work of God to our own works. For there is a much more splendid appearance when a Carthusian does many great and difficult works; and we all think much more of that which we do and merit ourselves. But the Scriptures teach thus: Even though we collect in one mass the works of all the monks, however splendidly they may shine, they would not be as noble and good as if God should pick up a straw. Why? Because the person is nobler and better. Here, then, we must not estimate the person according to the works, but the works according to the person, from whom they must derive their nobility. But insane reason will not regard this, and because baptism does not shine like the works which we do, it is to be esteemed as nothing.

From this now learn a proper understanding of the subject, and how to answer the question what baptism is, namely thus, that it is not mere ordinary water, but water comprehended in God's word and command, and sanctified thereby, so that it is nothing else than a divine water; not that the water in itself is nobler than other water, but that God's word and command are added. [LC IV.11–14]

Meditation:

1. Why does the devil want us to focus on our own works, rather than the work of God? What evidence do you see of his success in this among Christians?
2. Why are the smallest works of God greater than the greatest works of humans? What makes it difficult for most people to recognize this?
3. What turns baptism into something other than mere ordinary water? How can God's word and command make such a difference?

Prayer:

Dear Lord, forgive me for often focusing on my own works and the works of others. Help me to recognize instead your great work in me and in them. Amen.

Week Twenty-one – Monday

The Sacrament of Holy Baptism

First: What is baptism?—Answer. Baptism is not simple water only, but it is the water comprehended in God's command and connected with God's word.

Which is that word of God?—Answer. Christ, our Lord, says in the last chapter of Matthew: "Go ye into all the world and teach all nations, baptizing them in the name of the Father, and of the Son, and of the Holy Ghost."

Therefore it is pure wickedness and blasphemy of the devil that now our new spirits, to mock at baptism, omit from it God's word and institution, and look upon it in no other way than as water which is taken from the well, and then blather and say: "How is a handful of water to help the soul?" Aye, my friend, who does not know that water is water if tearing things asunder is what we are after? But how dare you thus interfere with God's order, and tear away the most precious treasure with which God has connected and enclosed it, and which he will not have separated? For the kernel in the water is God's word or command and the name of God, which is a treasure greater and nobler than heaven and earth.

Comprehend the difference, then, that baptism is quite another thing than all other water; not on account of the natural quality but because something more noble is here added; for God himself stakes his honor, his power and might on it. Therefore it is not only natural water, but a divine, heavenly, holy, and blessed water, and in whatever other terms we can praise it—all on account of the word, which is a heavenly, holy word, that no one can sufficiently extol, for it has, and is able to do, all that God is and can do. Hence also it derives its essence as a sacrament, as St. Augustine also taught: "When the word is joined to the element or natural substance, it becomes a sacrament," that is, a holy and divine matter and sign. [LC IV.15–18]

Meditation:

1. What happens to the water of baptism when God's word and institution are omitted? Why would anyone do such a thing?
2. Why is the name of God such a great and noble treasure? What is the connection between baptism and the Second Commandment?
3. How can God's word make something ordinary into something so powerful? What are some examples of great things that God has done with his word?

Prayer:

Father, thank you for your word, by which you created me and my faith. Help me to recognize that it has, and is able to do, all that you are and can do. Amen.

Week Twenty-one – Tuesday

The Sacrament of Holy Baptism

First: What is baptism?—Answer. Baptism is not simple water only, but it is the water comprehended in God's command and connected with God's word.

Which is that word of God?—Answer. Christ, our Lord, says in the last chapter of Matthew: "Go ye into all the world and teach all nations, baptizing them in the name of the Father, and of the Son, and of the Holy Ghost."

Therefore we always teach that the sacraments and all external things which God ordains and institutes should not be regarded according to the coarse, external mask, as we regard the shell of a nut, but as the word of God is included therein. For thus we also speak of the parental estate and of civil government. If we propose to regard them in as far as they have noses, eyes, skin, and hair, flesh and bones, they look like Turks and heathen, and someone might start up and say: "Why should I esteem them more than others?" But because the commandment is added: "Honor thy father and thy mother," I behold a different man, adorned and clothed with the majesty and glory of God. The commandment (I say) is the chain of gold about his neck, yea, the crown upon his head, which shows to me how and why one must honor this flesh and blood.

Thus, and much more even, you must honor baptism and esteem it glorious on account of the word, since he himself has honored it both by words and deeds; moreover, confirmed it with miracles from heaven. For do you think it was a jest that, when Christ was baptized, the heavens were opened and the Holy Ghost descended visibly, and everything was divine glory and majesty?

Therefore I exhort again that these two, the water and the word, by no means be separated from one another and parted. For if the word is separated from it, the water is the same as that with which the servant cooks, and may indeed be called a bathkeeper's baptism. But when it is added, as God has ordained, it is a sacrament, and is called Christ-baptism. Let this be the first part, regarding the essence and dignity of the holy sacrament. [LC IV.19–22]

Meditation:

1. What effect does the word of God have on external things? How does the Fourth Commandment illustrate this? What does this imply about baptism?
2. How has God honored and confirmed baptism? What happened when Christ was baptized? What does this imply about baptism?
3. What can we say about water that is separated from God's word? What must we say about it when God's word is added?

Prayer:

Lord God, thank you for using ordinary things like water, and like me, to accomplish your purposes. Help me to trust in the power of your word. Amen.

Week Twenty-one – Wednesday

The Sacrament of Holy Baptism

Secondly: What does baptism give or profit?—Answer. It works forgiveness of sins, delivers from death and the devil, and gives eternal salvation to all who believe this, as the words and promises of God declare.

Which are such words and promises of God?—Answer. Christ, our Lord, says in the last chapter of Mark: "He that believeth and is baptized shall be saved; but he that believeth not shall be damned."

In the second place, since we know now what baptism is, and how it is to be regarded, we must also learn why and for what purpose it is instituted; that is, what it profits, gives, and works. And this also we cannot discern better than from the words of Christ above quoted: "He that believeth and is baptized shall be saved." Therefore state it most simply thus, that the power, work, profit, fruit, and end of baptism is this, namely, to save. For no one is baptized in order that he may become a prince, but, as the words declare, that he be saved. But to be saved, we know, is nothing else than to be delivered from sin, death, and the devil, and to enter into the kingdom of Christ, and to live with him forever.

Here you see again how highly and precious we should esteem baptism, because in it we obtain such an unspeakable treasure, which also indicates sufficiently that it cannot be ordinary mere water. For mere water could not do such a thing, but the word does it, and (as said above) the fact that the name of God is comprehended therein. But where the name of God is, there must be also life and salvation, that it may indeed be called a divine, blessed, fruitful, and gracious water; for by the word such power is imparted to baptism that it is a laver of regeneration, as St. Paul also calls it, Titus 3:5. [LC IV.23–27]

Meditation:

1. What three things does baptism accomplish? Is it primarily a matter of law, what we do; or gospel, what God does for us?
2. When did each of us enter into the kingdom of Christ? Do we have to wait until death before we can begin living with him?
3. What is the source of baptism's power to save? Why it is important to keep emphasizing this over and over?

Prayer:

Jesus, thank you for saving me by my baptism—delivering me from sin, death, and the devil, and taking me into your kingdom to live with you forever. Amen.

Week Twenty-one – Thursday

The Sacrament of Holy Baptism

Secondly: What does baptism give or profit?—Answer. It works forgiveness of sins, delivers from death and the devil, and gives eternal salvation to all who believe this, as the words and promises of God declare.

Which are such words and promises of God?—Answer. Christ, our Lord, says in the last chapter of Mark: "He that believeth and is baptized shall be saved; but he that believeth not shall be damned."

But as our would-be wise new spirits assert that faith alone saves, and that works and external things avail nothing, we answer: It is true, indeed, that nothing in us is of any avail but faith, as we shall hear still further. But these blind guides are unwilling to see this, namely, that faith must have something which it believes, that is, of which it takes hold, and upon which it stands and rests. Thus faith clings to the water, and believes that it is baptism, in which there is pure salvation and life; not through the water (as we have sufficiently stated), but through the fact that it is embodied in the word and institution of God, and the name of God inheres in it. Now, if I believe this, what else is it than believing in God as in him who has given and planted his word into this ordinance, and proposes to us this external thing wherein we may apprehend such a treasure?

Now, they are so mad as to separate faith, and that to which faith clings and is bound, though it be something external. Yea, it shall and must be something external, that it may be apprehended by the senses, and understood and thereby be brought into the heart, as indeed the entire gospel is an external, verbal preaching. In short, what God does and works in us he proposes to work through such external ordinances. Wherever, therefore, he speaks, yea, in whichever direction or by whatever means he speaks, thither faith must look, and to that it must hold.

Now here we have the words: "He that believeth and is baptized shall be saved." To what else do they refer than to baptism, that is, to the water comprehended in God's ordinance? Hence it follows that whoever rejects baptism rejects the word of God, faith, and Christ, who directs us thither and binds us to baptism. [LC IV.28–31]

Meditation:

1. Is it true that faith alone saves? How, then, can we also say that baptism saves? What is the key difference between saving faith and generic faith?
2. To what does faith cling in baptism? In whom are we thus believing? Why is something external necessary and beneficial for such faith?
3. Why might some people reject baptism or its saving power? What else are they rejecting by doing so? Why is this a serious matter?

Prayer:

Dear God, thank you for giving me faith through baptism and sustaining it ever since. Help me to recognize and cling to your external means of grace. Amen.

The Lutheran Catechism

Week Twenty-one – Friday

The Sacrament of Holy Baptism

Secondly: What does baptism give or profit?—Answer. It works forgiveness of sins, delivers from death and the devil, and gives eternal salvation to all who believe this, as the words and promises of God declare.

Which are such words and promises of God?—Answer. Christ, our Lord, says in the last chapter of Mark: "He that believeth and is baptized shall be saved; but he that believeth not shall be damned."

In the third place, since we have learned the great benefit and power of baptism, let us see further who is the person that receives what baptism gives and profits. This is again most beautifully and clearly expressed in the words: "He that believeth and is baptized shall be saved." That is, faith alone makes the person worthy to receive profitably the saving, divine water. For, since these blessings are here presented and promised in the words in and with the water, they cannot be received in any other way than by believing them with the heart. Without faith it profits nothing, notwithstanding it is in itself a divine superabundant treasure. Therefore this single word ("He that believeth") effects this much that it excludes and repels all works which we can do, in the opinion that we obtain and merit salvation by them. For it is determined that whatever is not faith avails nothing nor receives anything.

But if they say, as they are accustomed: "Still baptism is itself a work, and you say works are of no avail for salvation; what, then, becomes of faith?" Answer: "Yes, our works, indeed, avail nothing for salvation; baptism, however, is not our work, but God's (for, as was stated, you must put Christ-baptism far away from a bathkeeper's baptism)." God's works, however, are saving and necessary for salvation, and do not exclude, but demand, faith; for without faith they could not be apprehended. For by suffering the water to be poured upon you, you have not yet received baptism in such a manner that it benefits you anything; but it becomes beneficial to you if you have yourself baptized with the thought that this is according to God's command and ordinance, and besides in God's name, in order that you may receive in the water the promised salvation. Now, this the fist cannot do, nor the body; but the heart must believe it. [LC IV.32–36]

Meditation:
1. Who is the person that receives what baptism gives and profits? Why does faith alone make the person worthy?
2. What does someone else's promise accomplish for you if you do not believe it? What is the application of this to baptism?
3. What role do our own works play in obtaining and meriting our salvation? Why is it a mistake to view baptism as our own work?

Prayer:

Heavenly Father, thank you for your gracious promise of salvation through your word and baptism. Help me to trust in your works, rather than my own. Amen.

Week Twenty-one – Saturday

The Sacrament of Holy Baptism

Secondly: What does baptism give or profit?—Answer. It works forgiveness of sins, delivers from death and the devil, and gives eternal salvation to all who believe this, as the words and promises of God declare.

Which are such words and promises of God?—Answer. Christ, our Lord, says in the last chapter of Mark: "He that believeth and is baptized shall be saved; but he that believeth not shall be damned."

Thus you see plainly that there is here no work done by us, but a treasure which he gives us, and which faith apprehends; just as the Lord Jesus Christ upon the cross is not a work, but a treasure comprehended in the word, and offered to us and received by faith. Therefore they do us violence by exclaiming against us as though we preach against faith; while we alone insist upon it as being of such necessity that without it nothing can be received nor enjoyed.

Thus we have these three parts which it is necessary to know concerning this sacrament, especially that the ordinance of God is to be held in all honor, which alone would be sufficient, though it be an entirely external thing, like the commandment, "Honor thy father and thy mother," which refers to bodily flesh and blood. Therein we regard not the flesh and blood, but the commandment of God in which they are comprehended, and on account of which the flesh is called father and mother; so also, though we had no more than these words, "Go ye and baptize," etc., it would be necessary for us to accept and do it as the ordinance of God. Now there is here not only God's commandment and injunction, but also the promise, on account of which it is still far more glorious than whatever else God has commanded and ordained, and is, in short, so full of consolation and grace that heaven and earth cannot comprehend it. But it requires skill to believe this, for the treasure is not wanting, but this is wanting that men apprehend it and hold it firmly. [LC IV.37–40]

Meditation:

1. How is baptism similar to the Lord Jesus Christ upon the cross? What did he accomplish there? How do we receive the benefits?
2. Why is it necessary for us to accept and do what God has commanded regarding baptism? What might otherwise hinder us?
3. Why does it require skill to believe what God has promised regarding baptism? How does studying the catechism help us to develop that skill?

Prayer:

Jesus, thank you for redeeming me upon the cross and giving me faith through baptism. Help me to obey your commands and believe your promises. Amen.

Week Twenty-two – Sunday

The Sacrament of Holy Baptism

Secondly: What does baptism give or profit?—Answer. It works forgiveness of sins, delivers from death and the devil, and gives eternal salvation to all who believe this, as the words and promises of God declare.

Which are such words and promises of God?—Answer. Christ, our Lord, says in the last chapter of Mark: "He that believeth and is baptized shall be saved; but he that believeth not shall be damned."

Therefore every Christian has enough in baptism to learn and to practice all his life; for he has always enough to do to believe firmly what it promises and brings: victory over death and the devil, forgiveness of sin, the grace of God, the entire Christ, and the Holy Ghost with his gifts. In short, it is so transcendent that if timid nature could realize it, it might well doubt whether it could be true.

For consider, if there were somewhere a physician who understood the art of saving men from dying, or, even though they died, of restoring them speedily to life, so that they would thereafter live forever, how the world would pour in money like snow and rain, so that because of the throng of the rich no one could find access! But here in baptism there is brought free to everyone's door such a treasure and medicine as utterly destroys death and preserves all men alive.

Thus we must regard baptism and make it profitable to ourselves, that when our sins and conscience oppress us, we strengthen ourselves and take comfort and say: "Nevertheless I am baptized; but if I am baptized, it is promised me that I shall be saved and have eternal life, both in soul and body." For that is the reason why these two things are done in baptism, namely, that the body, which can apprehend nothing but the water, is sprinkled, and, in addition, the word is spoken for the soul to apprehend. Now, since both, the water and the word, are one baptism, therefore body and soul must be saved and live forever: the soul through the word which it believes, but the body because it is united with the soul and also apprehends baptism as it is able to apprehend it. We have, therefore, no greater jewel in body and soul,

The Lutheran Catechism

for by it we are made holy and are saved, which no other kind of life, no work upon earth, can attain.

Let this suffice respecting the nature, blessing, and use of baptism, for it answers the present purpose. [LC IV.41–46]

Meditation:
1. How is baptism like being saved from dying? To what lengths do people go to extend their earthly lives? Why is baptism so much less valued?
2. When your sins and conscience oppress you, what should you say to yourself? Why "I *am* baptized," rather than "I *was* baptized"?
3. How does baptism offer salvation in a way that both body and soul can apprehend? Why is this important? Is eternal life only for the soul?

Prayer:

Dear Lord, thank you for saving my body and soul through baptism. When trials and temptations come, comfort me by reminding me that I am baptized. Amen.

Week Twenty-two – Monday

The Sacrament of Holy Baptism

Thirdly: How can water do such great things?—Answer. It is not the water indeed that does them, but the word of God which is in and with the water, and faith, which trusts such word of God in the water. For without the word of God the water is simple water and no baptism. But with the word of God it is a baptism, that is, a gracious water of life and a washing of regeneration in the Holy Ghost, as St. Paul says, Titus, chapter 3: "By the washing of regeneration and renewing of the Holy Ghost, which he shed on us abundantly through Jesus Christ, our Savior, that, being justified by his grace, we should be made heirs according to the hope of eternal life. This is a faithful saying."

Here a question occurs by which the devil, through his sects, confuses the world, namely, of infant baptism, whether children also believe, and are justly baptized. Concerning this we say briefly: Let the simple dismiss this question from their minds, and refer it to the learned. But if you wish to answer, then answer thus:

That the baptism of infants is pleasing to Christ is sufficiently proved from his own work, namely, that God sanctifies many of them who have been thus baptized, and has given them the Holy Ghost; and that there are yet many even today in whom we perceive that they have the Holy Ghost both because of their doctrine and life; as it is also given to us by the grace of God that we can explain the Scriptures and come to the knowledge of Christ, which is impossible without the Holy Ghost. But if God did not accept the baptism of infants, he would not give the Holy Ghost nor any of his gifts to any of them; in short, during this long time unto this day no man upon earth could have been a Christian. [LC IV.47–50a]

Meditation:

1. Why is it a mistake to focus only on the water of baptism? What must be added? What does the water then become?
2. Why do some Christians question whether infants are justly baptized? How would you answer them?
3. Since infant baptism has been the church's practice from the very beginning, what would be the case if it were not accepted by God?

Prayer:

Lord God, thank you for adding your word to the water so that every baptism is a gracious water of life and a washing of regeneration in the Holy Spirit. Amen.

Week Twenty-two – Tuesday

The Sacrament of Holy Baptism

Thirdly: How can water do such great things?—Answer. It is not the water indeed that does them, but the word of God which is in and with the water, and faith, which trusts such word of God in the water. For without the word of God the water is simple water and no baptism. But with the word of God it is a baptism, that is, a gracious water of life and a washing of regeneration in the Holy Ghost, as St. Paul says, Titus, chapter 3: "By the washing of regeneration and renewing of the Holy Ghost, which he shed on us abundantly through Jesus Christ, our Savior, that, being justified by his grace, we should be made heirs according to the hope of eternal life. This is a faithful saying."

Now, since God confirms baptism by the gifts of his Holy Ghost, as is plainly perceptible in some of the church fathers, as St. Bernard, Gerson, John Hus, and others, who were baptized in infancy, and since the holy Christian church cannot perish until the end of the world, they must acknowledge that such infant baptism is pleasing to God. For he can never be opposed to himself, or support falsehood and wickedness, or for its promotion impart his grace and Spirit. This is indeed the best and strongest proof for the simpleminded and unlearned. For they shall not take from us or overthrow this article: "I believe a holy Christian church, the communion of saints."

Further, we say that we are not so much concerned to know whether the person baptized believes or not; for on that account baptism does not become invalid; but everything depends upon the word and command of God. This now is perhaps somewhat acute, but it rests entirely upon what I have said, that baptism is nothing else than water and the word of God in and with each other, that is, when the word is added to the water, baptism is valid, even though faith be wanting. For my faith does not make baptism, but receives it. Now, baptism does not become invalid even though it be wrongly received or employed; since it is not bound (as stated) to our faith, but to the word. [LC IV.50b–53]

Meditation:

1. At what point in life were many of the church fathers baptized? How is it evident that God gave them the gifts of his Holy Spirit?
2. What does this indicate about infant baptism? Should we then expect everyone who has been baptized as an infant to be saved? Why not?
3. Does the validity of baptism depend on the faith of the recipient? To what is it bound instead? Why is this important?

Prayer:

Father, thank you for blessing those baptized as infants with the gifts of your Holy Spirit to assure us that your promise applies to all of your children. Amen.

Week Twenty-two – Wednesday

The Sacrament of Holy Baptism

Thirdly: How can water do such great things?—Answer. It is not the water indeed that does them, but the word of God which is in and with the water, and faith, which trusts such word of God in the water. For without the word of God the water is simple water and no baptism. But with the word of God it is a baptism, that is, a gracious water of life and a washing of regeneration in the Holy Ghost, as St. Paul says, Titus, chapter 3: "By the washing of regeneration and renewing of the Holy Ghost, which he shed on us abundantly through Jesus Christ, our Savior, that, being justified by his grace, we should be made heirs according to the hope of eternal life. This is a faithful saying."

For even though a Jew should today come dishonestly and with evil purpose, and we should baptize him in all good faith, we must say that his baptism is nevertheless genuine. For here is the water together with the word of God, even though he does not receive it as he should, just as those who unworthily go to the Sacrament receive the true Sacrament, even though they do not believe.

Thus you see that the objection of the sectarians is vain. For (as we have said) even though infants did not believe, which, however, is not the case, yet their baptism as now shown would be valid, and no one should rebaptize them; just as nothing is detracted from the sacrament though someone approach it with evil purpose, and he could not be allowed on account of his abuse to take it a second time the selfsame hour, as though he had not received the true sacrament at first; for that would mean to blaspheme and profane the sacrament in the worst manner. How dare we think that God's word and ordinance should be wrong and invalid because we make a wrong use of it? [LC IV.54–55]

Meditation:

1. Why would even the baptism of a dishonest unbeliever be genuine? Does this mean that the person would then be saved without faith?
2. What are the only two elements required for a valid baptism? Why does it not depend on anything on the part of the recipient?
3. How does recognizing this help to refute the opponents of infant baptism? What serious mistake are they making?

Prayer:

Dear God, I praise you for saving me by your word and ordinance in baptism. Help me to trust in your promises, rather than anything within myself. Amen.

Week Twenty-two – Thursday

The Sacrament of Holy Baptism

Thirdly: How can water do such great things?—Answer. It is not the water indeed that does them, but the word of God which is in and with the water, and faith, which trusts such word of God in the water. For without the word of God the water is simple water and no baptism. But with the word of God it is a baptism, that is, a gracious water of life and a washing of regeneration in the Holy Ghost, as St. Paul says, Titus, chapter 3: "By the washing of regeneration and renewing of the Holy Ghost, which he shed on us abundantly through Jesus Christ, our Savior, that, being justified by his grace, we should be made heirs according to the hope of eternal life. This is a faithful saying."

Therefore I say, if you did not believe then, believe now and say thus: "The baptism indeed was right, but I, alas! did not receive it aright." For I myself also, and all who are baptized, must speak thus before God: "I come hither in my faith and in that of others, yet I cannot rest in this, that I believe, and that many people pray for me; but in this I rest, that it is thy word and command." Just as I go to the Sacrament trusting not in my faith, but in the word of Christ; whether I am strong or weak, that I commit to God. But this I know, that he bids me go, eat and drink, etc., and gives me his body and blood; that will not deceive me or prove false to me.

Thus we do also in infant baptism. We bring the child in the conviction and hope that it believes, and we pray that God may grant it faith; but we do not baptize it upon that, but solely upon the command of God. Why so? Because we know that God does not lie. I and my neighbor and, in short, all men, may err and deceive, but the word of God cannot err.

Therefore they are presumptuous, clumsy minds that draw such inferences and conclusions as these: "Where there is not the true faith, there also can be no true baptism." Just as if I would infer: "If I do not believe, then Christ is nothing"; or thus: "If I am not obedient, then father, mother, and government are nothing." Is that a correct conclusion, that whenever anyone does not do what he ought, the thing in itself shall be nothing and of no value? [LC IV.56–58]

Meditation:

1. Why is it a mistake to rest in our own faith and other people's prayers for us? In what should we rest instead? Why?
2. What is the only valid reason for baptizing infants or anyone else? Why can we be confident that the word of God cannot err?
3. Does the truth of the law depend on our obedience? Why not? Does the truth of the gospel depend on our faith? Why not?

Prayer:

Lord, forgive me for sometimes trusting more in my faith than in your promises. Thank you for giving me your inerrant word in law and gospel. Amen.

Week Twenty-two – Friday

The Sacrament of Holy Baptism

Thirdly: How can water do such great things?—Answer. It is not the water indeed that does them, but the word of God which is in and with the water, and faith, which trusts such word of God in the water. For without the word of God the water is simple water and no baptism. But with the word of God it is a baptism, that is, a gracious water of life and a washing of regeneration in the Holy Ghost, as St. Paul says, Titus, chapter 3: "By the washing of regeneration and renewing of the Holy Ghost, which he shed on us abundantly through Jesus Christ, our Savior, that, being justified by his grace, we should be made heirs according to the hope of eternal life. This is a faithful saying."

My dear, just invert the argument and rather draw this inference: For this very reason baptism is something and is right, because it has been wrongly received. For if it were not right and true in itself, it could not be misused nor sinned against. The saying is: "Abuse does not destroy the essence, but confirms it." For gold is not the less gold though a harlot wear it in sin and shame.

Therefore let it be decided that baptism always remains true, retains its full essence, even though a single person should be baptized, and he, in addition, should not believe truly. For God's ordinance and word cannot be made variable or be altered by men. But these people, the fanatics, are so blinded that they do not see the word and command of God, and regard baptism and the magistrates only as they regard water in the brook or in pots, or as any other man; and because they do not see faith nor obedience, they conclude that they are to be regarded as invalid. Here lurks a concealed seditious devil, who would like to tear the crown from the head of authority and then trample it under foot, and, in addition, pervert and bring to naught all the works and ordinances of God. Therefore we must be watchful and well armed, and not allow ourselves to be directed nor turned away from the word, in order that we may not regard baptism as a mere empty sign, as the fanatics dream. [LC IV.59–63]

Meditation:

1. How does recognizing the misuse of baptism confirm its objective value? Does wrongly receiving it the first time mean that it must be repeated?
2. Why can God's ordinance and word not be made variable or altered by men? What comfort can we draw from this?
3. Why do some Christians treat baptism as a mere empty sign? Whose agenda are they unwittingly advancing when they do so?

Prayer:

Father, thank you for the assurance that your word is eternal and unchanging, so that my baptism depends only on your promise, not on anything in me. Amen.

Week Twenty-two – Saturday

The Sacrament of Holy Baptism

Fourthly: What does such baptizing with water signify?—Answer. It signifies that the old Adam in us should, by daily contrition and repentance, be drowned and die with all sins and evil lusts, and, again, a new man daily come forth and arise, who shall live before God in righteousness and purity forever.

Where is this written?—Answer. St. Paul says, Romans, chapter 6: "We are buried with Christ by baptism into death, that, like as he was raised up from the dead by the glory of the Father, even so we also should walk in newness of life."

Lastly, we must also know what baptism signifies, and why God has ordained just such external sign and ceremony for the sacrament by which we are first received into the Christian church. But the act or ceremony is this, that we are sunk under the water, which passes over us, and afterwards are drawn out again. These two parts, to be sunk under the water and drawn out again, signify the power and operation of baptism, which is nothing else than putting to death the old Adam, and after that the resurrection of the new man, both of which must take place in us all our lives, so that a truly Christian life is nothing else than a daily baptism, once begun and ever to be continued. For this must be practiced without ceasing, that we ever keep purging away whatever is of the old Adam, and that that which belongs to the new man come forth. But what is the old man? It is that which is born in us from Adam, angry, hateful, envious, unchaste, stingy, lazy, haughty, yea, unbelieving, infected with all vices, and having by nature nothing good in it. Now, when we are come into the kingdom of Christ, these things must daily decrease, that the longer we live we become more gentle, more patient, more meek, and ever withdraw more and more from unbelief, avarice, hatred, envy, haughtiness. [LC IV.64–67]

Meditation:

1. How is the act or ceremony of baptism described here? Does this surprise you? Are most Lutherans baptized by immersion today? Does it matter?
2. What does being sunk under the water signify? What does being drawn out again signify? Why must both of these take place in us all our lives?
3. What is the old Adam in us? What is the new man? What should happen to each of them over time, as a believer matures?

Prayer:

Jesus, I am baptized into your death and resurrection. Daily drown the old Adam in me and call forth the new man, that I may live a truly Christian life. Amen.

Week Twenty-three – Sunday

The Sacrament of Holy Baptism

Fourthly: What does such baptizing with water signify?—Answer. It signifies that the old Adam in us should, by daily contrition and repentance, be drowned and die with all sins and evil lusts, and, again, a new man daily come forth and arise, who shall live before God in righteousness and purity forever.

Where is this written?—Answer. St. Paul says, Romans, chapter 6: "We are buried with Christ by baptism into death, that, like as he was raised up from the dead by the glory of the Father, even so we also should walk in newness of life."

This is the true use of baptism among Christians, as signified by baptizing with water. Where this, therefore, is not practiced, but the old man is left unbridled, so as to continually become stronger, that is not using baptism, but striving against baptism. For those who are without Christ cannot but daily become worse, according to the proverb which expresses the truth, "Worse and worse—the longer, the worse." If a year ago one was proud and avaricious, then he is much prouder and more avaricious this year, so that the vice grows and increases with him from his youth up. A young child has no special vice; but when it grows up, it becomes unchaste and impure, and when it reaches maturity, real vices begin to prevail, the longer, the more.

Therefore the old man goes unrestrained in his nature if he is not checked and suppressed by the power of baptism. On the other hand, where men have become Christians, he daily decreases until he finally perishes. That is truly to be buried in baptism, and daily to come forth again. Therefore the external sign is appointed not only for a powerful effect, but also for a signification. Where, therefore, faith flourishes with its fruits, there it has no empty signification, but the work accompanies it; but where faith is wanting, it remains a mere unfruitful sign. [LC IV.68–73]

Meditation:

1. What happens daily to those who are without Christ? What keeps the old man in us from likewise continually becoming stronger?
2. Why are we unable to be completely free of the old man in this life? When will he finally perish? What should happen daily in the meantime?
3. What is the evidence that the external sign of baptism has a powerful effect, not merely an empty signification?

Prayer:

Dear Lord, as I remember my baptism, empower my faith to flourish with its fruits so that the old man in me daily decreases until he finally perishes. Amen.

Week Twenty-three – Monday

The Sacrament of Holy Baptism

Fourthly: What does such baptizing with water signify?—Answer. It signifies that the old Adam in us should, by daily contrition and repentance, be drowned and die with all sins and evil lusts, and, again, a new man daily come forth and arise, who shall live before God in righteousness and purity forever.

Where is this written?—Answer. St. Paul says, Romans, chapter 6: "We are buried with Christ by baptism into death, that, like as he was raised up from the dead by the glory of the Father, even so we also should walk in newness of life."

And here you see that baptism, both in its power and signification, comprehends also the third sacrament, which has been called repentance, as it is really nothing else than baptism. For what else is repentance but an earnest attack upon the old man and entering upon a new life? Therefore, if you live in repentance, you walk in baptism, which not only signifies such a new life, but also produces, begins, and exercises it. For therein are given grace, the Spirit, and power to suppress the old man, so that the new man may come forth and become strong.

Therefore our baptism abides forever; and even though someone should fall from it and sin, nevertheless we always have access thereto, that we may again subdue the old man. But we need not again be sprinkled with water; for though we were put under the water a hundred times, it would nevertheless be only one baptism, although the operation and signification continue and remain. Repentance, therefore, is nothing else than a return and approach to baptism, that we repeat and practice what we began before, but abandoned.

This I say lest we fall into the opinion in which we were for a long time, imagining that our baptism is something past, which we can no longer use after we have fallen again into sin. The reason is that it is regarded only according to the external act once performed. [LC IV.74–80]

Meditation:
1. What is the third sacrament? Why is it really nothing else than baptism? What does it mean to live in repentance? How does baptism enable this?
2. In what sense is repentance an earnest attack upon the old man and entering upon a new life? How often do we need it? Why?
3. Why is it not necessary to be sprinkled with water again every time we fall into sin? What should we do instead?

Prayer:

God, please forgive me for falling from my baptism and sinning despite your grace toward me. Help me to live in repentance by daily returning to my baptism. Amen.

Week Twenty-three – Tuesday

The Sacrament of Holy Baptism

Fourthly: What does such baptizing with water signify?—Answer. It signifies that the old Adam in us should, by daily contrition and repentance, be drowned and die with all sins and evil lusts, and, again, a new man daily come forth and arise, who shall live before God in righteousness and purity forever.

Where is this written?—Answer. St. Paul says, Romans, chapter 6: "We are buried with Christ by baptism into death, that, like as he was raised up from the dead by the glory of the Father, even so we also should walk in newness of life."

And this arose from the fact that St. Jerome wrote that repentance is the second plank by which we must swim forth and cross over after the ship is broken, on which we step and are carried across when we come into the Christian church. Thereby the use of baptism has been abolished so that it can profit us no longer. Therefore the statement is not correct, or at any rate not rightly understood. For the ship never breaks, because (as we have said) it is the ordinance of God, and not a work of ours; but it happens, indeed, that we slip and fall out of the ship. Yet if anyone fall out, let him see to it that he swim up and cling to it till he again come into it and live in it, as he had formerly begun.

Thus it appears what a great, excellent thing baptism is, which delivers us from the jaws of the devil and makes us God's own, suppresses and takes away sin, and then daily strengthens the new man; and is and remains ever efficacious until we pass from this estate of misery to eternal glory.

For this reason let everyone esteem his baptism as a daily dress in which he is to walk constantly, that he may ever be found in the faith and its fruits, that he suppress the old man and grow up in the new. For if we would be Christians, we must practice the work whereby we are Christians. But if anyone fall away from it, let him again come into it. For just as Christ, the mercy seat, does not recede from us or forbid us to come to him again, even though we sin, so all his treasure and gifts also remain. If, therefore, we have once in baptism obtained forgiveness of sin, it will remain every day, as long as we live, that is, as long as we carry the old man about our neck. [LC IV.81–86]

Meditation:
1. How is baptism like a ship that carries us through this life to eternal life? Why is it a mistake to think that we break the ship by sinning?
2. What should we do when we slip and fall out of the ship of baptism? What will happen to us if we try to keep swimming instead?
3. What does it look like for someone to walk constantly in his or her baptism as a daily dress? Is such a person sinless, or forgiven?

Prayer:

Father, please use my baptism to deliver me from the jaws of the devil, make me your own, suppress and take away sin, and daily strengthen the new man. Amen.

Week Twenty-three – Wednesday

Confession

What is confession?

Confession embraces two parts: the one is, that we confess our sins; the other, that we receive absolution, or forgiveness, from the confessor, as from God himself, and in no wise doubt, but firmly believe that our sins are thereby forgiven before God in heaven.

The keys are an office and power given by Christ to the church for binding and loosing sin, not only the gross and well-known sins, but also the subtle, hidden, which are known only to God, as it is written in Psalm 19:13: "Who can understand his errors?" And in Romans 7:25, St. Paul himself complains that with the flesh he serves the law of sin. For it is not in our power, but belongs to God alone, to judge which, how great, and how many the sins are, as it is written in Psalm 143:2: "Enter not into judgment with thy servant; for in thy sight shall no man living be justified." And Paul says, 1 Corinthians 4:4: "For I know nothing by myself; yet am I not hereby justified." . . .

Since absolution or the Power of the Keys is also an aid and consolation against sin and a bad conscience, ordained by Christ in the gospel, confession or absolution ought by no means to be abolished in the church, especially on account of timid consciences and on account of the untrained young people, in order that they may be examined, and instructed in the Christian doctrine. [SA III.VII.1–3, III.VIII.1]

Meditation:

1. What are the two parts of confession? Which one corresponds to the law? Which one corresponds to the gospel? Why are both essential?
2. Why are we unable to judge which, how great, and how many our own sins are? How does the regular practice of confession address this?
3. Whose absolution is administered by the confessor? How does this serve as an aid and consolation against sin and a bad conscience?

Prayer:

Lord, I confess that I have sinned. Thank you for the absolution that you offer through my pastor. Help me to seek it regularly and receive it in faith. Amen.

Week Twenty-three – Thursday

Confession

What sins should we confess?

Before God we should plead guilty of all sins, even of those which we do not know, as we do in the Lord's Prayer. But before the confessor we should confess those sins alone which we know and feel in our hearts.

Here we must confess, as Paul says in Romans 5:12, that sin originated from one man Adam, by whose disobedience all men were made sinners, subject to death and the devil. This is called original or capital sin.

The fruits of this sin are afterwards the evil deeds which are forbidden in the Ten Commandments, such as unbelief, false faith, idolatry, to be without the fear of God, presumption, despair, blindness, and, in short, not to know or regard God; furthermore to lie, to swear by God's name, not to pray, not to call upon God, not to regard God's word, to be disobedient to parents, to murder, to be unchaste, to steal, to deceive, etc.

This hereditary sin is so deep a corruption of nature that no reason can understand it, but it must be believed from the revelation of Scriptures, Psalm 51:5; Romans 6:12ff; Exodus 33:3; Genesis 3:7ff. . . .

But the enumeration of sins ought to be free to everyone, as to what he wishes to enumerate or not to enumerate. For as long as we are in the flesh, we shall not lie when we say: "I am a poor man, full of sin." Romans 7:23: "I see another law in my members," etc. For since private absolution originates in the Office of the Keys, it should not be despised, but greatly and highly esteemed, as all other offices of the Christian church. [SA III.I.1–3a, III.VIII.2]

Meditation:

1. Of which sins should we plead guilty before God? What is our condition as natural descendants of Adam? Why is it important to recognize this?
2. What are the fruits of original sin? Why are we readily capable of such evil deeds? How deep does Scripture reveal the corruption of our nature to be?
3. Which sins should we enumerate when speaking privately to a pastor or other confessor? Why is doing so, and then receiving absolution, beneficial?

Prayer:

God, help me to recognize and confess not only my actual sins of commission and omission, but also my sinful condition as revealed by your word. Amen.

Week Twenty-three – Friday

Confession

Which are these?

Here consider your station according to the Ten Commandments, whether you are a father, mother, son, daughter, master, mistress, a manservant or maidservant; whether you have been disobedient, unfaithful, slothful; whether you have grieved anyone by words or deeds; whether you have stolen, neglected, or wasted aught, or done other injury.

Here we hold that the law was given by God, first, to restrain sin by threats and the dread of punishment, and by the promise and offer of grace and benefit. But all this miscarried on account of the wickedness which sin has wrought in man. For thereby a part were rendered worse, those, namely, who are hostile to the law, because it forbids what they like to do, and enjoins what they do not like to do. Therefore, wherever they can escape punishment, they do more against the law than before. These, then, are the rude and wicked men, who do evil wherever they have the opportunity.

The rest become blind and arrogant, and conceive the opinion that they observe and can observe the law by their own powers, as has been said above concerning the scholastic theologians; thence come the hypocrites and false saints.

But the chief office or force of the law is that it reveal original sin with all its fruits, and show man how very low his nature has fallen, and has become utterly corrupted; as the law must tell man that he has no God nor regards God, and worships other gods, a matter which before and without the law he would not have believed. In this way he becomes terrified, is humbled, desponds, despairs, and anxiously desires aid, but sees no escape; he begins to be an enemy of God, and to murmur, etc. This is what Paul says, Romans 4:15: "The law worketh wrath." And Romans 5:20: "Sin is increased by the law." [SA III.II.1–5]

Meditation:

1. Why is considering our station in life helpful for recognizing the kinds of actual sins that we should enumerate in private confession?
2. Why are many people hostile to the law? Why do many others blindly believe that they can and do observe the law by their own powers?
3. What is the chief office of the law? How does it reveal original sin? How does it reveal the actual sins that are its fruits? What effects does this have?

Prayer:

Lord, forgive me for sometimes being hostile to your law or wrongly thinking that I can obey it by my own powers. Thank you for revealing the truth. Amen.

Week Twenty-three – Saturday

Confession

Which are these?

Here consider your station according to the Ten Commandments, whether you are a father, mother, son, daughter, master, mistress, a manservant or maidservant; whether you have been disobedient, unfaithful, slothful; whether you have grieved anyone by words or deeds; whether you have stolen, neglected, or wasted aught, or done other injury.

This office [of the law] the New Testament retains and urges, as St. Paul, Romans 1:18 does, saying: "The wrath of God is revealed from heaven against all ungodliness and unrighteousness of men." Again, Romans 3:19: "All the world is guilty before God. No man is righteous before him." And Christ says, John 16:8: "The Holy Ghost will reprove the world of sin."

This, then, is the thunderbolt of God by which he strikes in a heap both manifest sinners and false saints, and suffers no one to be in the right, but drives them all together to terror and despair. This is the hammer, as Jeremiah 23:29 says: "Is not my word like a hammer that breaketh the rock in pieces?" This is not "active contrition" or manufactured repentance, but "passive contrition," true sorrow of heart, suffering and sensation of death.

This, then, is what it means to begin true repentance; and here man must hear such a sentence as this: "You are all of no account, whether you be manifest sinners or saints; you all must become different and do otherwise than you now are and are doing, whether you are as great, wise, powerful, and holy as you may [be]. Here no one is godly," etc. [SA III.III.1–3]

Meditation:

1. Do law and gospel simply correspond to the Old and New Testaments? Why does the New Testament retain and urge the chief office of the law?
2. How is the law like a thunderbolt? How is it like a hammer? What effects does it have on sinners? Is anyone exempt?
3. What is contrition? Which kind of contrition, active or passive, does the law produce? Why does God want us to experience true sorrow of heart?

Prayer:

Father, I am of no account before you. Help me to become different and do otherwise, not by my own efforts, but by your Holy Spirit working in me. Amen.

Week Twenty-four – Sunday

Confession

Which are these?

Here consider your station according to the Ten Commandments, whether you are a father, mother, son, daughter, master, mistress, a manservant or maidservant; whether you have been disobedient, unfaithful, slothful; whether you have grieved anyone by words or deeds; whether you have stolen, neglected, or wasted aught, or done other injury.

But to this office [of the law] the New Testament immediately adds the consolatory promise of grace through the gospel, which must be believed, as Christ declares, Mark 1:15: "Repent and believe the gospel," i.e., become different and do otherwise, and believe my promise. And John, preceding him, is called a preacher of repentance, however, for the remission of sins, i.e., John was to accuse all, and convict them of being sinners, that they might know what they were before God, and might acknowledge that they were lost men, and might thus be prepared for the Lord, to receive grace, and to expect and accept from him the remission of sins. Thus also Christ himself says, Luke 24:47: "Repentance and remission of sins must be preached in my name among all nations."

But whenever the law alone, without the gospel being added, exercises this its office, there is death and hell, and man must despair, like Saul and Judas; as St. Paul, Romans 7:10, says: "Through sin the law killeth." On the other hand, the gospel brings consolation and remission not only in one way, but through the word and sacraments, and the like, as we shall hear afterward in order that there is with the Lord plenteous redemption, as Psalm 130:7 says against the dreadful captivity of sin. [SA III.III.4–8]

Meditation:

1. What does the New Testament immediately add to the office of the law? Does this mean that there was no gospel in the Old Testament?
2. Why is the gospel a consolatory promise of grace? What is the only way for a promise to benefit someone who hears it?
3. What is the role of the gospel in confession? What happens when someone only ever hears the law, or refuses to believe the gospel?

Prayer:

God, thank you for your law that reveals my sin and your gospel that reveals your salvation. Help me to find consolation in believing your promises. Amen.

Week Twenty-four – Monday

The Sacrament of the Altar

What is the Sacrament of the Altar?

It is the true body and blood of our Lord Jesus Christ, under the bread and wine, for us Christians to eat and to drink, instituted by Christ himself.

In the same manner as we have heard regarding Holy Baptism, we must speak also concerning the other sacrament, namely, these three points: What is it? What are its benefits? and, Who is to receive it? And all these are established by the words by which Christ has instituted it, and which everyone who desires to be a Christian and go to the Sacrament should know. For it is not our intention to admit to it and to administer it to those who know not what they seek, or why they come....

Here also we do not wish to enter into controversy and contend with the traducers and blasphemers of this sacrament, but to learn first (as we did regarding baptism) what is of the greatest importance, namely, that the chief point is the word and ordinance or command of God. For it has not been invented nor introduced by any man, but without anyone's counsel and deliberation it has been instituted by Christ. Therefore, just as the Ten Commandments, the Lord's Prayer, and the Creed retain their nature and worth, although you never keep, pray, or believe them, so also does this venerable sacrament remain undisturbed, so that nothing is detracted or taken from it, even though we employ and dispense it unworthily. What do you think God cares about what we do or believe, so that on that account he should suffer his ordinance to be changed? Why, in all worldly matters everything remains as God has created and ordered it, no matter how we employ or use it. This must always be urged, for thereby the prating of nearly all the fanatical spirits can be repelled. For they regard the sacraments, aside from the word of God, as something that we do. [LC V.1–2, 4–7]

Meditation:
1. What three questions must be answered about the Lord's Supper? Why is it essential that those receiving it know what they seek and why they come?
2. Who instituted the Sacrament of the Altar? Why is this significant? What is the most important thing for us to recognize about it?
3. Why are the nature and worth of the catechism not dependent on our use of it? Why is it a mistake to regard the sacraments as something that we do?

Prayer:

Lord, thank you for the assurance that your good gifts to us do not depend on anything we do. Help me to receive the Sacrament in faith accordingly. Amen.

Week Twenty-four – Tuesday

The Sacrament of the Altar

What is the Sacrament of the Altar?

It is the true body and blood of our Lord Jesus Christ, under the bread and wine, for us Christians to eat and to drink, instituted by Christ himself.

Now, what is the Sacrament of the Altar? Answer: It is the true body and blood of our Lord Jesus Christ, in and under the bread and wine which we Christians are commanded by the word of Christ to eat and to drink. And as we have said of baptism that it is not simple water, so here also we say the sacrament is bread and wine, but not mere bread and wine, such as are ordinarily served at the table, but bread and wine comprehended in, and connected with, the word of God.

It is the word (I say) which makes and distinguishes this sacrament, so that it is not mere bread and wine, but is, and is called, the body and blood of Christ. For it is said: "If the word be joined to the element, it becomes a sacrament." This saying of St. Augustine is so properly and so well put that he has scarcely said anything better. The word must make a sacrament of the element, else it remains a mere element. Now, it is not the word or ordinance of a prince or emperor, but of the sublime Majesty, at whose feet all creatures should fall, and affirm it is as he says, and accept it with all reverence, fear, and humility. [LC V.8–11]

Meditation:

1. Why do we say that the Sacrament of the Altar is the *true* body and blood of our Lord Jesus Christ? What other views do some Christians hold?
2. Why do we say that the body and blood of Christ are *in and under* the bread and wine? Can we explain *how* this happens? Does it matter?
3. What was St. Augustine's definition of a sacrament? Why is the word of God an essential ingredient? What makes his word so powerful?

Prayer:

Jesus, thank you for giving us your true body and blood, in and under the bread and wine. Help me to receive them with all reverence, fear, and humility. Amen.

Week Twenty-four – Wednesday

The Sacrament of the Altar

Where is this written?

The holy evangelists Matthew, Mark, Luke, and St. Paul, write thus: "Our Lord Jesus Christ, the same night in which he was betrayed, took bread: and when he had given thanks, he brake it, and gave it to his disciples, and said, 'Take, eat; this is my body, which is given for you. This do in remembrance of me.' After the same manner also he took the cup, when he had supped, gave thanks, and gave it to them, saying, 'Take, drink ye all of it. This cup is the new testament in my blood, which is shed for you for the remission of sins. This do ye, as oft as ye drink it, in remembrance of me.'"

With this word you can strengthen your conscience and say: If a hundred thousand devils, together with all fanatics, should rush forward, crying, "How can bread and wine be the body and blood of Christ?" etc., I know that all spirits and scholars together are not as wise as is the Divine Majesty in his little finger. Now here stands the word of Christ: "Take, eat; this is my body; Drink ye all of it; this is the new testament in my blood," etc. Here we abide, and would like to see those who will constitute themselves his masters, and make it different from what he has spoken. It is true, indeed, that if you take away the word or regard it without the words, you have nothing but mere bread and wine. But if the words remain with them, as they shall and must, then, in virtue of the same, it is truly the body and blood of Christ. For as the lips of Christ say and speak, so it is, as he can never lie or deceive. [LC V.12–14]

Meditation:

1. Where in Scripture do we find the words that Jesus spoke when he instituted this sacrament? Why do you suppose that they appear in four places?
2. Why does human reason question the idea that the bread and wine are the body and blood of Christ? On what basis do we affirm it?
3. What makes the bread and wine be the body and blood of Christ? Did he give any indication that he intended his words to be taken figuratively?

Prayer:

God, thank you for the assurance that you can never lie or deceive. Help me to cling to your word in faith, rather than relying on my own human reason. Amen.

Week Twenty-four – Thursday

The Sacrament of the Altar

Where is this written?

The holy evangelists Matthew, Mark, Luke, and St. Paul, write thus: "Our Lord Jesus Christ, the same night in which he was betrayed, took bread: and when he had given thanks, he brake it, and gave it to his disciples, and said, 'Take, eat; this is my body, which is given for you. This do in remembrance of me.' After the same manner also he took the cup, when he had supped, gave thanks, and gave it to them, saying, 'Take, drink ye all of it. This cup is the new testament in my blood, which is shed for you for the remission of sins. This do ye, as oft as ye drink it, in remembrance of me.'"

Hence it is easy to reply to all manner of questions about which men are troubled at the present time, such as this one: Whether even a wicked priest can minister at, and dispense, the Sacrament, and whatever other questions like this there may be. For here we conclude and say: Even though a knave takes or distributes the Sacrament, he receives the true Sacrament, that is, the true body and blood of Christ, just as truly as he who administers it in the most worthy manner. For it is not founded upon the holiness of men, but upon the word of God. And as no saint upon earth, yea, no angel in heaven, can make bread and wine to be the body and blood of Christ, so also can no one change or alter it, even though it be misused. For the word by which it became a sacrament and was instituted does not become false because of the person or his unbelief. For he does not say: "If you believe or are worthy, you receive my body and blood," but: "Take, eat and drink; this is my body and blood." Likewise: "Do this" (namely, what I now do, institute, give, and bid you take). That is as much as to say, "No matter whether you are worthy or unworthy, you have here his body and blood by virtue of these words which are added to the bread and wine." Only note and remember this well; for upon these words rest all our foundation, protection, and defense against all errors and deception that have ever come or may yet come. [LC V.15–19]

Meditation:

1. Does the presence of the body and blood of Christ in the Sacrament depend on the worthiness of the one who administers or receives it? Why not?
2. Who alone is capable of making bread and wine to be the body and blood of Christ? By what means does he cause this to happen?
3. What assurance does this provide about the efficacy of the Sacrament? What misconceptions do some Christians have about it?

Prayer:

Jesus, thank you for the power of your word that makes simple bread and wine to be your holy and precious body and blood, given and shed for me. Amen.

Week Twenty-four – Friday

The Sacrament of the Altar

What is the benefit of such eating and drinking?

That is shown us in these words: "Given, and shed for you, for the remission of sins"; namely, that in the Sacrament forgiveness of sins, life, and salvation are given us through these words. For where there is forgiveness of sins, there is also life and salvation.

Thus we have briefly the first point which relates to the essence of this sacrament. Now examine further the efficacy and benefits on account of which really the Sacrament was instituted; which is also its most necessary part, that we may know what we should seek and obtain there. Now this is plain and clear from the words just mentioned: "This is my body and blood, given and shed for you, for the remission of sins." Briefly that is as much as to say: For this reason we go to the Sacrament, because there we receive such a treasure by and in which we obtain forgiveness of sins. Why so? Because the words stand here and give us this; for on this account he bids me eat and drink, that it may be my own and may benefit me, as a sure pledge and token, yea, the very same treasure that is appointed for me against my sins, death, and every calamity. [LC V.20–22]

Meditation:

1. What three things are we given in the Sacrament? How are they related? Why do we need forgiveness of sins, life, and salvation?
2. What role do the words of Jesus, "given and shed for you, for the remission of sins," play in the Sacrament? What role do the bread and wine play?
3. Why is the Sacrament called a treasure? How does this suggest that we should view and value it? Why is it a sure pledge and token?

Prayer:

Jesus, thank you for coming to earth, giving your body, and shedding your blood for my sake, so that I may receive forgiveness of sins, life, and salvation. Amen.

Week Twenty-four – Saturday

The Sacrament of the Altar

What is the benefit of such eating and drinking?

That is shown us in these words: "Given, and shed for you, for the remission of sins"; namely, that in the Sacrament forgiveness of sins, life, and salvation are given us through these words. For where there is forgiveness of sins, there is also life and salvation.

On this account it is indeed called a food of souls, which nourishes and strengthens the new man. For by baptism we are first born anew; but (as we said before) there still remains, besides, the old vicious nature of flesh and blood in man, and there are so many hindrances and temptations of the devil and of the world that we often become weary and faint, and sometimes also stumble.

Therefore it is given for a daily pasture and sustenance, that faith may refresh and strengthen itself so as not to fall back in such a battle, but become ever stronger and stronger. For the new life must be so regulated that it continually increase and progress; but it must suffer much opposition. For the devil is such a furious enemy that when he sees that we oppose him and attack the old man, and that he cannot topple us over by force, he prowls and moves about on all sides, tries all devices, and does not desist, until he finally wearies us, so that we either renounce our faith or yield hands and feet and become listless or impatient. Now to this end the consolation is here given when the heart feels that the burden is becoming too heavy, that it may here obtain new power and refreshment. [LC V.23–27]

Meditation:
1. Why does a person require physical nourishment after being born? Why does a Christian require spiritual nourishment after being baptized?
2. What hindrances and temptations of the devil and of the world do you face in your daily battle against the old vicious nature of flesh and blood?
3. Why do we suffer such constant opposition to progress in the new life? How does receiving the Sacrament help us keep up the fight?

Prayer:
Father, I cannot defeat the devil, the world, or my sinful flesh on my own. Sustain my faith and give me strength through your word and sacrament. Amen.

Week Twenty-five – Sunday

The Sacrament of the Altar

How can bodily eating and drinking do such great things?

It is not the eating and drinking, indeed, that does them, but the words which stand here, namely: "Given, and shed for you, for the remission of sins." Which words are, beside the bodily eating and drinking, as the chief thing in the Sacrament; and he that believes these words has what they say and express, namely, the forgiveness of sins.

But here our wise spirits contort themselves with their great art and wisdom, crying out and bawling: "How can bread and wine forgive sins or strengthen faith?" Although they hear and know that we do not say this of bread and wine, because in itself bread is bread, but of such bread and wine as is the body and blood of Christ, and has the words attached to it. That, we say, is verily the treasure, and nothing else, through which such forgiveness is obtained. Now the only way in which it is conveyed and appropriated to us is in the words ("Given and shed for you"). For herein you have both truths, that it is the body and blood of Christ, and that it is yours as a treasure and gift. Now the body of Christ can never be an unfruitful, vain thing, that effects or profits nothing. Yet, however great is the treasure in itself, it must be comprehended in the word and administered to us, else we should never be able to know or seek it. [LC V.28–30]

Meditation:

1. What causes bodily eating and drinking to become spiritual nourishment? Why must we believe the words to receive the benefits of the Sacrament?
2. What two truths do we have in the words, "Given and shed for you"? Why is it important to recognize Christ's body and blood, and that they are for you?
3. Why is the Sacrament a great treasure and gift? Why can the body of Christ never be an unfruitful, vain thing?

Prayer:

Lord Jesus, grant me the faith to recognize in the Sacrament your true body and blood, given and shed for me. Thank you for this great treasure and gift. Amen.

Week Twenty-five – Monday

The Sacrament of the Altar

How can bodily eating and drinking do such great things?

It is not the eating and drinking, indeed, that does them, but the words which stand here, namely: "Given, and shed for you, for the remission of sins." Which words are, beside the bodily eating and drinking, as the chief thing in the Sacrament; and he that believes these words has what they say and express, namely, the forgiveness of sins.

Therefore also it is vain talk when they say that the body and blood of Christ are not given and shed for us in the Lord's Supper, hence we could not have forgiveness of sins in the Sacrament. For although the work is accomplished and the forgiveness of sins acquired on the cross, yet it cannot come to us in any other way than through the word. For what would we otherwise know about it, that such a thing was accomplished or was to be given us, if it were not presented by preaching or the oral word? Whence do they know of it, or how can they apprehend and appropriate to themselves the forgiveness, except they lay hold of and believe the Scriptures and the gospel? But now the entire gospel and the article of the Creed: "I believe a holy Christian church, the forgiveness of sin," etc., are by the word embodied in this sacrament and presented to us. Why, then, should we allow this treasure to be torn from the Sacrament when they must confess that these are the very words which we hear everywhere in the gospel, and they cannot say that these words in the Sacrament are of no use, as little as they dare say that the entire gospel or word of God, apart from the Sacrament, is of no use? [LC V.31–32]

Meditation:
1. Why do some Christians insist that we cannot and do not receive forgiveness of sins in the Lord's Supper? What mistake are they making?
2. When and where was the work of salvation accomplished and the forgiveness of sins acquired? How does it come to us today?
3. What is the purpose of both preaching and the sacraments? What is the connection between the Third Article and the Sacrament of the Altar?

Prayer:

God, grant me the faith to recognize and receive the forgiveness of my sins in both the oral word of the gospel and the visible word of the sacraments. Amen.

Week Twenty-five – Tuesday

The Sacrament of the Altar

Who, then, receives such sacrament worthily?

Fasting and bodily preparation is, indeed, a fine outward training; but he is truly worthy and well prepared who has faith in these words: "Given, and shed for you, for the remission of sins." But he that does not believe these words, or doubts, is unworthy and unfit; for the words "for you" require altogether believing hearts.

Thus we have the entire sacrament, both as to what it is in itself and as to what it brings and profits. Now we must also see who is the person that receives this power and benefit. That is answered briefly, as we said above of baptism and often elsewhere: Whoever believes it has what the words declare and bring. For they are not spoken or proclaimed to stone and wood, but to those who hear them, to whom he says: "Take and eat," etc. And because he offers and promises forgiveness of sin, it cannot be received otherwise than by faith. This faith he himself demands in the word when he says: "Given and shed for you." As if he said: "For this reason I give it, and bid you eat and drink, that you may claim it as yours and enjoy it." Whoever now accepts these words, and believes that what they declare is true, has it. But whoever does not believe it has nothing, as he allows it to be offered to him in vain, and refuses to enjoy such a saving good. The treasure, indeed, is opened and placed at everyone's door, yea, upon his table, but it is necessary that you also claim it, and confidently view it as the words suggest to you. This, now, is the entire Christian preparation for receiving this sacrament worthily. For since this treasure is entirely presented in the words, it cannot be apprehended and appropriated in any other way than with the heart. For such a gift and eternal treasure cannot be seized with the fist. [LC V.33–36]

Meditation:

1. Why does the question of worthiness to receive the Sacrament arise? Why do some Christians practice fasting and bodily preparation?
2. What is the only thing required to be worthy and well prepared? Why is faith the only way to receive a promise? What benefit does an unbeliever gain?
3. What is the difference between apprehending something with the heart and seizing it with the fist? Why are we often tempted toward the latter?

Prayer:

Lord, I am completely undeserving of forgiveness, life, and salvation. Thank you for giving me the faith that alone makes me worthy to receive these gifts. Amen.

Week Twenty-five – Wednesday

The Sacrament of the Altar

Who, then, receives such sacrament worthily?

Fasting and bodily preparation is, indeed, a fine outward training; but he is truly worthy and well prepared who has faith in these words: "Given, and shed for you, for the remission of sins." But he that does not believe these words, or doubts, is unworthy and unfit; for the words "for you" require altogether believing hearts.

Fasting and prayer, etc., may indeed be an external preparation and discipline for children, that the body may keep and bear itself modestly and reverently towards the body and blood of Christ; yet what is given in and with it, the body cannot seize and appropriate. But this is done by the faith of the heart, which discerns this treasure and desires it. This may suffice for what is necessary as a general instruction respecting this sacrament; for what is further to be said of it belongs to another time.

In conclusion, since we have now the true understanding and doctrine of the Sacrament, there is indeed need of some admonition and exhortation, that men may not let so great a treasure which is daily administered and distributed among Christians pass by unheeded, that is, that those who would be Christians make ready to receive this venerable sacrament often. For we see that men seem weary and lazy with respect to it; and there is a great multitude of such as hear the gospel, and, because the nonsense of the pope has been abolished, and we are freed from his laws and coercion, go one, two, three years, or even longer without the Sacrament, as though they were such strong Christians that they have no need of it; and some allow themselves to be prevented and deterred by the pretense that we have taught that no one should approach it except those who feel hunger and thirst, which urge them to it. Some pretend that it is a matter of liberty and not necessary, and that it is sufficient to believe without it; and thus for the most part they go so far that they become quite brutish, and finally despise both the Sacrament and the word of God. [LC V.37–41]

Meditation:

1. What do the words "for you" emphasize about the Lord's Supper? What does it mean to have altogether believing hearts? Why is this required?
2. Is it sufficient for Christian living to have the true understanding and doctrine? Why are admonition and exhortation also necessary?
3. Do we have to go to the Sacrament? Is any particular frequency mandated? Why not? What do we risk if we go without it for a while?

Prayer:

Dear Jesus, thank you for your body and blood, given and shed for me. Help me to hunger and thirst for righteousness, and to receive the Sacrament often. Amen.

The Lutheran Catechism

Week Twenty-five – Thursday

The Sacrament of the Altar

Who, then, receives such sacrament worthily?

Fasting and bodily preparation is, indeed, a fine outward training; but he is truly worthy and well prepared who has faith in these words: "Given, and shed for you, for the remission of sins." But he that does not believe these words, or doubts, is unworthy and unfit; for the words "for you" require altogether believing hearts.

Now, it is true, as we have said, that no one should by any means be coerced or compelled, lest we institute a new murdering of souls. Nevertheless, it must be known that such people as deprive themselves of, and withdraw from, the Sacrament so long a time are not to be considered Christians. For Christ has not instituted it to be treated as a show, but has commanded his Christians to eat and drink it, and thereby remember him.

And, indeed, those who are true Christians and esteem the Sacrament precious and holy will urge and impel themselves unto it. Yet that the simpleminded and the weak who also would like to be Christians be the more incited to consider the cause and need which ought to impel them, we will treat somewhat of this point. For as in other matters pertaining to faith, love, and patience, it is not enough to teach and instruct only, but there is need also of daily exhortation, so here also there is need of continuing to preach that men may not become weary and disgusted, since we know and feel how the devil always opposes this and every Christian exercise, and drives and deters therefrom as much as he can.

And we have, in the first place, the clear text in the very words of Christ: "Do this in remembrance of me." These are bidding and commanding words by which all who would be Christians are enjoined to partake of this sacrament. Therefore, whoever would be a disciple of Christ, with whom he here speaks, must also consider and observe this, not from compulsion, as being forced by men, but in obedience to the Lord Jesus Christ, and to please him. [LC V.42–45]

Meditation:

1. Why is it wrong to coerce or compel people to receive the Sacrament? Why might this lead to the murdering of souls?
2. How are we to consider people who deprive themselves of the Sacrament for a long time? Why? How does God desire that we treat non-Christians?
3. Why is partaking of the Lord's Supper expected of anyone who would be a disciple of Christ? Why does the devil try to deter us from this?

Prayer:

Dear Lord, help me consistently to obey your command to "Do this" as an act of discipleship. Protect me from the efforts of the devil to lead me astray. Amen.

Week Twenty-five – Friday

The Sacrament of the Altar

Who, then, receives such sacrament worthily?

Fasting and bodily preparation is, indeed, a fine outward training; but he is truly worthy and well prepared who has faith in these words: "Given, and shed for you, for the remission of sins." But he that does not believe these words, or doubts, is unworthy and unfit; for the words "for you" require altogether believing hearts.

However, if you say: But the words are added, "As oft as ye do it"; there he compels no one, but leaves it to our free choice, answer: "That is true, yet it is not written that we should never do so." Yea, just because he speaks the words, "As oft as ye do it," it is nevertheless implied that we should do it often; and it is added for the reason that he wishes to have the Sacrament free, not limited to special times, like the Passover of the Jews, which they were obliged to eat only once a year, and that just upon the fourteenth day of the first full moon in the evening, and which they must not vary a day. It is as if he would say by these words: "I institute a Passover or Supper for you which you shall enjoy not only once a year, just upon this evening, but often, when and where you will, according to everyone's opportunity and necessity, bound to no place or appointed time"; although the pope afterwards perverted it, and again made a Jewish feast of it.

Thus, you perceive, it is not left free in the sense that we may despise it. For that I call despising it if one allow so long a time to elapse and with nothing to hinder him yet never feels a desire for it. If you wish such liberty, you may just as well have the liberty to be no Christian, and neither have to believe nor pray; for the one is just as much the command of Christ as the other. But if you wish to be a Christian, you must from time to time render satisfaction and obedience to this commandment. For this commandment ought ever to move you to examine yourself and to think: "See, what sort of a Christian I am! If I were one, I would certainly have some little longing for that which my Lord has commanded to do." [LC V.46–50]

Meditation:

1. How often were the Jews obliged to eat the Passover feast? Why is the Sacrament of the Altar different? Why is this a good thing?
2. What does it indicate if someone goes without the Lord's Supper for a long time, yet never feels a desire for it? Has this ever happened to you?
3. Why did Christ command us to receive his body and blood often, rather than leaving it entirely up to us?

Prayer:

Dear God, forgive me for not always obeying your word and receiving the sacrament as you have commanded. Help me never to despise these gifts. Amen.

Week Twenty-five – Saturday

The Sacrament of the Altar

Who, then, receives such sacrament worthily?

Fasting and bodily preparation is, indeed, a fine outward training; but he is truly worthy and well prepared who has faith in these words: "Given, and shed for you, for the remission of sins." But he that does not believe these words, or doubts, is unworthy and unfit; for the words "for you" require altogether believing hearts.

And, indeed, since we act such strangers to it, it is easily seen what sort of Christians we were under the papacy, namely, that we went from mere compulsion and fear of human commandments, without inclination and love, and never regarded the commandment of Christ. But we neither force nor compel anyone; nor need anyone do it to serve or please us. But this should induce and constrain you by itself, that he desires it and that it is pleasing to him. You must not suffer men to coerce you unto faith or any good work. We are doing no more than to say and exhort you as to what you ought to do, not for our sake, but for your own sake. He invites and allures you; if you despise it, you must answer for it yourself.

Now, this is to be the first point, especially for those who are cold and indifferent, that they may reflect upon and rouse themselves. For this is certainly true, as I have found in my own experience, and as everyone will find in his own case, that if a person thus withdraw from this sacrament, he will daily become more and more callous and cold, and will at last disregard it altogether. To avoid this, we must, indeed, examine heart and conscience, and act like a person who desires to be right with God. Now, the more this is done, the more will the heart be warmed and enkindled, that it may not become entirely cold. [LC V.51–54]

Meditation:

1. What is wrong with using compulsion and fear of human commandments to get people to church so that they receive the Lord's Supper?

2. What is the proper motivation for anyone to come? Why do we have faith? Why do we perform good works? What makes us right with God?

3. Have you ever become cold and indifferent toward God for a time? How does frequent reception of the Sacrament help to prevent this?

Prayer:

Lord, thank you for pursuing me in love and offering your body and blood to keep my heart warm and enkindled. Help me not to neglect this great gift. Amen.

Week Twenty-six — Sunday

The Sacrament of the Altar

Who, then, receives such sacrament worthily?

Fasting and bodily preparation is, indeed, a fine outward training; but he is truly worthy and well prepared who has faith in these words: "Given, and shed for you, for the remission of sins." But he that does not believe these words, or doubts, is unworthy and unfit; for the words "for you" require altogether believing hearts.

But if you say: How if I feel that I am not prepared? Answer: That is also my scruple, especially from the old way under the pope, in which a person tortured himself to be so perfectly pure that God could not find the least blemish in us. On this account we became so timid that everyone was instantly thrown into consternation and said to himself: "Alas! you are unworthy!" For then nature and reason begin to reckon our unworthiness in comparison with the great and precious good; and then it appears like a dark lantern in contrast with the bright sun, or as filth in comparison with precious stones. Because nature and reason see this, they refuse to approach and tarry until they are prepared, so long that one week trails another, and one half year the other. But if you are to regard how good and pure you are, and labor to have no compunctions, you must never approach.

We must, therefore, make a distinction here among men. For those who are wanton and dissolute must be told to stay away; for they are not prepared to receive forgiveness of sin, since they do not desire it and do not wish to be godly. But the others, who are not such callous and wicked people, and desire to be godly, must not absent themselves, even though otherwise they be feeble and full of infirmities, as St. Hilary also has said: "If anyone have not committed sin for which he can rightly be put out of the congregation and esteemed as no Christian, he ought not stay away from the Sacrament, lest he may deprive himself of life." For no one will make such progress that he will not retain many daily infirmities in flesh and blood. [LC V.55–60]

Meditation:

1. Why might someone feel that he or she is not properly prepared to receive the Lord's Supper? Have you ever felt that way?
2. Is it true or false that we are unworthy in comparison with the great and precious good of the Sacrament? What makes us worthy in God's eyes?
3. What kind of person should indeed stay away? What is the difference between being wanton and dissolute versus full of daily infirmities?

Prayer:

Lord Jesus, I am unworthy of the great and precious good that you offer. Thank you for giving me faith and forgiveness, despite my daily infirmities. Amen.

Week Twenty-six – Monday

The Sacrament of the Altar

Who, then, receives such sacrament worthily?

Fasting and bodily preparation is, indeed, a fine outward training; but he is truly worthy and well prepared who has faith in these words: "Given, and shed for you, for the remission of sins." But he that does not believe these words, or doubts, is unworthy and unfit; for the words "for you" require altogether believing hearts.

Therefore such people must learn that it is the highest art to know that our Sacrament does not depend upon our worthiness. For we are not baptized because we are worthy and holy, nor do we go to confession because we are pure and without sin, but the contrary, because we are poor miserable men, and just because we are unworthy; unless it be someone who desires no grace and absolution nor intends to reform.

But whoever would gladly obtain grace and consolation should impel himself, and allow no one to frighten him away, but say: "I, indeed, would like to be worthy; but I come, not upon any worthiness, but upon thy word, because thou hast commanded it, as one who would gladly be thy disciple, no matter what becomes of my worthiness." But this is difficult; for we always have this obstacle and hindrance to encounter, that we look more upon ourselves than upon the word and lips of Christ. For nature desires so to act that it can stand and rest firmly on itself, otherwise it refuses to make the approach. Let this suffice concerning the first point.

In the second place, there is besides this command also a promise, as we heard above, which ought most strongly to incite and encourage us. For here stand the kind and precious words: "This is my body, given for you. This is my blood, shed for you, for the remission of sins." These words, I have said, are not preached to wood and stone, but to me and you; else he might just as well be silent and not institute a sacrament. Therefore consider, and put yourself into this *you*, that he may not speak to you in vain. [LC V.61–65]

Meditation:

1. Are we baptized because we are worthy and holy? Do we go to confession because we are pure and without sin? What are we seeking in both cases?
2. What do we likewise seek from the Sacrament? Why are we tempted to look more upon ourselves than upon the word and lips of Christ?
3. What is contained in the words of Christ, besides a command? To whom is his promise directed? What does it mean to put yourself into this *you*?

Prayer:

Dear God, thank you for granting forgiveness in baptism, absolution, and the Lord's Supper, not just for sinners in general, but for me in particular. Amen.

Week Twenty-six – Tuesday

The Sacrament of the Altar

Who, then, receives such sacrament worthily?

Fasting and bodily preparation is, indeed, a fine outward training; but he is truly worthy and well prepared who has faith in these words: "Given, and shed for you, for the remission of sins." But he that does not believe these words, or doubts, is unworthy and unfit; for the words "for you" require altogether believing hearts.

For here he offers to us the entire treasure which he has brought for us from heaven, and to which he invites us also in other places with the greatest kindness, as when he says in St. Matthew 11:28: "Come unto me, all ye that labor and are heavy laden, and I will give you rest." Now it is surely a sin and a shame that he so cordially and faithfully summons and exhorts us to our highest and greatest good, and we act so distantly with regard to it, and permit so long a time to pass that we grow quite cold and hardened, so that we have no inclination or love for it. We must never regard the Sacrament as something injurious from which we had better flee, but as a pure, wholesome, comforting remedy imparting salvation and comfort, which will cure you and give you life both in soul and body. For where the soul has recovered, the body also is relieved. Why, then, is it that we act as if it were a poison, the eating of which would bring death?

To be sure, it is true that those who despise it and live in an unchristian manner receive it to their hurt and damnation; for nothing shall be good or wholesome to them, just as with a sick person who from caprice eats and drinks what is forbidden him by the physician. But those who are sensible of their weakness, desire to be rid of it and long for help, should regard and use it only as a precious antidote against the poison which they have in them. For here in the Sacrament you are to receive from the lips of Christ forgiveness of sin, which contains and brings with it the grace of God and the Spirit with all his gifts, protection, shelter, and power against death and the devil and all misfortune. [LC V.66–70]

Meditation:

1. What is the treasure that Christ has brought for us from heaven? What kind of rest does he give to those who labor and are heavy laden?
2. Why might a person regard the Sacrament as something injurious? How should we regard it instead? What comfort do you receive from it?
3. What effect does the Lord's Supper have on those who despise it and live in an unchristian manner? What effect does it have on those who long for it?

Prayer:

Dear Lord, help me to recognize the poison of sin that I have in me and earnestly seek the only antidote, your gift of forgiveness in word and sacraments. Amen.

Week Twenty-six – Wednesday

The Sacrament of the Altar

Who, then, receives such sacrament worthily?

Fasting and bodily preparation is, indeed, a fine outward training; but he is truly worthy and well prepared who has faith in these words: "Given, and shed for you, for the remission of sins." But he that does not believe these words, or doubts, is unworthy and unfit; for the words "for you" require altogether believing hearts.

Thus you have, on the part of God, both the command and the promise of the Lord Jesus Christ. Besides this, on your part, your own distress which is about your neck, and because of which this command, invitation, and promise are given, ought to impel you. For he himself says [Matt. 9:12]: "They that be whole need not a physician, but they that be sick"; that is, those who are weary and heavy laden with their sins, with the fear of death, temptations of the flesh and of the devil.

If, therefore, you are heavy laden and feel your weakness, then go joyfully to this sacrament and obtain refreshment, consolation, and strength. For if you would wait until you are rid of such burdens, that you might come to the Sacrament pure and worthy, you must forever stay away. For in that case he pronounces sentence and says: "If you are pure and godly, you have no need of me, and I, in turn, none of thee." Therefore those alone are called unworthy who neither feel their infirmities nor wish to be considered sinners.

But if you say: "What, then, shall I do if I cannot feel such distress or experience hunger and thirst for the Sacrament?" Answer: For those who are so minded that they do not realize their condition I know no better counsel than that they put their hand into their bosom to ascertain whether they also have flesh and blood. And if you find that to be the case, then go, for your good, to St. Paul's Epistle to the Galatians [5:19–21], and hear what sort of a fruit your flesh is: "Now the works of the flesh are manifest, which are these: Adultery, fornication, uncleanness, lasciviousness, idolatry, witchcraft, hatred, variance, emulations, wrath, strife, seditions, heresies, envyings, murders, drunkenness, revelings, and such like." [LC V.71–75]

Meditation:

1. What two kinds of statements do we find throughout God's word and connected with each of the sacraments? Why are both important?
2. What should you do when you are heavy laden with your sins and feel your weakness? What does the Lord offer you in his Supper?
3. What should you do when you do not feel a desire for the Sacrament? How does being reminded of our flesh demonstrate our need for it?

Prayer:

Father, thank you for giving me both your commands and your promises. Help me to obey and believe, since I cannot do either by my own strength. Amen.

Week Twenty-six – Thursday

The Sacrament of the Altar

Who, then, receives such sacrament worthily?

Fasting and bodily preparation is, indeed, a fine outward training; but he is truly worthy and well prepared who has faith in these words: "Given, and shed for you, for the remission of sins." But he that does not believe these words, or doubts, is unworthy and unfit; for the words "for you" require altogether believing hearts.

Therefore, if you cannot feel it, at least believe the Scriptures; they will not lie to you, and they know your flesh better than you yourself. Yea, St. Paul further concludes in Romans 7:18: "I know that in me, that is, in my flesh, dwelleth no good thing." If St. Paul may speak thus of his flesh, we do not propose to be better nor more holy. But that we do not feel it is so much the worse; for it is a sign that there is a leprous flesh which feels nothing, and yet rages and keeps spreading. Yet, as we have said, if you are quite dead to all sensibility, still believe the Scriptures, which pronounce sentence upon you. And, in short, the less you feel your sins and infirmities, the more reason have you to go to the Sacrament to seek help and a remedy.

In the second place, look about you and see whether you are also in the world, or if you do not know it, ask your neighbors about it. If you are in the world, do not think that there will be lack of sins and misery. For only begin to act as though you would be godly and adhere to the gospel, and see whether no one will become your enemy, and, moreover, do you harm, wrong, and violence, and likewise give you cause for sin and vice. If you have not experienced it, then let the Scriptures tell you, which everywhere give this praise and testimony to the world. [LC V.76–79]

Meditation:

1. Why are our feelings an unreliable basis for ascertaining whether we need the Sacrament? What should we consult and believe instead?
2. What did Paul say about his flesh? Is yours any different? If your skin was leprous, yet you felt no pain, would you ignore it on that basis? Why not?
3. What do you see when you look about you at the world? What happens to godly believers? Why should this drive us to the Lord's Supper?

Prayer:

God, forgive me for trusting my fallible feelings, rather than your sure word. Help me to overcome my sinful flesh and the opposition of the world. Amen.

Week Twenty-six – Friday

The Sacrament of the Altar

Who, then, receives such sacrament worthily?

Fasting and bodily preparation is, indeed, a fine outward training; but he is truly worthy and well prepared who has faith in these words: "Given, and shed for you, for the remission of sins." But he that does not believe these words, or doubts, is unworthy and unfit; for the words "for you" require altogether believing hearts.

Besides this, you will also have the devil about you, whom you will not entirely tread underfoot, because our Lord Christ himself could not entirely avoid him. Now, what is the devil? Nothing else than what the Scriptures call him, a liar and murderer. A liar, to lead the heart astray from the word of God, and to blind it, that you cannot feel your distress or come to Christ. A murderer, who cannot bear to see you live one single hour. If you could see how many knives, darts, and arrows are every moment aimed at you, you would be glad to come to the Sacrament as often as possible. But there is no reason why we walk so securely and heedlessly, except that we neither think nor believe that we are in the flesh, and in this wicked world or in the kingdom of the devil.

Therefore, try this and practice it well, and do but examine yourself, or look about you a little, and only keep to the Scriptures. If even then you still feel nothing, you have so much the more misery to lament both to God and to your brother. Then take advice and have others pray for you, and do not desist until the stone be removed from your heart. Then, indeed, the distress will not fail to become manifest, and you will find that you have sunk twice as deep as any other poor sinner, and are much more in need of the Sacrament against the misery which unfortunately you do not see, so that, with the grace of God, you may feel it more and become the more hungry for the Sacrament, especially since the devil plies his force against you, and lies in wait for you without ceasing to seize and destroy you, soul and body, so that you are not safe from him one hour. How soon can he have brought you suddenly into misery and distress when you least expect it! [LC V.80–84]

Meditation:

1. How did the devil behave toward Jesus while he was on earth? How should we expect the devil to behave toward us?
2. In what sense is the devil a liar and murderer? Why does he desire to lead us astray and bring us harm? How does the Sacrament protect us from him?
3. What do you observe when you examine yourself, the world, and the devil in accordance with the Scriptures? What can you do about it?

Prayer:

Saving Lord, remind me daily that the devil is truly out to get me. Thank you for providing your word and sacraments to inform me and protect me. Amen.

Week Twenty-six – Saturday

The Sacrament of the Altar

Who, then, receives such sacrament worthily?

Fasting and bodily preparation is, indeed, a fine outward training; but he is truly worthy and well prepared who has faith in these words: "Given, and shed for you, for the remission of sins." But he that does not believe these words, or doubts, is unworthy and unfit; for the words "for you" require altogether believing hearts.

Let this, then, be said for exhortation, not only for those of us who are old and grown, but also for the young people, who ought to be brought up in the Christian doctrine and understanding. For thereby the Ten Commandments, the Creed, and the Lord's Prayer might be the more easily inculcated to our youth, so that they would receive them with pleasure and earnestness, and thus would practice them from their youth and accustom themselves to them. For the old are now well-nigh done for, so that these and other things cannot be attained, unless we train the people who are to come after us and succeed us in our office and work, in order that they also may bring up their children successfully, that the word of God and the Christian church may be preserved. Therefore let every father of a family know that it is his duty, by the injunction and command of God, to teach these things to his children, or have them learn what they ought to know. For since they are baptized and received into the Christian church, they should also enjoy this communion of the Sacrament, in order that they may serve us and be useful to us; for they must all indeed help us to believe, love, pray, and fight against the devil. [LC V.85–87]

The Lutheran Catechism

Meditation:
1. Why is it important that young people be brought up in the Christian doctrine and understanding? How does the catechism facilitate this?
2. At the same time, is anyone too old or too wise to benefit from reviewing the Ten Commandments, the Creed, and the Lord's Prayer? Why not?
3. Who is primarily responsible for teaching these things? Why is it best done within the family, rather than at church?

Prayer:

God, thank you for the summary of your word and sacraments in the catechism. Help me to use it daily to believe, love, pray, and fight against the devil. Amen.

The Lutheran Catechism

Daily Prayers

Morning Prayer

In the morning, when you rise, you shall bless yourself with the holy cross and say: In the name of God the Father, Son, and Holy Ghost. Amen.

Then, kneeling or standing, repeat the Creed and the Lord's Prayer. If you choose, you may, in addition, say this little prayer:

I thank thee, my heavenly Father,
through Jesus Christ, thy dear Son,
that thou hast kept me this night from all harm and danger;
and I pray thee to keep me this day also from sin and all evil,
that all my doings and life may please thee.
For into thy hands I commend myself,
my body and soul, and all things.
Let thy holy angel be with me,
that the wicked foe may have no power over me. Amen.

Then go to your work with joy, singing a hymn, such as the Ten Commandments, or what your devotion may suggest.

Evening Prayer

In the evening, when you go to bed, you shall bless yourself with the holy cross and say:

In the name of God the Father, Son, and Holy Ghost. Amen.
Then, kneeling or standing, repeat the Creed and the Lord's Prayer. If you choose, you may, in addition, say this little prayer:
I thank thee, my heavenly Father,
through Jesus Christ, thy dear Son,
that thou hast graciously kept me this day,
and I pray thee to forgive me all my sins, where I have done wrong,
and graciously keep me this night.
For into thy hands I commend myself,
my body and soul, and all things.
Let thy holy angel be with me,
that the wicked foe may have no power over me. Amen.
Then go to sleep promptly and cheerfully.

Asking a Blessing

The children and servants shall go to the table with folded hands and reverently, and say:

The eyes of all wait upon thee, O Lord;
and thou givest them their meat in due season;
thou openest thine hand,
and satisfiest the desire of every living thing.

Note: To satisfy the desire means that all animals receive so much to eat that they are on this account joyful and of good cheer; for care and avarice hinder such satisfaction.

Then the Lord's Prayer, and the prayer here following:

Lord God, heavenly Father,
bless us and these thy gifts,
which we take from thy bountiful goodness,
through Jesus Christ, our Lord. Amen.

Returning Thanks

Likewise also after the meal they shall reverently and with folded hands say:

O give thanks unto the Lord, for he is good;
for his mercy endureth forever.
He giveth food to all flesh;
he giveth to the beast his food,
and to the young ravens which cry.
He delighteth not in the strength of the horse;
he taketh not pleasure in the legs of a man.
The Lord taketh pleasure in them that fear him,
in those that hope in his mercy.

Then the Lord's Prayer and the prayer here following:

We thank thee, Lord God, Father,
through Jesus Christ, our Lord,
for all thy benefits,
who livest and reignest forever and ever. Amen.

Table of Duties

Certain passages of Scripture for various holy orders and positions, admonishing them about their duties and responsibilities.

Sunday
For Bishops, Pastors, and Preachers: A bishop must be blameless, the husband of one wife, vigilant, sober, of good behavior, given to hospitality, apt to teach; not given to wine, no striker, not greedy of filthy lucre; but patient, not a brawler, not covetous; one that ruleth well his own house, having his children in subjection with all gravity; not a novice; holding fast the faithful word as he hath been taught, that he may be able by sound doctrine both to exhort and to convince the gainsayers. (1 Tim. 3:2ff; Titus 1:6)

Monday
Concerning Civil Government: Let every soul be subject unto the higher powers. For the power which exists anywhere is ordained of God. Whosoever resisteth the power resisteth the ordinance of God; and they that resist shall receive to themselves damnation. For he beareth not the sword in vain; for he is the minister of God, a revenger to execute wrath upon him that doeth evil. (Rom. 13:1–4)

Tuesday
For Husbands: Ye husbands, dwell with your wives according to knowledge, giving honor unto the wife, as unto the weaker vessel, and as being heirs together of the grace of life, that your prayers be not hindered. (1 Pet. 3:7) And be not bitter against them. (Col. 3:9)

For Wives: Wives, submit yourselves unto your own husbands, as unto the Lord, even as Sarah obeyed Abraham, calling him lord; whose daughters ye are, as long as ye do well, and are not afraid with any amazement. (1 Pet. 3:6; Eph. 5:22)

Wednesday
For Parents: Ye fathers, provoke not your children to wrath, but bring them up in the nurture and admonition of the Lord. (Eph. 6:4)

For Children: Children, obey your parents in the Lord; for this is right. Honor thy father and mother; which is the first commandment with promise: that it may be well with thee, and thou mayest live long on the earth. (Eph. 6:1–3)

Thursday

For Male and Female Servants, Hired Men, and Laborers: Servants, be obedient to them that are your masters according to the flesh, with fear and trembling, in singleness of your heart, as unto Christ; not with eyeservice, as men-pleasers, but as the servants of Christ, doing the will of God from the heart; with good will doing service as to the Lord, and not to men; knowing that whatsoever good thing any man doeth, the same shall he receive of the Lord, whether he be bond or free. (Eph. 6:5ff ; Col. 3:22)

Friday

For Masters and Mistresses: Ye masters, do the same things unto them, forbearing threatening, knowing that your Master also is in heaven; neither is there respect of persons with him. (Eph. 6:9; Col. 4:1)

For Young Persons in General: Likewise, ye younger, submit yourselves unto the elder. Yea, all of you be subject one to another, and be clothed with humility; for God resisteth the proud, and giveth grace to the humble. Humble yourselves, therefore, under the mighty hand of God that he may exalt you in due time. (1 Pet. 5:5–6)

Saturday

For Widows: She that is a widow indeed, and desolate, trusteth in God, and continueth in supplications and prayers night and day. But she that liveth in pleasure is dead while she liveth. (1 Tim. 5:5–6)

For All in Common: Thou shalt love thy neighbor as thyself. Herein are comprehended all the commandments. (Rom. 13:8ff) And persevere in prayer for all men. (1 Tim. 2:1–2)

Let each his lesson learn with care,
And all the household well shall fare.

www.ingramcontent.com/pod-product-compliance
Lightning Source LLC
Chambersburg PA
CBHW071108160426
43196CB00013B/2502